Drawing on a wealth of international experiei ... policing
fascinating and important insight into contempo ..., migration, police
and sex work. Covering, as it does, issues such as I....
integrity, vigilantism, and morality, the book makes a significant contribution
to much wider debates within criminology and sociology. Students, academics,
policy-makers and concerned citizens will find much insight in this impressive
book.

Mike Rowe, Professor of Criminology, Northumbria University, UK

Prostitution continues to attract varied policy responses, from prohibitionism to
decriminalisation. Focusing on the pivotal role of the police, this book provides
an authoritative international overview of the enforcement of these policies and
demonstrates the importance of policing in shaping the well-being of sex workers,
their clients and the communities in which they work. Recognising the complexity
and increasing plurality of police practices, this collection offers real insight into
the models of policing which effectively protect sex workers whilst penalising
those who seek to exploit or harm them. An important and timely collection that
demands to be read by all those involved in the formulation and evaluation of
prostitution policy.

Phil Hubbard, Professor of Urban Studies, Kings College London, UK

Sanders and Laing have assembled an absorbing collection that serves as an
important intervention in the sex-work debate. United by a rigorous yet passionate
approach to the subject of sex work, these chapters are as lucid as they are thought-
provoking. A must read for anyone interested in the sex work debate.

Chris Ashford, Professor of Law and Society, Director of Research
and Innovations and Law, Northumbria University, UK

The growing demand for high quality research on sex work is well served by this
unrivalled collection of chapters on policing. It is an impressive and coherent
collection which gives great insight into the complex world of contemporary
policing. By reaching across the globe, the editors have produced an articulate
cross-cultural compendium of modern policing as applied to sexual labour. It is
both highly theorised and at the same time highly readable so that scholars, not
just of sexuality, but also of community policing and personal safety will find this
far-reaching collection invaluable.

Belinda Brooks-Gordon, Reader in Psychology,
University of London, UK

Policing the Sex Industry

The exponential growth of sexual commerce, migration and movement of people into the sex industry, as well as localised concerns about transactional sex, are key areas of interest across the urban west. Given the complex regulatory frameworks under which the sex industry manifests, the role of the police is significant.

Policing the Sex Industry draws on the research and expertise of academics and practitioners, presenting advanced scholarship across a range of countries and spaces. Unpicking the relationship between police practice and commercial sex whilst speaking to the current policy agendas, *Policing the Sex Industry* explores key issues including: trafficking, decriminalisation, localised impacts of punitive policing approaches, uneven policing approaches, hate-crime approaches and the impact of policing on trans sex workers.

A dynamic and incisive contribution to existing research, *Policing the Sex Industry* will appeal to undergraduate and postgraduate students, as well as researchers at all levels, interested in fields including Criminology, Sociology, Gender Politics and Women's Studies.

Teela Sanders is Professor of Criminology at the University of Leicester, UK.

Mary Laing is a Senior Lecturer in Criminology at Northumbria University, UK.

Interdisciplinary Studies in Sex for Sale

https://www.routledge.com/Interdisciplinary-Studies-in-Sex-for-Sale/
book-series/ISSS\

Interdisciplinary Studies in Sex for Sale is a new and exciting series emphasising innovative work on the complexities of sex for sale, its practices, the policies designed to regulate it and their effects. It covers both recent and historical developments with an aim to explore multidisciplinary and international perspectives, expand theoretical approaches, and analyse matters which are the subject of controversy and debate in this field.

We welcome submissions of single and co-authored books, as well as edited collections that address sex for sale, its practices and regulation, including those with a focus on: comparative analysis; multi-scalar approaches; methodological perspectives; cultural and economic contexts; and the policies concerned with the regulation of sex for sale.

This series emerges from and intends to expand the work of the European Concerted Research COST Action IS1209 'Comparing European Prostitution Policies: Understanding Scales and Cultures of Governance (*ProsPol*)', a European network funded under Horizon 2020 (www.prospol.eu).

Isabel Crowhurst is Lecturer in Sociology and Criminology at the University of Essex, UK, and coordinator (Chair) of *ProsPol*.

Rebecca Pates, is Professor of Political Theory at Leipzig University, Germany.

May-Len Skilbrei is Professor in Criminology at the University of Oslo, Norway, and Vice Chair of *Prospol*.

Books:

Erotic Performance and Spectatorship
Katy Pilcher

Assessing Prostitution Policies in Europe
Edited by Hendrik Wagenaar and Synnøve Økland Jahnsen

Policing the Sex Industry
Protection, Paternalism and Politics
Edited by Teela Sanders and Mary Laing

Policing the Sex Industry

Protection, Paternalism and Politics

**Edited by Teela Sanders
and Mary Laing**

Routledge
Taylor & Francis Group

LONDON AND NEW YORK

First published 2018 by Routledge

2 Park Square, Milton Park, Abingdon, Oxfordshire OX14 4RN

52 Vanderbilt Avenue, New York, NY 10017

Routledge is an imprint of the Taylor & Francis Group, an informa business

First issued in paperback 2019

British Library Cataloguing-in-Publication Data
A catalogue record for this book is available from the British Library

Library of Congress Cataloging-in-Publication Data
A catalog record for this book has been requested

ISBN: 978-1-138-71662-9 (hbk)
ISBN: 978-0-367-37514-0 (pbk)

Typeset in Times New Roman
by Apex CoVantage, LLC

Contents

PART II
Policing Operations, Enforcement and Austerity 107

Contributors

Lynzi Armstrong is a Lecturer in Criminology at Victoria University of Wellington in New Zealand. Her PhD research explored the management of risks of violence among female street-based sex workers in Wellington and Christchurch, exploring the significance of these experiences in the context of decriminalisation. Her ongoing research interests include legislative responses to sex work, sex worker rights, violence against sex workers, stigma, the impacts of anti-trafficking policies, and migration for sex work.

Del Campbell worked as The Community Engagement Manager at Terrence Higgins Trust for eight years where he managed the SWISH project (sex workers into sexual health) developing a unique service for male, female and transgender sex workers across seven London boroughs, supporting them on their safety, sexual health and well-being. In 2016 he joined National Ugly Mugs, a charity which empowers sex workers to warn each other about potential violent offenders. The charity also encourages sex workers who are the victims of crime to report to the police. His role is specifically around training the police on best practice when sex workers come into contact with the criminal justice system, placing particular emphasis on the barriers trans sex workers face on accessing services and reporting crime.

Rosie Campbell OBE is a Researcher in the Department of Criminology, University of Leicester and a Visiting Research Fellow, Sociology, University of York. She holds a PhD from Durham University. Her research areas of interest include: sex work, violence and policing, multi-agency responses to sex work, online sex work and participatory action approaches. She was a founder of UK Network of Sex Work Projects which established National Ugly Mugs, of which she is a board member. She has been involved in the front-line delivery of a number of sex work projects in the UK, coordinating Armistead Street and Portside projects in Merseyside, when Merseyside Police introduced the approach of treating crimes against sex workers as hate crime which she went on to research.

Alex Feis-Bryce, National Ugly Mugs, Northumbria University Alex was the founding (former) CEO of National Ugly Mugs, an organisation which supports sex workers throughout the UK when they become victims of crime, from April 2012 to May 2017. He came to post to oversee the set-up of the organisation and was instrumental in its development from a small pilot project to a multi-award-winning national organisation which has supported thousands of sex workers and has contributed significantly to local and national policy. During this time, Alex has been at the forefront of policy and practice in the UK. He was also an influential member of the National Police Working Group on Sex Work which advises the National Police Chiefs Council on policy and guidelines. He was runner-up both as "Influencer" in the 2014 DSC Social Change Awards and as "Rising Star CEO" in the 2016 Charity Times Awards. He also featured on the most recent Independent on Sunday Rainbow List of the most influential LGBTI people in the UK. He is also a postgraduate research student at Northumbria University and is a board member of Survivors Manchester.

Synnøve Jahnsen is a Postdoctoral Research Fellow at the Uni Research Rokkan Centre. Jahnsen studied sociology and gender studies at the University of Bergen, where she obtained her PhD degree in 2014. Her primary research interests are in globalisation, gender, migration, border control, organised crime, police reform, professionalisation and organisational borders. She is also a co-editor of a forthcoming themed edition of the *Nordic Journal of Policing Studies* 'Policing High-Trust Societies' and an edited book assessing European prostitution policy in 22 different countries, which is one of the outcomes of COST Action IS1209 'Comparing European Prostitution Policies: Understanding Scales and Cultures of Governance' (ProsPol), where she is a member of the Management Committee.

Debbie Jones is a Senior Lecturer in Criminology and Director of Undergraduate Studies for Criminology, College of Law and Criminology, Swansea University. Prior to beginning her academic career, Debbie was a police officer with the Metropolitan Police specialising in major crimes and child protection. Since 2008 Debbie has been researching regulation of the sex industry and has brought a unique vision to the methodological approaches to researching sex which has led to transformational understanding. Debbie is also academic advisory to Cardiff Sex Work Forum and one of the founding members of the All Wales Sex Work Group. She is Co-Director of the Consortium for Sexuality Studies: Research Innovation and Practice at Swansea University.

Matthew Jones is Senior lecturer in Criminology at Northumbria University. His research explores contemporary intersections between gender and sexuality with crime/criminal justice. His work has a strong social justice focus and he is passionate about providing minority voices within the criminal justice system space through empirical research. Matthew is deputy-Chair of the British Society of Criminology Policing Network.

Mary Laing is a Senior Lecturer in Criminology at Northumbria University interested in the regulation and criminalisation of sex work and the sex industry. She is on the Board of National Ugly Mugs and is currently undertaking participatory research with practitioners and sex workers identifying as trans or in other gender diverse ways, utilising digital technologies with Open Lab, Newcastle University.

Julia Leser is a researcher at the department of political sciences at the University of Leipzig, Germany, where she is teaching courses on issues of security and policing practices. She is a member of the German National Research Council funded project 'ProsCrim: Institutionalizing Human Trafficking', where she is currently finishing her PhD on emotion management techniques in bureaucracies and policing agencies. Her research interests lie in governmental migration control, prostitution and human trafficking as well as the transformation processes of statehood, national security and police.

Lucy Neville is a Lecturer in Criminology at the University of Leicester. She is a feminist and activist, and one of the founding members of the FemGenSex network of feminist scholars interested in investigating areas around women, gender and sexuality. Her research interests relate to understanding women's engagement with pornography, sex and sex work; sex work policy in the UK and internationally; violence towards women; domestic violence; violent crime; and the impacts of austerity on responses to violent crime.

Tracey Sagar is Professor of Criminology and Head of the Department of Criminology, College of Law and Criminology, Swansea University. Tracey is a leading expert on sex work research – undertaking empirical research projects both locally and nationally which have transformed policy and practice responses to sex work in Wales. Tracey is also a Co-Director of the Consortium for Sexuality Studies: Research, Innovation and Practice at Swansea University which provides an innovative research and service development environment where academics, stakeholder organisations and policy makers collaborate to identify sexuality needs/concerns of the community and strive to deliver positive social change.

Teela Sanders is Professor of Criminology at the University of Leicester specialising in the cross sections between gender, crime and justice. She has researched areas relating to the sex industry for twenty years producing eight books and many articles. Her current projects look at digital technologies and the sex industry (www.beyond-the-gaze.com) with a strong impact agenda around netreach and safety guidance for sex workers. She is a strong supporter of Participatory Action Research methods which underpin her research endeavours, working alongside the sex work community to ensure evidence-based policy speaks to the rights agenda. Other work focuses on homicide and mental health with sex workers. The National Ugly Mugs are collaborative partners with her research activities, enabling impact into grassroots activities.

Erin Sanders-McDonagh is a Lecturer in Criminology at the University of Kent. She is a feminist public scholar with a commitment to radical and engaged pedagogic practices. Her research explores inequality in different forms, and she has worked with a range of marginalised groups in recent research projects. She has a strong commitment to working with scholars from across disciplinary boundaries and to moving research findings into the public arena.

Andrew L. Spivak is Associate Professor of Sociology at the University of Nevada, Las Vegas. A graduate of The University of Oklahoma (PhD, 2007), he previously worked in corrections for 10 years. He teaches courses in criminology, penology, demography, research methods and statistics, and supervises a prison casework internship programme. He is a recipient of several university and state teaching awards, and his published scholarship relates to topics including prison recidivism, suicide and violent behaviour, social deviance, juvenile justice processing, tobacco regulation and residential segregation.

Angelika Strohmayer is an interdisciplinary researcher exploring the ways in which digital technologies are utilised by and designed with sex work support services to facilitate support in fragmented and centralised contexts. Currently she is based at Open Lab, Newcastle University.

Acknowledgements

We would like to dedicate this book to sex workers across the globe, and hope that, in some small way, this research contributes to ensuring better access to social and criminal justice for all.

We would like to recognise the tireless work that Alex Feis-Bryce has dedicated to his former role as CEO at the National Ugly Mugs and the work of the staff there who are at the forefront of sex worker rights and the prevention of violence and crimes.

Introduction –
Policing the sex industry

Tackling exploitation, facilitating safety?

Teela Sanders and Mary Laing

The role of the police in the regulation and facilitation of sex work is increasingly highlighted and discussed in policy initiatives, media exposes and in the context of the front line work carried out by specialist services for sex workers. This introduction to the edited collection shines a light on the complexities of policing the sex industry, drawing particularly on the dual role of the police to both enforce the law and protect victims. In some jurisdictions where commercial sex is heavily criminalised, there is evidence of various types, and alarming levels, of police mistreatment of sex workers, which jeopardises the role of the police as protectors and/or facilitators of justice. In other instances, it is clear that the police are compromised in trying to apprehend exploiters, traffickers and perpetrators of violence, yet at the same time their actions and responses often inhibit the rights of sex workers to operate in a safe environment.

This introduction maps out the complex issues at play in relation to policing which are evident across the globe. We examine key themes such as the lack of awareness of crimes against sex workers and responses (attitudinal and relational) by police; the shifting political climates around the place of commercial sex in the criminalised legal framework and the role of the police in facilitating community relations; the difficulties of policing crimes against sex workers whilst enforcing laws against exploiters; and the gathering momentum around decriminalisation and the existing plurality of policing.

The theoretical spectrum considering the sex industry

Sex work is a divisive issue within feminism. The ideological and theoretical foundations of this debate are discussed widely in the extant literature, and are often described as the 'sex wars' (Weitzer 2000, 2010b). Despite this wide recognition and understanding, it is important to explore these discussions in this introduction, as not only are they theoretically important to research on the sex industry, but discursive constructions of sex work can have a very real impact on policing practice.

In most basic terms, two key opposing theoretical frameworks dominate the feminist debate. These are used, not just to define the practices of commercial sex, but to give meaning to the performative aspects of the commercial sexual exchange. The first is sometimes coined 'prohibitionism', 'abolitionism', 'neo-abolitionism' or the 'oppression paradigm' (Weitzer 2010b). Although there are some nuanced differences between these approaches, they are fundamentally informed by radical feminist views of the sex industry. At its core, radical feminism positions all commercial sexual transactions as violent and inevitably exploitative. The argument is that even if actual violence is not part of the transaction, the exchange of money, or receiving some sort of remuneration for a sexual service (of whatever type) is exploitation. As reinforced by Dworkin (1993/1994: np emphasis added) who states: 'Prostitution *in and of itself* is an abuse of a woman's body'.

Within this perspective, prostitution is positioned as a central and scaffolding factor in the wider subordination of women; it is intrinsic to endemic gender oppression. Prostitution enables and embeds patriarchy within the fabric of society. It is oppressive, abusive and violent for all women. Because of the inextricable link between unequal gender relations and prostitution, radical feminism positions the male identities within debates on prostitution as violent and abusive – whether their positionality is of the client, abuser, pimp or trafficker. Within these discourses these identities are rarely interrogated through an empirical lens and thus become caricatures of violence and exploitation (see Kingston 2010 for a discussion of how this plays out in policy). It is through the process of the (male) purchase of (female) sex that the passive body of the female victim becomes objectified, commodified and essentially dehumanised. With sex workers described as 'generic embodiment[s]' of women, they are positioned as passive to the whole experience. Prostitution is positioned as something which is done to women by men; and women are simply 'prostituted' (Dworkin 1993/1994: np). The sex of prostitution is described as non-consensual and rape; as Barry (1996: 11) describes, prostitution is 'the most extreme and crystallized form of all sexual exploitation'.

The narrative of the passive victim is something which is challenged by liberal or sex positive feminists who do not see the sex of prostitution as intrinsically exploitative. This approach, also known as the 'empowerment paradigm' (Weitzer 2010a) recognises the complex and dynamic social-cultural-political-economic contexts in which some people make a 'rational choice' (Chapkis 1997: 67) to engage in the sale of sex. This means that for that person, at that time and in that space the sale of sex is either the best or favourable option for them. Sex work may look and be experienced differently by different people in different contexts. Notably, people will have more or less control over their situation, but this perspective recognises the agency of individuals providing sexual services. There is a varied and vast empirical evidence base, which exists alongside materials written by sex workers, demonstrating not only the diversity of experiences of those engaging in sex work but also what this entails and how this labour is managed and practised (see for example collections by van der Meulen et al. and Laing et al.). Thus, for many engaged in sex work, sexual labour is able to provide flexible and favourable working conditions and economic reward. One recent UK-based survey of 240 sex workers revealed that amongst the sample, job satisfaction was high, with 91% of people describing sex work as flexible, (many utilise sex work as a secondary or 'dual' stream of income, Bowen 2016), 66% as fun and over 50% as rewarding, skilful, sociable and empowering (Sanders et al. 2016). In addition, further research has demonstrated the comparability of sex work, with other non-sexualised forms of labour. Phoenix and Oerton (2001) looked at the experiences of home-based sex workers and therapeutic massage practitioners, and found that although there were differences, there were also similarities in terms of bodily contact and touching; skin to skin encounters; undressing; and no-go areas. Others have explored the emotional labour and body work utilised by sex workers (for example Sanders 2005), which are arguably also commonplace in other types of service sector performative work.

Sex positive and liberal feminists recognise the diversity and heterogeneity of experience (Pitcher 2015) in the sex industry, and although in some sectors and spaces, experiences of violence are relatively few and far between (O'Doherty 2011), sex workers being targeted and victimised in the context of their work remains a key area of concern. Rather than violence however being something intrinsic to the sexual exchange, sex positive and liberal feminists focus on actual experiences of violence and seek to understand these within the socio-legal context in which the work takes place. The historic criminalisation of sex workers and their positionality within moral discourse has led to the creation of a stigmatic identity, although stigma is not always and evenly felt by all sex workers, (Redman 2016); and this varies culturally and globally. Stigma has been evidenced to directly contribute to violence and criminality, for example in the manifestation of hate crime (Campbell 2014 and also see Chapter 3 in this collection) and further marginalisation of sex workers. Thus, in many contexts individuals and communities have little resource to rights and services, as well as associated criminal justice and public protections – mostly notably from the police.

Discursive constructions of the sex worker body are also clearly visible in policy and policing settings. For example in Sweden where the purchase of sex is criminalised, prostitution is described as 'a serious form of oppression of women and children and that efforts must be made to combat it' (cited in Scoular 2010: 18). The harm described here is linked to broader notions of societal and patriarchal oppression; thus this approach is clearly informed by a radical feminist perspective.

Policy approach in Sweden shapes practices of policing. The Network for Sex Work Projects (NSWP hereafter) (2014) report that one of the outcomes of the criminalisation of the purchase of sex is that police enforcement often focuses on street-based sex workers. Sustained enforcement against street-based sex workers has reportedly led to a drop in the number of clients, meaning women have fewer options in terms of customers and may feel unable to reject those they might have otherwise (NSWP 2014). It was also reported some sex workers may have felt they had to offer services they would not have if there had been more choice of clients, and charge less given the fewer number of clients which also leads to increased competition. Further, evidence suggests that individuals who have moved off street but continue to sell sex are operating in less visible spaces and away from the purview of services (NSWP 2014).

Comparatively, evidence from New Zealand, where sex work has been decriminalised and a more rights-based approach has been taken, demonstrates a more progressive model of policing. The New Zealand Prostitutes Collective played an important role in the process which led to the implementation of the Prostitution Reform Act (PRA) and the decriminalisation of prostitution (Radačić 2017). Evident of the agentic, liberal approach, the process of decriminalisation meant that 'prostitution was discussed within the framework of human rights and equality (of treatment), rather than violence against women or rehabilitation' during the process which is reflective of 'the ethos of fairness in New Zealand' (Radačić 2017: 10). Thus, the diversity and heterogeneity of the experience of sex workers was recognised, reflecting a more liberal/sex positive feminist approach.

Given that in New Zealand the exchange of sex between consenting adults in a variety of spaces and contexts is no longer a criminal matter, policing plays out in very different ways to Sweden. Although decriminalisation should not be posited as a panacea, and changes in national legal framework will not impact on negative societal attitudes towards the sex industry and entrenched stigma overnight, a change in legal framework does have the potential to shape the relationship between sex workers and law enforcement in progressive ways. Armstrong reported in 2010 that, although there were some negative aspects of the change in law in relation to policing for street sex workers (fewer street clients; increased police presence frightening clients away; reluctance to report violence), a decriminalised framework enabled important first steps towards the police playing a role in ensuring the well-being of sex workers. Since 2010, relationships between sex workers and the police have reported to have improved even further. Armstrong (2016) reports that decriminalisation provides space for sex workers to challenge negative or inappropriate police behaviour, facilitate information sharing and foster a positive and proactive relationship to facilitate safety (see also Chapter 4 this collection).

Perhaps one of the key issues through which practices of policing law and sex work coalesce is trafficking. Radical feminist theorisations construct trafficking as an exploitative practice which is intrinsic to sex work – migrant sex workers are not considered within this paradigm. Liberal feminists explore the nuances of the debate and recognise the complex and dynamic ways in which people move nationally and internationally, with or without the intention of selling sex but ultimately end up working in the industry – as part of which people have myriad experiences (see Mai 2009). The policing of trafficking and the search for trafficked victims are something which is discussed by contributors in this volume, but is also an important theme in the literature internationally. Jahnsen and Skilbrei (2017: 14) have explored this in Norway, specifically analysing how national criminal and immigration penal frameworks intersect with state provisions around welfare, with victims of trafficking being excluded from such benefits unless they are 'willing to be rehabilitated' and . . . comply with standards of responsible victimhood.' They also describe how police tactics are used in a carte blanche fashion to seek out victims of trafficking. For example, in Oslo, *Operasjon Husløs* (Operation Houseless) was a pre-emptive operation targeting trafficking as part of which indoor prostitution venues were identified and sex workers and clients questioned. Landlords were contacted, and venues where Eastern European, Asian and African women worked were particularly targeted.

These tactics are also reflected in policing practices elsewhere: for example, the raids on brothels in Soho and Chinatown in London in October 2016 wherein six massage parlours were stormed by police, 'bringing to justice those who seek to profit from the exploitation of vulnerable people' (Metropolitan Police 2016: np). At the same time, as it was 'anti-slavery week', other indoor spaces across the UK were also raided. Sex workers and allies protested the raids and in a Joint Statement described the police action of raiding as 'alarming' and paying 'scant regard for welfare despite claims to be addressing vulnerability' (NUM et al. 2016: np). The fact that the media were present at the raids taking photographs was especially troubling. No victims of trafficking were found through the raids. This is not to say that police intervention is not required to tackle the very serious crime of sex trafficking – but that responses should be appropriate, proportionate, evidence-based and in line with national guidelines (NPCC 2016).

The contemporary role of the police

Understanding how the police intersect with the operation of the sex industry must be placed in the broader context of policing sexuality. The contemporary landscape of policing sexuality has been documented (Johnson and Dalton 2012) where discussions ensue about the policing of private consensual sexual behaviour and practices. Indeed, those aspects of private life that have generally been left outside the law in liberal democratic societies are now being included in legal regulation and public policing. The regulation of sex more generally has been noted as a growing concern for neoliberal governments (Phoenix and Oreton 2001), and identified as an area of intense policy and legal intervention. Whilst there are areas which have traditionally been heavily outlawed and policed such as sex between men and public sex, cultural and legal approaches to other types of non-normative sex have been subjected to state interventions through laws and criminal justice processes. Whilst it is often assumed that the policing of 'deviant' sexualities is tied closely with religiously dominated nation states, where morality is the daily business of the police, the ways in which sexuality is policed in modern democratic states has in some regards become a problematic issue of human rights. There have evidently been massive changes to how some sexualities are treated by the state – Moran's (2012) analysis of the 'minor revolution' that has taken place for men who have sex with men in the UK regarding their place as legitimate citizens who should have the same access to safety and justice as all other citizens, is a sound example of such revolutionary changes in the policing of sexuality. Yet in many ways, as this collection of new empirical evidence testifies, the shift in policing sexualities has not had the same effects for those engaged in commercial sex, either as sellers, buyers or organisers.

Political debate, media coverage and on-the-ground practice interventions have been increasingly concerned with how the sex industry is policed and by whom. The state's role in regulating the sex industry is rarely off the political radar as governments wrestle with the exponential growth of sexual commerce, global issues such as sex trafficking and the migration of people for voluntary entry into sex work, as well as localised policies which demand new and different solutions to old, endemic gendered issues. Media attention straddles troubling accounts of police misconduct in relation to dishonest and abusive engagement with sex workers, and championing innovative (as well as politically risky) policing methods used to keep sex workers safe and confront victimisation and crime. The police walk a difficult line of enforcement and enabling, as the complexities of the law and neoliberal sex markets means the sex industry is one of the most difficult terrains to navigate because of the legal/illegal nexus where much commercial sex work sits. Within this complex landscape there are crimes of exploitation, violence and trafficking which demand the attention of law enforcement agencies to protect the most vulnerable in society and bring the full force of the law down upon perpetrators. Yet there is also much professional practice, with groups and individual sex workers operating under entrepreneurial business models despite their quasi-criminalised status, which can be equally challenging for police services to manage due to the very blunt and outdated tools they have at their discretion. This collection addresses these complexities in terms of examining the role of the police in relation to the regulation of sex work by drawing on cutting edge research and commentary about policing activities and policy initiatives which enable the development of policing scholarship in this area.

Police abuses, mistreatments and malpractices

Dynamics between the police and sex workers have been documented over time, demonstrating the strained power relations, tensions and intersectional gender abuses which have become commonplace in many jurisdictions. The publication Research for Sex Work in 2005 (an output from the Global Network of Sex Work Projects) provides a comprehensive example of the lived experiences of sex workers from different parts of the world who were encountering mainly difficult relationships and practices with the police. Crago et al. (2010) have since provided some detailed statistics and qualitative data across 11 countries in Europe and Central Asia which document the continued police harassment and mistreatment experienced by male, female and transgender sex workers (also see Odinokova et al. 2014 regarding Russia).

Research also shows that even where there is no direct harassment and mistreatment, the presence of heavy policing and crackdowns creates a dangerous environment for sex workers, particularly on the streets (Sanders 2004) but also for those who work from indoor environments (O'Doherty 2011). Latest evidence from Canada (Vancouver) where police changed their policy approach to focus on customers and not sex workers still demonstrates the negative effects of criminalisation through rushed negotiations due to police presence, resulting in notably high levels of vulnerability for the street-based workers (Landsberg et al. 2017). Huang and Pan (2014) note the range of responses that sex workers had to intense raids on their premises and work locations in China. Reporting on what was to date one of the largest Chinese government enforcements of prostitution laws in 2010, their study documents several strategies employed by sex workers in response to police actions, including increasing mobility and visibility of their sex work and taking more sexual health risks to accommodate clients. Other research suggests that the 'policing' goes beyond the formal state controls and is hijacked by community residents and groups who use their own methods of policing prostitution (Sagar 2005; Kingston 2013), some of which result in vigilantism and crimes against sex workers due to severe levels of intolerance and hatred (Hubbard 1998; Kinnell 2008). As Kunkel (2017) describes through the policing of prostitution in the legalised county of Frankfurt in Germany, the 'contested visibility' of commercial sex, evident through community protests, is one of the diversions for the police who must attend to public order occurrences which are at odds with the protection of sex workers who are working legally in brothels.

There are other concerns around policing practices which relate to the specific treatment of transgender sex workers (covered in this collection in Chapter 2). Whilst documented more readily by NGO organisations and activist groups over many years, research findings have begun to expose the treatment of transgender sex workers by the police and notifiable differences have been logged. Nichols (2010) flags up the victimisation of male-to-female transgender sex workers in Sri Lanka who often experience mistreatment at the hands of the police (building on work from others such as Kulick 1998 and Miller 2002). Targeted for both their feminine gender expression and their homosexuality, this group experiences unequal police treatment, as well as accounts of verbal, physical and sexual abuse.

Using condoms as part of police raids and evidence-gathering protocols is increasingly being reported across the world. Whilst there are some elements of expectation that such draconian activities would be happening in countries where there are strict laws and punishments around commercial sex, it is somewhat shocking to note how this practice is spreading in Western territories. Open Societies Foundation (2012) in their publication *Criminalizing Condoms* reports how the condom is considered contraband specifically in Kenya, Namibia, Russia, South Africa, the United States and Zimbabwe. Respondents reported a range of police behaviours from intimidation and harassment for doing sex work. Because of extortion, taking or destroying condoms and using condoms as evidence of sex work, many are afraid to carry them because of these potential consequences. Some of this behaviour was officially sanctioned by the police in these jurisdictions; in other countries, using condoms as evidence for law breaking was considered part of the police culture and abusive disregard for sex workers. This trend is evidenced throughout the world and is turning into a prolific activity in jurisdictions where sex work is criminalised. The Human Rights Watch (McLemore 2012) in the United States produced a detailed piece of research interviewing 200 sex workers about their relationships and experiences with the police across four cities – New York, Washington, D.C., Los Angeles and San Francisco. The findings suggest:

> police stop, search, and arrest sex workers using condoms as evidence to support prostitution charges. For many sex workers, particularly transgender women, arrest means facing degrading treatment and abuse at the hands of the police. For immigrants, arrest for prostitution offenses can mean detention and removal from the United States.

In our collection, Jahnsen continues with this theme, demonstrating how policing activities in Norway are adopting these practices as part of their everyday policing (see Chapter 8).

The public health implications of such practices have caused alarm amongst medical practitioners and associations, noting the relationships between policing practices and public health successes with marginalised and vulnerable groups.

Footer et al. (2016) note from a systematic review of 137 articles where 14 studies were found to yield some data on policing practices and HIV, *'there is a strong relationship between police practices and sex workers' HIV risk behaviours and HIV and STI infection'* (2016: 11). Such findings have been supported in the past by the UNAIDS Advisory Group on HIV and Sex Work (UNAIDS 2009) who have evaluated the evidence and summarised that criminalisation leaves sex workers open to more vulnerability and abuse and does not have the desired effects of reducing demand or removing sex work from the streets. Studies across individual countries show starkly the links between police practices, abuses and sex worker vulnerability to HIV and STIs. One example from a team working in India, Erausquin et al. (2011), conducted logistical regressions on survey data from 835 female sex workers which indicated that police-related experiences were heavily connected to HIV risk behaviours and violence. The study found that reports of having sex with police to avoid interventions, giving gifts to police, having police take condoms away and being arrested were all associated with contraction of STIs, inconsistent condom use, acceptance of more money for sex without a condom and experience of client violence (Erausquin et al. 2011: S1223).

Cultural and policy changes within the police

The recognition of violence (Deering et al. 2014), targeted hate crime (Campbell 2014) and the continual risks embedded in criminalised environments (Kinnell 2008) have slowly begun to infiltrate policing practices in the UK. Chapters in this collection from Feis-Bryce and Campbell begin to show the small changes which are happening in policy and practice, but the lack of legal strength and compliance at a national level means that sex work continues to operate in a criminalised framework. The need for policing partnerships to be at the fore of new forms of working with the sex industry, particularly where the agenda is protectionist in the face of client violence, has been evidence-based for over a decade (Penfold et al. 2004). These themes are picked up by Armstrong in the context of decriminalisation in New Zealand (Chapter 4) and Sagar and Jones in the Welsh context (Chapter 5). Having a strong message that sex work should be policed through the lens of protection rather than enforcement wherein sex workers are constructed as offenders is now established in policy in the UK, but as Feis-Bryce identifies, the plurality of policing across the 43 forces in England means that there are different models in operation from hard level enforcement to innovative models of legalisation and decriminalisation. We see innovation taking place in the city of Leeds in the UK (Brown and Sanders 2017), where through consultation with the residents, business community, police, local authority and allied support projects, a 'free from arrest' managed area has been in operation since 2015. This example of an effective partnership in terms of multiple agencies coming together to create a workable model where protection is prioritised, suggests that with official support cultural attitudes within the organisation of the police can shift. There are other reports across the world (from Canada for example) where policing shifts have been noted despite the criminalised frameworks persisting. Krusi et al. (2016) note how in Vancouver, Canada, the shift from arrest-based policing strategies to those which prioritised safety of sex workers has resulted in a notable change on the ground in terms of how sex workers experience police attitudes and practices. Yet still there is a persistent concern that changes are rhetoric and that policy does not translate into practice: Krusi et al. (2016) report how police continued to deny sex workers their citizenship rights leading to a responsibilisation of their own victimisation. The disjunction between policy and practice is explored throughout the chapters in this collection.

The momentum for decriminalisation

Despite further criminalisation and enforcement-led policing, there has been momentum forward to halt the penalisation of sex workers through the promotion of human rights models of approaching the sex industry. Usually relying on a wealth of evidence from over a decade of decriminalisation in New Zealand (Abel et al. 2010; Armstrong 2015, 2016), supporting the rights of sex workers through occupational and health legislation and policy rather than criminal frameworks has produced a different type of environment and attitude for sex work to happen. Whilst there is no immediate quick fix to centuries' old cultural discourses around stigma and sex work and simply changing the law to decriminalise sex work does not dissipate violence immediately, the evidence for enabling the rights of sex workers to be accessed within a decriminalisation model is evident.

Since full decriminalisation of sex work in New Zealand in 2003, momentum for the decriminalisation of sex work gathered pace in 2015 when, after lengthy global consultation and evidence gathering, Amnesty International adopted a policy of decriminalisation which they argued would serve to protect the human rights of sex workers. The dominance of the neo-abolitionist approach towards sex work is being tackled in the UK through political channels, making small inroads to legal change. At a local level in the UK the movement for decriminalisation is evident with a consultation lead by MEP Jean Urquhart in 2016 to decriminalise sex work in Scotland following on from the English Collective of Prostitutes holding a consultation and evidence-giving event in parliament in 2015. This event showcased the support of MPs John McDonnell, Jeremy Corbyn (Leader of the Labour Party), and the Green Party who have stated that they would introduce decriminalisation if in power. Equally, the other main political party in the UK – the Liberal Democrats – also have passed a policy supporting decriminalisation. Other political will is evident: in 2016, the Home Affairs Select Committee cross party consultation on prostitution published an interim report supporting the decriminalisation of sex work in terms of removing soliciting offences and allowing sex workers to share working premises. Individual sex workers are also leading the way on challenges to problematic laws that harm them. Laura Lee, an activist sex worker, challenged the law in Northern Ireland that makes it a crime to pay for sex and in September 2016 she was granted the right to a judicial review of the law. Various elements of the campaign to remove problematic laws which lead to problematic policing of a group of sex workers, some of whom are vulnerable, demonstrates the complexity of both the politics of prostitution and policing. We can see this in the plurality of policing activities that are evident within one jurisdiction as well as between neighbouring nations.

Structure of the collection and methodological considerations

Within the context of what we know about the relationship between the police and the sex industry, this edited collection provides room for recent research and commentary that interrogates, exposes and discusses the complexities of policing operations in relation to the sex industry. More contemporary reflections and evidence are needed to document how the police approach sex workers, how they engage with the sex industry and take forward intelligence to intersect serious transnational crimes such as sex trafficking. There are also examples of where policing approaches surpass domestic law due to calls for decentralisation, with local partnership agreements coming up with innovative policies based on principles of protection and welfare. These are often least talked about amidst the political discourses that aim to 'eradicate prostitution' and 'reduce the demand for purchasing'.

This edited collection provides the opportunity to fill these gaps in knowledge by showcasing new research in policing studies which contributes important knowledge about policing to a range of disciplines and audiences. The timeliness of this topic is key given the centrality of the criminalisation of the sex industry on the agendas of many European countries, as the banning of the purchase of sex (originating in Sweden in 1999) with accompanying abolitionist ideology sweeps across Northern Ireland (2015) and France (2016). The governance of sex work is steeped in fractious politics as various lobbies fight for their corner of the 'sex wars', resulting in a complex global politics of the governance of the sex industry (see Sanders and Campbell 2014). The legal reforms and political wrangling about the rights and wrongs of prostitution mean that the role of the police and how policing is done will effectively come under more scrutiny. With this in mind, this edited collection draws on research from the UK, Europe and the United States to offer new insights into the complex and conditional role of the police in regulating the complexities of commercial sex in the 21st century.

The collection is divided into two parts to reflect the key themes emerging from the research here. Not only does the diversity of chapters make for important and rich reading, but the range of methodologies utilised by authors as well as their varied positionalities also make for a particularly dynamic collection.

Part 1 *'Protection through Policing: Plurality and Pragmatism'* explores some developments – particularly in the UK – which are pushing the boundaries of traditional policing around sex work and moving practice forward. Alex Feis-Bryce, as former CEO of National Ugly Mugs (NUM), a national organisation seeking to end violence against sex workers through the provision of a life-saving alerting system, discusses the inconsistent ways in which sex work is policed in Britain. Being a key actor in national policy and policing discussions since the launch of NUM in 2012, this chapter draws not only on Feis-Bryce's practice-centred knowledge, but also reflects on his first-hand experiences of supporting around 50 sex workers per month. Offering an analytical discussion through NUM data, criminal justice data and policy analysis in this chapter, it offers a discussion of the complex legislation in the UK which determines policing, whilst also hinting at the cultural and policy changes that are slowly taking place.

Drawing on the varied experiences of the authors, with Laing, Jones and Strohmayer being academics whose experiences cross into practice and Campbell being a leading practitioner nationally in the area of male and trans sex workers, Chapter 2 provides one of the first published overviews in relation to the policing and practices of trans sex workers in the UK. Providing an overview of the academic literature, a review of service needs and a discussion of crime data pertaining to the experiences of trans sex workers from National Ugly Mugs, it concludes by making recommendations for future research with, by and for trans sex workers. In Chapter 3, Campbell draws on her knowledges as an expert practitioner delivering front-line services to sex workers in the UK and her vital empirical research on the policing of sex work to explore police powers to position crimes committed against sex workers as hate crimes. Utilising interview data, she considers the experiences of sex workers, situating crimes committed against them within both conceptual and policy frameworks.

The next two chapters in this part reflect on the model and consequences of decriminalisation. Armstrong (Chapter 4) looks at how the police have responded to the decriminalisation of sex work in New Zealand. She offers a critical policy-centred discussion of the impacts of decriminalisation and also the legacy of criminalisation in the context of policing, noting especially how this can impact on the safety of sex workers and reporting violence. Following this, Sagar and Jones (Chapter 5) expose the voices who demand this model in the face of a series of criminalisation laws in Wales. Drawing on findings from a large-scale research project 'Sex Work Research Wales', they find that regulating sex work is not a policing or community priority, strengthening arguments for decriminalisation as opposed to punitive modes of control.

The second part of the collection, '*Policing Operations, Enforcement and Austerity*', focuses on the operational side of policing sex work, using examples from Germany, United States, Norway and the UK to interrogate the ways in which laws are enforced. Relying on innovative methods to expose the realities of policing activities, Leser (Chapter 6) shares her findings of a trafficking raid on a brothel in Germany utilising an ethnographic approach in this area of work to explore the 'absent victim' and the 'problematic sex worker'. High levels of enforcement are discussed by Spivak (Chapter 7) in the context of the United States and his discussion of pimping, coercion and violence amongst street sex workers in Las Vegas. Drawing on a large interview sample, he considers the policing practices and anti-prostitution enforcement approaches used against sex workers. In Chapter 8, Jahnsen takes the reader on the journey of how in Norway condoms are used as evidence in two divergent police districts; and considers how they could be considered a site of 'conflict, interaction and exchange'. Finally, in the UK we hear about the use of Anti Social Behaviour Orders as a tool used for sanctioning individual sex workers in London (Neville and Sanders-McDonagh, Chapter 9). Utilising a mixed-methods approach, Neville and Sanders-McDonagh draw on ethnography, mobile interviews, GIS mapping and semi-structured interviews with a range of actors to inform their analysis. The range of techniques drawn upon reflects the day-to-day practices of the organisations they connected with and their service users.

The collection showcases a range of methodological approaches and tools throughout the chapters, enabling rich and new data to surface, be analysed and made sense of in relation to existing literature and policy contexts. There is extensive academic literature reviewed through the chapters, often bringing together small pools of evidence around seldom-discussed subjects (such as Laing, Campbell, Jones and Strohmayer on trans sex work and Feis-Bryce on policing in the UK). Other contributors have used traditional qualitative interview techniques to speak with marginalised groups – those who are often not asked about their opinions and ideas (see Armstrong, Campbell, Sagar and Jones, Spivak, Neville and Sanders-McDonagh). These tried and tested methods have been applied in different ways to elicit information regarding sensitive topics and experiences of doing sex work (or criminal justice). What this collection brings in terms of innovative methodology is the three chapters by Jahnsen, Leser and Neville and Sanders-McDonagh who have individually applied ethnographic techniques to access often hidden policing activities (a brothel raid in Germany, a police investigation in Norway and street outreach in the UK) to consider the long-term policing activities and interventions into the policing of sex work. More innovative mixed-methods approaches, such as Neville and Sanders-McDonagh in Chapter 9, using GIS mapping to plot routes taken by outreach staff, show the fertile methodological designs that these complex questions demand. It is these original empirical projects and the analysis of data which has enabled this collection to shed new light on the complex issues relating to sex work, policing and criminal justice. We hope this brings new information to diverse audiences and continues to spark the campaign for social justice for sex workers.

References

Abel, G., Fitzgerald, L., Healy, C., and Taylor, A. (Eds.) (2010) *Taking the crime out of sex work: New Zealand sex workers' fight for decriminalisation*. Bristol, UK: Policy Press, p. 271.

Amnesty International. (2015) *Global movement votes to adopt policy to protect human rights of sex workers*. Available at: www.amnesty.org/en/latest/news/2015/08/global-movement-votes-to-adopt-policy-to-protect-human-rights-of-sex-workers/ (Accessed 16 May 2017).

Armstrong, L. (2010) 'Out of the shadows (and into a bit of light): Decriminalisation, human rights and street-based sex work in New Zealand', in Hardy, K., Kingston, S., and Sanders, T. (Eds.) *New sociologies of sex work*. Surrey: Ashgate, pp. 39–56.

Armstrong, L. (2015) '"Who's the slut, who's the whore?" Street harassment in the workplace among female sex workers in New Zealand', *Feminist Criminology*, 11 (3), 285–303.

Armstrong, L. (2016) 'From law enforcement to protection? Interactions between sex workers and police in a decriminalized street-based sex industry', *British Journal of Criminology*, 57 (3), 570–588.

Barry, K. (1996) *The prostitution of sexuality*. New York: New York University Press.

Bowen, R. (2016) 'Squaring up: Experiences of transition from off-street sex work to square work and duality – concurrent involvement in both – in Vancouver BC', *Canadian Review of Sociology*, 52 (4), 429–449.

Brown, K., and Sanders, T. (2017) 'Pragmatic, progressive, problematic: Addressing vulnerability through a local street sex work partnership initiative', *Social Policy and Society*.

Available at: www.cambridge.org/core/journals/social-policy-and-society/article/div-classtitlepragmatic-progressive-problematic-addressing-vulnerability-through-a-local-street-sex-work-partnership-initiativediv/C9F1CFBE4864D848478F37087D67A2DB (Accessed 16 May 2017).

Campbell, R. (2014) 'Not getting away with it: Linking sex work and hate crime in Merseyside', in Chakraborti, N., and Garland, J. (Eds.) *Responding to hate crime: The case for connecting policy and research.* Bristol: Policy Press, pp. 55–70.

Chapkis, W. (1997) *Live sex acts: Women performing erotic labour.* Abingdon: Taylor and Francis.

Crago, A., Rakhmetova, A., and Sheilds, A. (2010) 'The police beat you up, demand money and will detain you if you don't pay: Police violence against sex workers in eleven countries in Europe and Central Asia', *Research for Sex Work*, 12, 3–8.

Deering, K. N., Shovelller, J., Nesbitt, A., Garcia-Moreno, C., Duff, P., Argento, E., and Shannon, K. (2014) 'A systematic review of the correlates of violence against sex workers', *American Journal of Public Health*, 104 (5), 42–54.

Dworkin, A. (1993/1994) *Prostitution and male supremacy.* Available at: www.nostatus quo.com/ACLU/dworkin/MichLawJourI.html (Accessed 11 July 2017).

Erausquin, J. T., Reed, E., and Blakenship, K. M. (2011) 'Police-related experiences and HIV risk among female sex workers in Andhra Pradesh, India', *The Journal of Infectious Diseases*, 1 (204), 1223–1228.

Footer, K., Siberzahn, B. E., Tormohlen, K. N., and Sherman, S. G. (2016) 'Policing practices as a structural determinant for HIV among sex workers: A systematic review of empirical findings', *Journal of International AIDS Society*, 19 (3), 1–13.

Huang, Y., and Pan, S. (2014) 'Government crackdown of sex work in China: Responses from female sex workers and implications for their health', *Global Public Health*, 9 (9), 1067–1079.

Hubbard, P. (1998) 'Community action and the displacement of street prostitution: Evidence from British cities', *Geoforum*, 29 (3), 269–286.

Jahnsen, S., and Skilbrei, M. (2017) 'Leaving no stone unturned: The borders and orders of transnational prostitution', *British Journal of Criminology.* Available at: https://academic.oup.com/bjc/article/doi/10.1093/bjc/azx028/3813353/Leaving-no-stone-unturned-The-borders-and-orders#.WRWPniQi6AQ.facebook (Accessed 16 May 2017).

Johnson, P., and Dalton, D. (Eds.) (2012) *Policing sex.* London: Routledge.

Kingston, S. (2010) 'Intent to criminalize: Men who buy sex and prostitution policy in the UK', in Kingston, S., Hardy, K., and Sanders, T. (Eds.) *New sociologies of sex work.* Surrey: Ashgate, pp. 23–28.

Kingston, S. (2013) *Prostitution in the community: Attitudes, action and resistance.* Oxon: Routledge.

Kinnell, H. (2008) *Violence and sex work in Britain.* Cullompton: Willan.

Krusi, A., Kerr, T., Taylor, C., Rhodes, T., and Shannon, K. (2016) '"They won't change it back in their heads that we're trash": The intersection of sex work-related stigma and evolving policing strategies', *Sociology of Health and Illness*, 38 (7), 1137–1150.

Kulick, D. (1998) *Travesti.* Chicago: Chicago University Press.

Kunkel, J. (2017) 'Gentrification and the flexibilization of spatial control: Policing sex work in Germany', *Urban Studies*, 54 (3), 730–746.

Laing, M., Pilcher, K., and Smith, N. (Eds.) (2015) *Queer sex work.* London: Routledge.

Landsberg, A., Shannon, K., Krusi, A., DeBeck, K., Milloy, M.-J., Nosova, E., Kerr, T., and Hayashi, K. (2017) 'Criminalizing sex work clients and rushed negotiations among sex workers who use drugs in a Canadian setting', *Journal of Urban Health*, 1–9. Available at: doi: 10.1007/s11524-017-0155-0.

Mai, N. (2009) *Migrant workers in the UK sex industry: Final policy-relevant report*. London: ESRC.

McLemore, M. (2012) *Condoms as evidence of prostitution in four cities in the USA*. Available at: www.hrw.org/report/2012/07/19/sex-workers-risk/condoms-evidence-prostitution-four-us-cities (Accessed 16 May 2017).

Metropolitan Police. (2016) *UPDATE: Police arrest 10 people in Soho and Chinatown operation*. Available at: http://news.met.police.uk/news/police-arrest-18-people-in-soho-and-chinatown-operation-193026 Accessed 16/05/17 (Accessed 11 July 2017).

Miller, J. (2002) 'Violence and coercion in Sri Lanka's commercial sex industry: Intersections of gender, sexuality, culture and the law', *Violence Against Women*, 8, 1044–1073.

Moran, L. J. (2012) 'The changing landscape of policing male sexualities: A minor revolution?', in Johnson, P., and Dalton, D. (Eds.) *Policing sex*. London: Routledge, pp. 11–22.

National Ugly Mugs, English Collective of Prostitutes, Sex Worker Open University, Sex Work Research Hub, SCOT-PEP and Basis (2016) *Joint statement expressing serious concerns about police and UK Border Agency actions targeting migrant sex workers*. Available at: https://uknswp.org/um/statement/ (Accessed 11 July 2017).

Nichols, A. (2010) 'Dance Ponnaya, dance! Police abuses against transgender sex workers in Sri Lanka', *Feminist Criminology*, 5 (2), 195–222.

NPCC. (2016) *National policing sex work guidance*. London: National Police Chiefs Council.

NSWP. (2014) *The real impact of the Swedish Model on sex workers*. Available at: www.nswp.org/sites/nswp.org/files/2.%20Impacts%20of%20the%20Sex%20Purchase%20Law%20-%20Street-Based%20Sex%20Work%20and%20Levels%20of%20Sex%20work%2C%20Swedish%20Model%20Advocacy%20Toolkit%2C%20NSWP%20-%20December%202014.pdf (Accessed 16 May 2017).

Odinokova, V., Rusakova, M., Urada, L., Silverman, J., and Raj, A. (2014) 'Police sexual coercion and its association with risky sex work and substance use behaviours among female sex workers in St. Petersburg and Orenburg, Russia', *International Journal of Drug Policy*, 25, 96–104.

O'Doherty, T. (2011) 'Criminalization and off-street sex work in Canada', *Canadian Journal of Criminology and Criminal Justice*, 53 (2), 217–245.

Oerton, S., and Phoenix, J. (2001) 'Sex/bodywork: Discourses and practices', *Sexualities*, 4 (4), 387–412.

Open Societies Foundation. (2012) *Criminalizing condoms*. Available at: www.opensocietyfoundations.org/reports/criminalizing-condoms (Accessed 16 May 2017).

Penfold, C., Hunter, G., Campbell, R., and Barham, L. (2004) 'Tackling client violence in female street prostitution: Inter-agency working between outreach agencies and the police', *Policing & Society*, 14 (4), 365–379.

Pitcher, J. (2015) 'Direct sex work in Great Britain: Reflecting diversity', *Graduate Journal of Social Sciences*, 11 (2), 76–100.

Radačić, I. (2017) 'New Zealand Prostitutes Collective – An example of a successful policy actor', *Social Sciences*, 6 (46), 1–12.

Redman, S. (2016) *Female and male escorts in the UK: A comparative analysis of working practices, stigma and relationships*. Ph.D. Leeds University, UK.

Research for sex work. (2005) www.nswp.org/sites/nswp.org/files/research-for-sex-work-8-english.pdf (Accessed 12/07/2017)

Sagar, T. (2005) 'Street watch: Concept and practice: Civilian participation in street prostitution control', *British Journal of Criminology*, 45 (1), 98–112.

Sanders, T. (2004) 'The risks of street prostitution: Punters, police and protesters', *Urban Studies*, 41 (9), 1703–1717.

Sanders, T. (2005) *Sex work: A risky business*. Cullompton: Willan.

Sanders, T., and Campbell, R. (2014) 'Criminalisation, protection and rights: Global tensions in the governance of commercial sex', *Criminology and Criminal Justice*, 14 (6), 535–548.

Sanders, T., Connelly, L., and King, L. J. (2016) 'On our own terms: The working conditions of internet-based sex workers in the UK', *Sociological Research Online*, 21 (4), 1–15.

Scoular, J. (2010) 'What's law got to do with it? How and why law matters in the regulation of sex work', *Journal of Law and Society*, 37 (1), 12–39.

UNAIDS. (2009) *United Nations guidance note on HIV and sex work*. Available at: www.unodc.org/documents/hiv-aids/publications/guidance_note_English.pdf (Accessed 9 May 2017).

Van der Meulen, E., Durisin, E. M., and Love, V. (Eds.) (2013) *Selling sex: Experience, advocacy and research on sex work in Canada*. Vancouver: UBC Press.

Weitzer, R. (Ed.) (2000) *Sex for sale: Prostitution, pornography and the sex industry*. London: Routledge.

Weitzer, R. (Ed.) (2010a) *Sex for sale: Prostitution, pornography and the sex industry* (2nd edn). London: Routledge.

Weitzer, R. (2010b) 'The mythology of prostitution: Advocacy research and public policy', *Sex Research Social Policy*, 7, 15–29.

Part I
Protection through policing
Plurality and pragmatism

1 Policing sex work in Britain

A patchwork approach

Alex Feis-Bryce

Introduction

Currently, neither the purchase nor the sale of sex is criminalised in Britain but there are various pieces of legislation that seek to regulate and forbid a range of acts associated with transactional sex in both an indoor and outdoor setting. These laws, in theory, seek to provide a mechanism for police both to minimise the impact sex work has on the wider community and penalise those who are seen to be either profiting from or exploiting sex workers.

The laws relating to prostitution in Britain have not radically changed in the 60 years since the introduction of the Sexual Offences Act 1956, which focuses on the perceived exploiters and the third parties who gain financially from transactional sex; and the 1959 Street Offences Act, primarily concerned with soliciting. The Wolfenden Report 1957, which preceded the 1959 Sexual Offences Act and provided the tone and justification for the laws we have today, was laden with moralistic language and primarily concerned with the impact of sex work on wider communities, but Hubbard argues that "alongside this desire for order was a concern that it was not the law's role to interfere in the private lives of citizens or to seek to enforce any particular pattern of behaviour" (Hubbard 2006).

The fact that there has not been a fundamental overhaul of the law in this area since the late 1950s, despite the dramatic change to sex work markets and the emergence of the internet as the most significant space in which clients and sex workers find one another, is remarkable and reveals the fear that successive Governments have had when it comes to announcing any meaningful policy changes in this area. Partly due to the dominance of the construction of sex work as a form of public nuisance, which was central to the Wolfenden Report, policy and policing does not always reflect the true nature and spread of sex work markets. This is arguably truer now than ever before, with the decline of traditionally predominant markets: there have been significant reductions in both street-based markets and in managed indoor premises for selling sex which typically take the form of brothels, flats or saunas (Brooks Gordon et al. 2015; Scoular and O'Neill 2007).

Trends and strategies in policing of sex work in Britain have historically been comprised of a number of approaches including regulationism, suppression and, from the late 1980s onwards, welfarism which can be seen as multi-agency responses to conflicting interests around the needs of local communities, sex workers and the front line services which support them (Matthews and O'Neill 2003; Scoular and O'Neill 2007). Sex work is commonly framed as problematic, particularly when it is present and visible in urban areas; consequently, sex workers are often targeted by a range of interventions from police and governing authorities (Laing and Cook 2014). The representation of sex workers in the media and, in particular, the propagation of certain damaging myths justifies law and order strategies designed to exclude and deliberately marginalise sex workers as discussed in O'Neill et al. (2008).

As Sagar and Jones in this collection expose, local approaches to policing sex work are driven by several complex factors. These include: political pressure, often driven by the vocal concerns of residents (Sagar and Croxall 2012); national trends in policing; ideological positions influenced by the media and Government, such as the conflation of sex work with trafficking; the construction of sex work as problematic and inherently exploitative (Laing and Cook 2014); and, more recently, the redefining of sex work as anti-social behaviour (Scoular and O'Neill 2007).

Beyond New Labour

Key legacies of the New Labour Government, in the context of policing sex work and the redefining of sex work as anti-social behaviour, include Anti-Social Behaviour Orders (ASBOs) and Engagement and Support Orders (ESOs) – both of which have been seen to impact negatively on social welfare and access to support services (Sagar 2007; Scoular and Carline 2014). Legislation intended to curb so-called anti-social behaviour was streamlined by the *Anti-Social Behaviour, Crime and Policing Act 2014* which replaced ASBOs with Criminal Behaviour Orders and civil injunctions which increased police powers to use legislation to disrupt and displace sex workers through dispersal orders.

The New Localism agenda, which is now central to the current political consensus, has a significant impact on approaches to policing. This can be problematic for sex workers, leading to insular nimbyism (not in my back yard syndrome), which excludes minority voices, becoming a driving force to local strategies (Sagar and Croxall 2012), particularly in the case of street sex work and visible brothels in residential areas. The paradox of localism is that in theory it seeks to redress marginalisation and social exclusion but, in reality, further marginalises minorities who are not seen as embodying an active citizenship and are therefore often denied a voice (Sagar and Croxall 2012).

Since the departure from office of the New Labour Government, which was heavily influenced by a radical feminist construction of sex work and the 'victim and victimizer' narrative, a more nuanced understating of sex workers' vulnerability has emerged at national policy level (Sanders and Campbell 2014; Brown and Sanders 2017). Neither the Coalition Government, nor its Conservative predecessor, has been forthcoming in attempting to establish a single national narrative on sex work. Instead, the localism agenda has retained its prominence along with the rhetorical commitment of policy makers to a community policing model with local accountability which culminated in introduction of Police and Crime Commissioners, the first of which were elected in November 2012, representing a significant constitutional step towards local policing. In addition, while the legislation was not drafted by the Government with sex workers in mind, the Anti-Social Behaviour, Crime and Policing Act 2014 increased the powers of police to issue dispersal orders to sex workers and increased the length of time of a person's exclusion from a particular area to 48 hours.

Perhaps the most significant direct intervention by the Coalition Government into this policy area was in providing financial support for the establishment of National Ugly Mugs (NUM) to support sex workers when they're victims of crime. A central element of the service offered is a third-party reporting mechanism so sex workers can report crimes to NUM who produce alerts or warnings which are circulated to other sex workers to prevent crime. Although local information sharing schemes have existed in the UK and throughout the world since the 1980s, NUM was the first to be established on a national scale, funded by Government and with formal links to police intelligence systems. In a sense, this intervention can be seen as a move away from the muscular liberal welfarist approach which characterised the New Labour years to a tacit support for a harm reduction agenda and an acknowledgement that sex workers often do not report serious crimes to the police. Following on from the Home Office-funded pilot, NUM has been a huge success, demonstrating that it regularly prevents crimes against sex workers, leads to the conviction of violent serial offenders (NUM Impact Report 2016/17) and has become a strong advocate for evidence-based policy and policing and for the decriminalisation of sex work.

Certain national trends, which emerged during the New Labour years, have retained their prominence in the debate and continue to influence both policing policy and practice throughout Britain. The conflation of sex work and human trafficking combined with the Government's commitment to their flagship modern slavery policy agenda are still persistent drivers of police enforcement in relation to sex work.

The position of the Home Office on the policing of prostitution, recently outlined in a submission to the Home Affairs Select Committee (HASC) Prostitution Inquiry, is that, "Local areas are in the best position to identify and respond to specific issues" (Home Office 2016: 2). With the absence of legislation built on strategic or ethical principles, whether based on the rights and safety of sex workers or the notion that sex work should be eradicated, police forces retain discretion in applying and enforcing the existing laws and are influenced by the range of competing factors outlined above. However, as I will outline in this chapter, the Modern Slavery Agenda, which gained even greater prominence when Theresa May became Prime Minister, has resulted in central pressure from the Government, the National Crime Agency and the National Police Chiefs Council being imposed on local police forces to take action to disrupt indoor sex work markets in an attempt to be seen to be taking action to 'rescue victims of modern slavery'.

Policing in practice

In practice, for as long as the state has sought to police sex work, it has been more common in Britain for enforcement to focus on sex workers than clients or third parties. According to Crown Prosecution Service (CPS) Data, curiously grouped together with Human Trafficking in their Violence Against Woman and Girls Crime Report, in 2013/14 there were more charges for loitering and soliciting than for control offences, brothel keeping offences and kerb-crawling put together. In 2014/15, the number of prosecutions for loitering and soliciting was more than double those for kerb-crawling (456 versus 227). In 2015/16, this gap narrowed but the number of prosecutions for soliciting was still greater than for kerb crawling offences (163 versus 153). In addition, based on data between 2002 and 2012 relating to cautions and prosecutions for soliciting and loitering offences, by far the most common outcome for sex workers who are prosecuted is a financial penalty (see Figure 1.1) which seems counter-productive and inconsistent with the stated aims of most police forces to 'exit' street-based sex workers (Ministry of Justice Freedom Of Information request).

In 2015/16 as compared to 2014/15, there was an increase in prosecutions for control offences (100 from 83), brothel keeping (211 from 182) and a fall in prosecutions for kerb crawling (153 from 227) and soliciting (163 from 456) which could be a sign that the focus of enforcement is shifting in many areas (see Figure 1.2) to the indoor sex work markets or merely a reflection of where the majority of transactional sex takes place (Brooks Gordon et al. 2015). The most likely hypothesis is that the increased use of other legislation, such as Sections 34–42 of the Anti-Social Behaviour, Crime and Policing Act 2014, has led to a reduction in the enforcement of soliciting laws which means that the true level of criminalisation faced by sex workers is often hidden from statistics. The use of these orders in a particular area can be authorised by a relatively low ranking police inspector and failure to comply is a criminal offence. On this basis, the use of such orders, which can be issued with impunity and are only held to the criminal burden of proof if they are breached, is a way of effectively displacing sex workers without being held accountable in court for whether the legislation is being used appropriately.

When it comes to criminal sanctions suffered by sex workers, Government datasets can be misleading, particularly when offences relating to control, soliciting, brothel keeping, advertising and kerb crawling are all grouped together under

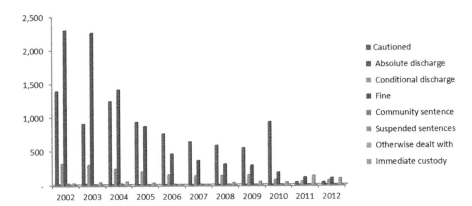

Figure 1.1

(Source: FOI request, Justice Statistics Analytical Services – Ministry of Justice)

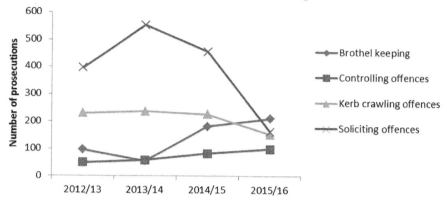

Figure 1.2
(Source: Crown Prosecution Service data)

the violence against women and girls banner. Offences are often introduced, based on a moral objection to sex work, and labelled misleadingly in both the legislation and CPS data. Take 'controlling' offences, for example. As pointed out by Luke Gittos, Law Editor of Spiked, according to the Court of Appeal, the so-called 'control offences' introduced in the Sexual Offences Act 2003 do not actually require force or compulsion and can be successfully prosecuted even if the sex worker is exercising free will (Gittos 2013). Brothel keeping legislation is broad and without nuance, making no distinction between brothel owners or managers and sex workers themselves or people they employ for security, safety or general business support which means that many of those prosecuted under the legislation are, in fact, sex workers.

There is also the notorious 'prostitute caution' – this has become a legal anomaly because regular police cautions require both sufficient evidence to give a realistic prospect of conviction and an admission of guilt by the offender (Mullin 2015). The 'prostitute caution' does not require any evidence of a criminal offence or an admission of guilt from the alleged offender and there is no right to appeal. It is also not merely criminal legislation that is used to restrict and criminalise sex work with civil legislation, which requires a lower burden of proof, being increasingly used against sex workers by local authorities and police. If breached, these orders can lead to fines and imprisonment. The Sex Worker Open University (SWOU), in their written submission to the HASC Prostitution Inquiry, cite Ilford as an example, taken from the Ilford Recorder.

> Ilford police station arrested no fewer than 100 sex workers, handed out 236 cautions and issued 6 ASBOs in the year to September 2013.
>
> (SWOU 2016)

With 43 relatively autonomous police forces in England and Wales, each of which has a Police and Crime Commissioner and a Chief Constable, we are left with a patchwork approach which can vary considerably from one area to the next and is driven by a wide range of factors, many of which are not related to the fundamental role of the police to protect the public from harm. An enforcement-based approach in a particular area may be underpinned by a concerted strategic effort to either eradicate the constructed 'problem' of sex work or move it to another area or it could merely be a series of reactionary responses to public outcry or community complaints. Equally, an approach that avoids enforcing legislation against sex workers or their clients could be based on an acknowledgement that enforcement against either rarely achieves its objectives or it could be due to a lack of resources to commit to what may be seen as a low priority area. Thus, in the British context, policing of sex work is as often determined by default as it is by design.

In many areas police adopt their own interpretations of spacial and sexual morality and how this impacts on the wider public which informs their approach to policing sex work. In response, sex workers themselves often develop their own understanding of how their spaces will be policed and adjust their working habits accordingly (Hubbard 2005; Hubbard and Sanders 2003). In areas with street-based sex work spaces this can create a balance whereby police and sex workers can communicate with each other and share information for mutual benefit. This approach founded on engagement within certain boundaries is incompatible with heavy police enforcement but if cultivated can significantly improve the trust that sex workers have in the police. However, these relationships are often dependent on particular individuals and are rarely built on a solid foundation or enshrined in policy. On this basis, they can be fraught with complexities and can be easily undermined by a change in approach by the police driven by other factors such as recent 'immigration stings'.

Raids of brothels, most often justified by police as a response to intelligence about human trafficking and a desire to 'rescue victims', usually take the form of heavy enforcement. In December 2013, during Operation Companion, more than 200 police dressed in riot gear smashed down the doors of a number of brothels and massage parlours, and sex workers were dragged out onto the streets and photographed by journalists who had been invited along by the police. Police Commander Alison Newcomb was quoted in the Observer justifying the raids on the grounds that it was important to 'close brothels where we have evidence of very serious crimes happening, including rape and human trafficking' but she subsequently stated that 'no specific number of women were suspected of being trafficked' (Townsend 2014), bringing into question whether there was, in fact, any intelligence relating to human trafficking or whether a moral panic instigated by media hysteria had led to certain assumptions being made. Sex workers, after enduring the frightening experience of having their doors smashed down by police in riot gear then being dragged onto the streets in their underwear were asked to complete 'welfare questionnaires'. This extreme manifestation of forced welfarism, which is not atypical in brothel raids, seems more congruent with the state oppression masked by caring rhetoric described by Scoular and O'Neill (2007) that the positive step towards a multi-agency approach described by Matthews (2005).

No victims of trafficking were found and sex workers successfully appealed the closure orders issued by police to a number of the premises on the grounds that 'control' was taking place and 18 of the 20 flats were reopened. In one case, heard at Isleworth Crown Court, the police attempted to use a sign which advertised the premises as proof that there was an unknown individual profiting from the premises. The sex workers successfully convinced the Judge that they themselves had clubbed together to purchase the sign (McLennan 2014). In his written judgement, quoted in the West End Reporter, Recorder John Kingston said:

> [The Met] says that, taking the evidence together, it is clear that, on the balance of probabilities, someone was controlling the activities of the appellants. . . . We disagree. In our view, the furthest the evidence goes is to show that the appellants used the first and second floor flats for prostitution by arrangement with other sex workers at mutually convenient and agreed times. That does not constitute control.
>
> (McLennan 2014)

It was hoped by sex workers and projects supporting sex workers in Westminster that the Metropolitan Police had learned from the mistakes of Operation Companion but in October 2016 they launched Operation Lanhydrock to coincide with a national 'week of action' to combat modern slavery and human trafficking. Six massage parlours were raided and the Metropolitan Police justified their actions as such: 'The operation is aimed at bringing to justice those who seek to profit from the exploitation of vulnerable people'.[1] According to answers to written questions answered by the Mayor of London, 105 police officers were involved in the operation, 24 arrests were made, none of which were for human trafficking related offences and no victims of trafficking were found. Of the arrests made, 17 were for immigration matters which resulted in four people being detained, four voluntarily deported and nine forcibly deported (Mayor of London 2016). So, once again, an operation justified under the guise of rescuing victims of trafficking found none and resulted in sex workers being detained and deported. The two aforementioned operations in Soho, as well as the infamous Operations Pentameter 1 and 2 in 2006 where 822 brothels were raided throughout the country and only 11 people were found to be genuine 'victims' of human trafficking who wanted or needed police help, all highlight how spectacularly unsuccessful brothel raids are when it comes to identifying victims of human trafficking (Boff 2012).

The NUM has evidenced how the use of brothel raids to deport migrant sex workers is becoming an increasingly common trend in Britain fuelled by Brexit and the growing populist, anti-immigration narrative (https://uknswp.org/um/statement/). Both non-EU and EU migrants are targeted; the latter are often deported for not adhering to their treaty obligations which require 'economic activity'. There is a certain tragic irony that sex workers are being arrested whilst they are working and deported for not being economically active. The forced deportation of those labelled as 'victims of trafficking' could, in itself, be seen as a form of abuse, justified under racist border control ideologies, which turns the police and the UK Government themselves into the trafficker (Connelly 2015).

---

1 Quote from Temporary Detective Superintendent Jane Corrigan, quoted in press http://news.met.police.uk/news/police-arrest-18-people-in-soho-and-chinatown-operation-193026

Perhaps the biggest challenge for police service in relation to policing sex work is that police forces are divided into various units which are each judged against different targets and often have competing priorities. For instance, in this context, the work of a detective from a sexual offences unit assigned to investigate the rape of a sex worker is made more difficult by the neighbourhood enforcement officer whose main responsibility is to respond to complaints from the public about 'nuisance' relating to the presence of sex work in a particular area. These competing priorities in what is a huge and diverse workforce characterise the complex relationship between sex workers and the police.

Commenting to the Guardian in the wake of the murder of migrant sex worker Mariana Popa in East London in October 2013, the Assistant Commissioner of the Metropolitan Police Martin Hewitt (at the time Deputy Assistant Commissioner) highlighted the challenges presented to police who are cast in a dual role as both the enforcers of complex laws criminalising many aspects of sex work and protectors of a group who are often vulnerable to being targeted by offenders.

> We are policing a 21st-century style of prostitution with legislation that's fairly dated. We have very contradictory actions. On the one hand we sit down with sex workers asking them to trust us and give us information. On the other hand we are doing enforcement actions. We are all working off outdated legislation.
>
> (Taylor and Townsend 2014)

Striving for consistency

In the context of the complex, confusing and fragmented legislation governing sex work in Britain, the existence of 44 autonomous police forces, and the role of the police as both enforcers against and protectors of sex workers, there is a need for some consistency in approach within a police force and from one force to the next. To respond to this the National Police Chiefs Council (NPCC), formerly the Association of Chief Police Officers (ACPO), produces guidance which is refreshed or rewritten every few years. The aim of NPCC Guidance is stated on the cover:

> Guidance produced by the NPCC should be used by chief officers to shape police responses to ensure that the general public experience consistent levels of service. The operational implementation of all guidance will require operational choices to be made at local level in order to achieve the appropriate police response and this document should be used in conjunction with Authorised Professional Practice (APP) produced by the College of Policing.
>
> (NPPC 2016)

The most recent guidance, launched in February 2016 represents a significant break from previous such documents with a strong emphasis on supporting sex workers when they become victims of crime and building trust to improve the likelihood that sex workers will report to the police (NPCC 2016). The launch of this new approach was described, somewhat misleadingly, in a Sky News report as "a step towards decriminalisation" (Hirsch 2016). There is also a clear message about enforcement and brothel raids:

> "Crackdowns" on either sex workers themselves or men in cars and on foot are at the very best, likely to prove only short-term palliatives and may result in displacement to other areas. Displacement is not a solution and will put sex workers at greater risk.
>
> (NPCC 2016)

The guidance is, to an extent, underpinned by vulnerability narratives, which have been ever present in discourse and policy around sex work (Brown and Sanders 2017) but rather than constructing sex workers as vulnerable per se, the focus is more nuanced and recognises that sex workers are vulnerable to being targeted by offers due to the context in which they work. A good example of the more nuanced tone adopted in the latest guidance is how the document warns against conflating sex work and trafficking and refers to an ACPO commissioned study (Jackson et al. 2010) to conclude that 'the majority of migrant sex workers are not trafficked'.

However, these progressive and evidence-based guidelines, which if utilised could significantly change the face of British policing in relation to sex work, are not enforceable and there is not any requirement to adopt them as policy or incorporate them into local strategies relating to prostitution. Furthermore, there are a wide range of guidance documents and no requirement that police officers receive training specific to them or even read them.

Del Campbell, Policing and Criminal Justice Policy Advocate for National Ugly Mugs, works proactively with police throughout London promoting the NPCC Guidelines and supporting police officers in incorporating them into their practice and policies. He has provided training to over 1000 officers in London across 17 of the 32 Metropolitan Police Borough Commands.

> The vast majority of the police officers I provide training and support to were not aware that the Guidance existed prior to us working with them. Most officers have limited knowledge of the needs of sex workers and the impact enforcement can have but there is a great deal of consensus that the Guidance is useful and will improve their practice. They can be useful for sex work projects to use with local police officer to try to challenge bad practices. However, given that officers aren't routinely made aware of them or expected to adhere to them their impact is limited. My work would in supporting police to improve their practices would be much easier if they were NPCC policy rather than just guidance.
>
> (Del Campbell 2017, personal communication)

Due to the fact that there is not a formal process by which officers are made aware of new guidance, then the responsibility falls upon an organisation like NUM and other sex work support services to proactively inform police forces of their existence. Given the dearth of specialist sex work support services in Britain and the lack of resources available within existing services to provide meaningful criminal justice support, the aim of the NPPC Guidance to 'ensure that the general public experience consistent levels of service' is unlikely to be achieved.

Sex workers as victims of crime

It is well established in the literature that sex workers are often targeted by offenders and for a variety of reasons are often unwilling to report crimes to the police (Barnard 1993; Campbell 2002; Church et al. 2001; Kinnell 2006; Kinnell 2008; Kinnell and Campbell 2001; Laing et al. 2013). Ward et al. (1999) estimated that sex workers are 12 times more likely to be murdered in the UK than non-sex workers. It is also well established that street sex workers face significantly higher levels of violence than those working indoors (Sanders and Campbell 2007). However, a survey of 240 sex workers, which found high levels of job satisfaction and autonomy amongst a sample of mostly indoor, internet-based workers, also found that 47% had been the victim of a crime and almost half (49%) were either 'unconfident' or 'very unconfident' that police would take their reports of crime seriously (Sanders et al. 2016).

Whilst sex work has long been constructed as both inherently violent and as a form of violence in and of itself in radical feminist discourse (Jeffreys 1997), Sanders (2016) argues that the environment and space in which sex workers operate, the modes of governance they are forced to work within, and the stigma and social status attached to what they do create a context in which they are targeted by violent perpetrators. Sanders (2016) also points out that the vast majority of transactions between sex workers and clients are nonviolent.

So far the discussion has focused predominantly on police enforcement against female sex workers but that is not due to any desire on my part to erase the experiences of male sex workers. The main reason for this is that male sex work tends to manifest itself in different physical spaces to female sex work and therefore receives far less attention from the police and authorities. There are a number of male street sex work beats in the UK but these are rarely as visible as their female equivalents, often existing alongside gay cruising grounds (Ellison and Weitzer 2016). Other factors such as the othering of sex workers or the construction of them as either the victims of exploitation or perpetrators of social nuisance seem to be most commonly applied to females. So, whilst the relative absence of male sex work in policy discussions, and to an extent in academic literature, is problematic for a range of reasons, there may be one advantage: that male sex workers are perhaps less likely to be subjected to police enforcement. However, that is not to say that male sex workers do not experience violence and when they do they are even less likely to report to the police than their female counterparts (Bryce et al. 2015).

Reporting crimes to the police

This chapter has thus far primarily focused on how sex work is policed in the UK and the many factors which drive policing in this complex area. In the remaining portion of this chapter, I will discuss, drawing on data from NUM, the impact of law enforcement on the safety of sex workers and, in particular, the likelihood that they will report to the police if they become the victim of a crime.

When a sex worker reports a crime to NUM (or a front line support services reports on their behalf), they are presented with two options in relation to the police: whether they consent for the information about the offender and the offence (but not the sex worker) to be shared with police anonymously as intelligence or whether they are willing to formally report to the police which would involve actually speaking to police and passing on their personal details.

Since NUM was founded in July 2012, there have been over 2,500 incidents reported and currently there are around 50 per month. Both the proportion of sex workers willing to share anonymous intelligence and formally report to the police have remained constant throughout at around 92% and 25% respectively. This clearly demonstrates that while the majority of sex workers are willing to pass on intelligence about the perpetrator, the majority do not want the police to have any information about them which could lead to their identification. The proportion willing to report formally to the police has barely fluctuated nationally since NUM was founded in July 2012, but there is significant variation from one area to the next.

Given that NUM collects data by police force area, it is possible to investigate whether there is any relationship between the approach a particular force adopts and the likelihood that sex workers will report crimes to the police.

As previously discussed, police enforcement activity is driven by a range of factors. Also significant is how sex work manifests itself in a particular area and which parts of the sex work markets are constructed by police, residents and local authorities as problematic. This makes it increasingly difficult to characterise whether an approach by a force is focused primarily on attempting to eradicate or reduce sex work through enforcement or on engagement with sex workers. To further complicate matters, the approach of a particular force may not be consistent within force boundaries and may have evolved organically rather than being part of an overarching strategy or documented as policy; there is no requirement for a force to even have a prostitution strategy. It is thus possible to have a patchwork approach to policing sex work within one particular force area.

A tale of two cities – engagement versus attempting to 'end demand' through enforcement

Lancashire Police is a strong example both of how policing approaches can vary within a force and of the impact a specific policing approach can have on the likelihood that sex workers will report to the police. The force's visible sex work profile is focused on the four urban areas of Blackpool, Preston, Burnley and Blackburn. Blackpool's sex work population is made up predominantly of indoor premises; Preston has some visible indoor and outdoor sex work; Burnley and Blackburn's visible sex work population is mainly comprised of relatively small street sex work beats. The force has a progressive prostitution strategy and most division units within the force have traditionally worked proactively with partners to safeguard sex workers, avoiding enforcement activities where possible.

However, in Blackburn prior to 2013, the police pursued a heavy enforcement approach aimed at reducing street sex work. In 2012/13 (see Figure 1.3) only

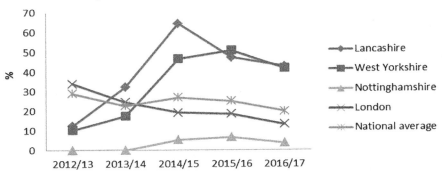

Figure 1.3
(Source: National Ugly Mugs reporting data)

around 12.5% of sex workers were willing to report to the police in Lancashire. If we interrogate the data further, in 2012/13 the majority of the incidents reported to NUM in Lancashire Force were from Blackburn and only one sex worker targeted in Blackburn was willing to report to the police in that period. The Jarman Centre, the local NHS support project, supported by NUM at strategic level, lobbied to change local policing practice in Blackburn to reflect the aims of the wider Force strategy. This change brought about a significant increase in the proportion of sex workers reporting to the police when they become the victim of a crime in Blackburn, from 17% in 2012/13, 35% in 2014/15 to 92% in 2014/15. Since the change in Blackburn, Lancashire Police has consistently been the area with the highest proportion of sex workers who report crimes to NUM being willing to formally report to the police (see Figure 1.3). In Cooper's (2016) research in Blackpool, which falls within Lancashire Police Force area, sex workers also reported positive relationships with police.

In contrast, a force with consistently the lowest levels of reporting to police is Nottinghamshire Police whose approach is based on enforcement. According to their submission of written evidence to the HASC Prostitution Inquiry, "It has always been a significant part of our approach to reduce prostitution by tackling the demand through enforcement". Clients of sex workers are frequently arrested and required to attend a 'rehabilitation' programme.

> Since 2004 we have dealt with 1590 men caught attempting to purchase a sexual act on the streets of Nottingham. Of these 945 have attended a one-day rehabilitation programme known as the Change Course intended to address the man's use of prostitution.
>
> (Nottinghamshire Police 2016)

As well as attempting to eradicate sex work, the Nottinghamshire Police approach is partly founded on a desire to acquire as much DNA as possible from sex buyers, which, they believe, could assist in identifying perpetrators of crimes in future.

Men attending the Change Course will receive a police caution at the end of the day and men attending court a conviction. This allows us to capture photographic, fingerprint and DNA identity evidence from all of these men.

(Nottinghamshire Police 2016)

In their submission to the HASC Inquiry, they claim that 'reporting of sexual offences and violence against those involved in prostitution has been improved' by their approach but provide no data which substantiates the claims. In fact, it is clear from NUM reporting data that the vast majority of sex workers who are victims of crime in Nottinghamshire do not want to report to the police. Since 2012, NUM has dealt with 62 incidents of crime against sex workers in Nottingham, including four rapes, four attempted rapes, nine other sexual assaults and 32 violent attacks. Only two of the sex workers targeted by offenders in these incidents were willing to report to the police (see Figure.1.3). So, the approach by Nottinghamshire Police, which focuses predominantly on attempting to use enforcement against the clients of street sex workers, has resulted in the vast majority of sex workers being unwilling to report often very serious crimes to the police. Thus, targeting clients has a direct impact on the trust sex workers themselves have in police.

The 'managed approach': from enforcement to engagement

Whilst the Nottinghamshire approach is influenced by more normative and less nuanced vulnerability narratives which construct the clients of sex workers as exploiters, Brown and Sanders (2017) point to the recent policy changes in Leeds as an example of a more inclusive and rights-based approach founded on a more nuanced interpretation of the vulnerability of sex workers.

West Yorkshire Police's (the Force jurisdiction in which Leeds sits) approach in this area had historically focused on enforcement and this was reflected by the fact that prior to 2013/14 only a very small proportion of sex workers were willing to report to the police when they became victims of crime (see Figure.1.3). However, the Leeds Strategic Partnership Group recognised that after 'a decade of complaints, a failed cycle of sanction and enforcement focused policing', it was necessary to reconsider their approach (Sanders and Sehmbi 2015). From 2014, there was a general move away from enforcement, combined with the establishment of a dedicated liaison officer who would never be involved in enforcement actions but would support sex workers if they become victims of crime. Perhaps the most significant, and certainly the most controversial, element of the Safer Leeds Strategy was the establishment of a 'managed area' comprised of streets away from residential houses in which street sex work could take place with specific operational rules and neither the sex workers nor the clients would be subject to arrest. In terms of improving the relationship between sex workers and the police and increasing the amount of intelligence about dangerous offenders being shared with the police, the policy has been a marked success and the independent evaluation found that:

A year on under the pilot scheme, 2014/2015, there has been a significant increase in reporting. From 1st April up until March 31st 2015, 73 reports had been taken by Basis Sex Work Project (formerly Genesis) . . . and an increase to 50% was reported with full details to the police. In first quarter of 2015/2016 100% of ugly mugs reports made were formally reported to the police.

(Sanders and Sehmbi 2015: 1)

This was founded on the fact that the change in policy had removed the fear of arrest allowing the women to focus on getting and conducting business in the safest possible way. Since the policy change, there have also been a number of convictions for serious offenders who targeted sex workers and whilst the proportion of offences reported to the police increased significantly, the number of incidents of crime reported to NUM and other supported services actually decreased in 2016, which could lead to the conclusion that sex workers are less frequently targeted by offenders in Leeds since the adoption of the managed area. In addition to improved levels of trust, there was a significant reduction in the number of complaints from residents and a better understanding from the community about street sex work.

The Safer Leeds strategy is an example of how a more nuanced approach, balancing the needs of the community, without overlooking the rights and safety of sex workers as members of that community, can achieve positive results relatively quickly and lead to a more effective use of police resources. However, recent actions by enforcement agencies, in this case the UK Border Agency, in the managed area represent a powerful reminder of how successful local practice can be undermined by interventions driven by broader political agendas fuelled by prevailing narratives such as the moral panic around sex trafficking or, in this case, the emerging anti-immigration populism. In Leeds on 21st October 2017, an operation by UK Border Agency accompanied by West Yorkshire Police targeted the managed area, resulting in the removal and detention of six EU migrant sex workers (NUM, ECP, SWOU, SWRH, Scot-PEP, Basis 2016) for not exercising their treaty rights.

Conclusion

In the context of the complex and often contradictory legislation in Britain and the absence of a consistent, evidence-based policing approach to sex work, we are forced to rely on innovative practice at the local level to uphold the human rights and safety of sex workers (Sanders 2016). It is clear that the pockets of positive policing practice in Britain, in places like Leeds and Lancashire, can significantly improve the trust that sex workers have in the police, thereby increasing the likelihood that serious crimes will be reported and offenders apprehended. Such approaches are often founded on a more nuanced understanding of sex workers as potential victims of crime who may need police protection rather than individuals who are vulnerable per se and without agency (Brown and Sanders 2017; Sanders 2016). The NPCC Guidelines, with the clear distinction between sex work and human trafficking, the recognition that the majority of sex workers are not coerced and the warnings that police action can entrench vulnerabilities and harm sex workers, also represents a significant move away from more simplistic victim narratives (Brown and Sanders 2017) and if adopted more consistently could have been a watershed moment for sex worker safety in the UK.

The NPCC Guidance also focuses on the importance of police forces working with support services to work proactively with sex workers and build trust. In fact, due to the lack of awareness among police officers that the Guidance exists, it often requires support services to make their local police officers aware of them as NUM is doing in London. Sanders (2016) argues that the partnerships between local services and police are key to establishing community responses involving sex workers and support agencies and putting the rights of sex workers at the heart of policy approaches. The vital role of local specialist services in meeting the diverse needs of a marginalised group is also emphasised as key by Grenfell et al. (2016).

However, at a time of writing when the funding for sex worker support services is being cut throughout Britain and changes to commissioning landscapes have resulted in many such services being commissioned not through public health but through violence against women and girls or drugs and community safety strategies, further complexity to the often blurred relationship between enforcement and support agencies has been introduced (Grenfell et al. 2016). Much of this funding is commissioned through Police and Crime Commissioners or local authorities, both of which can take the role of enforcers of laws against sex workers, which can make it much harder for services to remain independent. National Ugly Mugs, for example, who consistently speak out when policing compromises sex worker safety, rely on police funding to survive. It is crucial for services to strike the right balance between working constructively with police as partners but maintaining the critical friend role and not being expected to remain silent when police actions undermine the safety of sex workers. To do so would make support services complicit in state actions which criminalise and further marginalise those they were set up to support.

Connelly (2015: 154) refers to 'the blurred line between help and hindrance' in her research with NGOs involved in 'the rescue industry' which should act as a note of caution for sex work support services whose relationship with funders and commissioners can compromise their independence from law enforcers.

> One interviewee told me that her organisation employs a '*broad definition of trafficking*', one that essentially conflates trafficking and prostitution, in order to secure funding for vulnerable British sex workers. She explained that by applying the '*internal victim of trafficking*' label to vulnerable British national sex workers, they could attract donor funding for a group that would otherwise, because of the pervasive stigma surrounding voluntary prostitution, have been overlooked.
>
> (Connelly 2015: 156)

She argues that the 'victim of trafficking' label makes it easier for the state to exert some form of control over the women and, indeed, provides justification for this control; so by working uncritically in this framework, anti-trafficking NGOs are 'co-opted by the state' and 'their work serves to maintain the neoliberal status-quo', making them complicit in the oppression. By failing to mobilise 'a sustained campaign against restrictive border policies which push women into pursuing more 'risky' routes of migration', Connelly astutely observes that they are in fact justifying 'the anti-immigration agenda' (Connelly 2015: 157). This is what Agustin (2012) calls a 'soft form of imperialism' perpetrated by the rescue industry co-opted by the state.

The fact that the joint operations with police and the UK Border Agency in both Leeds and Soho, discussed earlier in this chapter, took place within a day of each other – both resulting in the detention and deportation of migrant sex workers – is perhaps a warning that the modern slavery agenda, which frequently undermines positive local policing practice and established partnerships, has merged with the prevailing anti-immigration agenda. This should be no surprise given that their goals, to return marginalised people to their country of origin, are often aligned. With police and UK Border Agency operations increasingly targeting sex workers throughout Britain, often with the stated aims of 'rescuing victims' but frequently resulting in the detention and deportation of those 'victims', the conflation of distinct concepts and interchangeable construction of sex workers by law enforcement agencies as either offenders or victims has taken on yet another dimension which can be applied whenever it suits: the sex worker as the illegal immigrant. This juxtaposition of vulnerability narratives with traditional enforcement and deportation of migrant sex workers illustrates just how contradictory policy and policing in this area can be. The same is true of the construction, which gained prominence during the New Labour years, of sex workers as both vulnerable victims and perpetrators of anti-social behaviour.

With the creeping dominance of the populist national trends of both the modern slavery and the anti-immigration agendas which leads to increased pressure on local police forces from national state agencies, such as the Home Office, the National Crime Agency and the NPCC, the principles of local policing, that an approach should be determined by local factors and intelligence, are undermined. With swinging cuts to police budgets, it can be difficult for forces to resist the temptation to tap into the seemingly abundant national resources set aside to combat modern slavery which can further skew policing priorities. This creates the paradoxical situation where local policing prevails, even at the expense of the evidence-based national NPCC Guidelines, except when there is pressure from central Government to pander to populist agendas. On this basis, consistency in British policing is rare and more often driven by ideology and moral panic than by evidence and public protection.

In the complex policy and legislative context outlined in this chapter, it is possible to establish local pockets of innovative policing practice founded on a nuanced understanding of the vulnerabilities of sex workers and constructive engagement with local partners that puts sex workers' rights and their voices at the heart of the process. However, these can, and often are, undermined by the need to pander to broader political narratives fed by hysteria rather than evidence. Thus, with the absence of binding national policing policy, a consistent approach which prioritises human rights and public protection creating a framework for sex workers to report crimes and abuses to the police is unachievable outside a decriminalised setting. We should look to New Zealand where (see Chapter 4 by Lynzi Armstrong) legislation was motivated by the desire to create safer working environments for sex workers. By removing the threat of arrest, more positive relationships with the police have been fostered, increasing the likelihood that sex workers will report crimes and seek help if they are attacked, harassed or exploited.

References

Agustin, L. (2012) 'The soft side of imperialism', *Counter Punch*. Available at: www. counterpunch.org/2012/01/25/the-soft-side-of-imperialism/ (Accessed 12 July 2017).

Barnard, M. (1993) 'Violence and vulnerability: Conditions of work for street working prostitutes', *Sociology of Health and Illness*, 15 (5), 683–705.

Boff, A. (2012) *'Silence on violence': Improving the safety of women*. Report from the Lord Mayor of London's Office. Available at: www.nswp.org/sites/nswp.org/files/Report-on-the-Safety-of-Sex-Workers-Silence-on-Violence.pdf (Accessed 12 July 2017).

Brooks Gordon, B., Perry, G., Mai, N., and Sanders, T. (2015) *Calculating the number of sex workers and contribution to non-observed economy in the UK for the Office for National Statistics*. London: Birkbeck College, University of London.

Brown, K., and Sanders, T. (2017) 'Pragmatic, progressive, problematic: Addressing vulnerability through a local street sex work partnership initiative', *Social Policy and Society*, 16 (3), 429–441.

Bryce, A., Campbell, R., Pitcher, J., Laing, M., Irving, A., Brandon, J., Swindells, K., and Safrazyan, S. (2015) 'Male escorting, safety and National Ugly Mugs: Queering policy and practice in the reporting of crimes against sex work', in Laing, M., Pitcher, K., and Smith, M. (Eds.) *Queer sex work*. London: Routledge, pp. 245–268.

Campbell, R. (2002) *Working on the street: An evaluation of the Linx Project, 1998–2001*. Liverpool: Liverpool Hope University.

Church, S., Henderson, M., Barnard, M., and Hart, G. (2001) 'Violence by clients towards female prostitutes in different work settings: Questionnaire survey', *British Medical Journal*, 322 (7285), 524–525.

Connelly, L. (2015) 'The "rescue industry": The blurred line between help and hindrance', *Graduate Journal of Social Science*, 11 (2), 154–160.

Cooper, E. (2016) 'It's better than daytime television: Questioning the socio-spatial impacts of massage parlours on residential communities', *Sexualities*, 19 (5–6), 547–566.

Crown Prosecution Service. (2014) *Violence against women and girls crime report 2013/14*. Available at: www.cps.gov.uk/publications/docs/cps_vawg_report_2014.pdf (Accessed 12 July 2017).

Crown Prosecution Service. (2015) *Violence against women and girls crime report 2014/15*. Available at: www.cps.gov.uk/publications/docs/cps_vawg_report_2015_amended_september_2015_v2.pdf (Accessed 12 July 2017).

Crown Prosecution Service. (2016) *Violence against women and girls crime report 2015/16*. Available at: www.cps.gov.uk/publications/docs/cps_vawg_report_2016.pdf (Accessed 12 July 2017).

Ellison, G., and Weitzer, R. (2016) 'The dynamics of male and female street prostitution in Manchester, England', *Men and Masculinities*, 20 (2), 181–203.

Gittos, L. (2013) *Britain's crazy prostitution laws*. Available at: www.spiked-online.com/newsite/article/britains_crazy_prostitution_laws/14291#.WJBhE_mLTIU (Accessed 12 July 2017).

Grenfell, P., Eastham, J., Perry, G., and Platt, L. (2016) 'Decriminalising sex work in the UK', *British Medical Journal (Clinical Research Edn)*, 354, i4459.

Hirsch, A. (2016) *Police could stop raids on suspected brothels*. Available at: http://news. sky.com/story/police-could-stop-raids-on-suspected-brothels-10160038 (Accessed 12 July 2017).

Home Office. (2016) *Written evidence submitted by the Home Office to the Home Affairs Select Committee*. Available at: http://data.parliament.uk/writtenevidence/committeee vidence.svc/evidencedocument/home-affairs-committee/prostitution/written/29590.pdf (Accessed 12 July 2017).

Hubbard, P. (2006) 'Out of touch and out of time', in Campbell, R., and O'Neill, M. (Eds.) *Sex work now*. Cullompton: Willan, pp. 1–32.

Hubbard, P., and Sanders, T. (2003) 'Making space for sex work', *International Journal of Urban and Regional Research*, 27 (1), 75–89.

Jackson, K., Jeffery, J., and Adamson, G. (2010) *Setting the record: The trafficking of migrant women in the England and Wales off-street prostitution sector*. Regional Intelligence Unit for the South West: Association of Chief Police Officers.

Jeffreys, S. (1997) *The idea of prostitution*. Victoria: Spinifex.

Kinnell, H. (2006) 'Murder made easy', in Campbell, R., and O'Neill, M. (Eds.) *Sex work now*. Cullompton: Willan, pp. 141–168.

Kinnell, H. (2008) *Violence and sex work in Britain*. Cullompton: Willan.

Kinnell, H., and Campbell, R. (2001) 'We shouldn't have to put up with this: Street sex work and violence', *Criminal Justice Matters*, 42, 12–13.

Laing, M., and Cook, I. R. (2014) 'Governing sex work in the city', *Geography Compass*, 8 (8), 505–515.

Laing, M., Pitcher, J., and Irving, A. (2013) *National Ugly Mugs pilot scheme evaluation report*. London: National Ugly Mugs.

Matthews, R. (2005) 'Policing prostitution ten years on', *British Journal of Criminology*, 45 (6), 877–895.

Mayor of London. (2016) *Answers to written questions*. London: London Assembly.

McLennan, W. (2014) 'Vicar says Soho community feels police "were not honest" about brothel raids operation', *West End Reporter*. Available at: www.westendextra. com/news/2014/feb/vicar-says-soho-community-feels-police-%E2%80%98were-not-honest%E2%80%99-about-brothel-raids-operation (Accessed 12 July 2017).

Ministry of Justice. *FOI data*. Available at: https://www.gov.uk/government/uploads/sys tem/uploads/attachment_data/file/246428/foi-83417-annex-a.xls

Mullin, F. (2015) *The specialist cautions don't require police to follow any of the normal rules, and once they're dished out they make it incredibly hard for women to find work elsewhere*. Available at: https://www.vice.com/en_uk/article/8gdzw3/uk-sex-work-care-jobs-235 (Accessed 1 October 2017).

Nottinghamshire Police. (2016) *Written evidence submitted to the Home Affairs Select Committee*. Available at: http://data.parliament.uk/writtenevidence/committeeevidence. svc/evidencedocument/home-affairs-committee/prostitution/written/29125.html (Accessed 12 July 2017).

NPCC. (2016) *National policing sex work guidance*. National Police Chiefs Council.

NUM. (2017) *National Ugly Mugs Impact report 2016/17*. National Ugly Mugs.

NUM, ECP, SWOU, SWRH, Scot-PEP, Basis. (2016) 'Joint Statement expressing serious concerns about police and UK Border Agency actions targeting migrant sex workers', *National Ugly Mugs, English Collective of Prostitutes, Sew Worker Open University, Sex Work Research Hub, Scot-PEP, Basis*. Available at: https://uknswp.org/um/statement/

O'Neill, M., Campbell, R., Hubbard, P., Pitcher, J., and Scoular, J. (2008) 'Living with the other: Street sex work, contingent communities and degrees of tolerance', *Crime, Media, Culture*, 4 (1), 73–93.

Sagar, T. (2007) 'Tackling on-street sex work anti-social behaviour orders, sex workers and inclusive inter-agency initiatives', *Criminology and Criminal Justice*, 7 (2), 153–168.

Sagar, T., and Croxall, J. (2012) 'New localism: Implications for the governance of street sex work in England and Wales', *Social Policy and Society*, 11 (4), 483–494.

Sanders, T. (2016) 'Inevitably violent? Dynamics of space, governance, and stigma in understanding violence against sex workers', *Studies in Law Politics and Society*, 71, 93–114.

Sanders, T., and Campbell, R. (2007) 'Designing out violence, building in respect: Violence, safety and sex work policy', *British Journal of Sociology*, 58 (1), 1–18.

Sanders, T., and Campbell, R. (2014) 'Criminalisation, protection and rights: Global tensions in the governance of commercial sex', *Criminology and Criminal Justice*, 14 (6), 535–548.

Sanders, T., Connelly, L., and King, L. J. (2016) 'On our own terms: The working conditions of internet-based sex workers in the UK', *Sociological Research Online*, 21 (4), 15.

Sanders, T., and Sehmbi, V. (2015) *Evaluation of the Leeds street sex working managed area*. Leeds University.

Scoular, J., and Carline, A. (2014) 'A critical account of a "creeping neo-abolitionism": Regulating prostitution in England and Wales', *Criminology and Criminal Justice*, 14 (5), 608–626.

Scoular, J., and O'Neill, M. (2007) 'Regulating prostitution social inclusion, responsibilization and the politics of prostitution reform', *British Journal of Criminology*, 47 (5), 764–778.

Sex Worker Open University. (2016) *Written evidence submitted to the Home Affairs Select Committee*. Available at: http://data.parliament.uk/writtenevidence/committeeevidence. svc/evidencedocument/home-affairs-committee/prostitution/written/29160.html

Taylor, D., and Townsend, M. (2014) 'Mariana Popa was killed working as a prostitute: Are the police to blame?', *The Observer*. Available at: www.theguardian.com/society/2014/ jan/19/woman-killed-prostitute-police-blame

Townsend, M. (2014) 'Closure of Soho brothels raises risks for women, says local priest', *The Observer*. Available at: www.theguardian.com/society/2014/feb/23/soho-brothel-sex-worker-raids-priest

Ward, H., Day, S., and Weber, J. (1999) 'Risky business: Health and safety in the sex industry over a 9 year period', *Sexually Transmitted Infections*, 75 (5), 340–343.

Wolfenden, J. (1957) *Report of the Departmental Committee on homosexual offences and prostitution*, Cmnd 247. London: HMSO.

2 Trans sex workers in the UK

Security, services and safety

Mary Laing, Del Campbell, Matthew Jones and Angelika Strohmayer

Introduction

Policy, debate and academic discourse around sex work has become increasingly gender nuanced, especially over past 10 years. This is not to say that the binary of male client/female sex worker does not continue to dominate, but there are an increasing number of voices and attempts to 'queer' sex work in a variety of spaces. Academic research on non-binary, queer and LGBTQ+ transactional sex and other commercialised sexualities has become more visible. The heteronormative, and arguably heterosexist (Smith 2012) binary of the female sex worker and male client which has dominated discussions in academia, policy and media spaces is being broken down by scholars exploring a plethora of performances and exchanges. These include for example the experiences of male sex workers; female clients; online avatars and their involvement in commercial sex; kink and BDSM amongst other practices (see inter alia Kingston et al., 2018; Minichiello and Scott 2014; Laing et al. 2015). Although there is an emergent and important literature on the experiences of trans sex workers internationally (see inter alia Infante et al. 2009; Sausa et al. 2007; Lyons et al. 2017; Poteat et al. 2015), there is very little literature (academic or otherwise) exploring the experiences of trans sex workers in the UK context (see Barton 2017; Mai 2012).

This chapter seeks to address this lacuna, and outline the extant knowledge on trans sex workers and sex work in the UK with a focus on security, services and safety. Starting with an academic overview, we give a snapshot of the existing knowledge base specifically on the policing and security risks faced by trans sex workers. We discuss the myriad and complex issues often faced by, or experienced by trans sex workers in the context of gender, sexualities and stigma. Following this, Campbell, as an expert practitioner having worked with male and trans sex workers in various contexts since 2005, offers an overview of the potential and varied service needs of trans people who engage in transactional sex. Finally, we consider safety through a discussion of data from National Ugly Mugs (NUM),[1] which details violence and crimes committed against trans sex workers. To

---

1 National Ugly Mugs is an organisation seeking to end violence against, and tackle stigma experienced by sex workers, by providing a national reporting and alert system of crimes experienced by sex workers.

conclude, we make some suggestions about where future research might usefully contribute to enhance knowledge and practice around trans sex work in the UK, as well as how spaces might be created for trans sex workers to share their experiences and voices opinions as to what is most needed from future scholarship.

Throughout this chapter, we have purposefully chosen to use the term 'trans sex worker' and 'trans sex work'. We also recognise that a trans identity can be performed, lived and experienced in a multiplicity of ways both inside and outside of the sex industry. As Nicki Smith notes in the footnotes of her 2012 article, drawing upon Browne (2004), recognition of the complex, fluid and stretchy boundaries of gender and sex(uality) is absolutely vital; but in order to present discussion in an accessible way, the importance of also being 'intelligible' must also not be underestimated. The terminology we use of 'trans sex work' and 'trans sex workers' is therefore not intended to be reductionist in any sense; we use it so we can be understood by as wide an audience as possible. In addition, we use 'trans' as an accessible umbrella term to include rather than exclude a diverse range of positionalities, which do not conform to the normative binary positions.

Academic overview

Existing research documents the sophisticated ways sex workers manage their work: from police engagement, to personal safety and negotiating commercial intimacy (Wolkowitz et al. 2013). In addition, there is a growing, sophisticated literature theorising and exploring the lives and experiences of trans and non-binary people (Hines 2010; Hines and Sanger 2010; Stryker and Whittle 2006; Stryker and Aizura 2013). Although these debates are hugely valuable, the experiences and needs of trans sex workers remain largely invisible within these literatures (although see Barton 2017; Gregory 2010; Fitzgerald 2015; Nuttbrock 2017). This is especially the case in the UK. As Smith et al. (2015) note, the erasure of queer, non-normative LGBTQ+ identities from sex work discourse problematically entrenches heterosexist gender dualisms, which do not reflect the diverse realities of sex workers. Despite the lack of empirical insight into the experiences of trans sex workers in England and Wales, there is a developing international knowledge base in this area – some of the dominant themes from which will now be explored.

First, internationally, trans sex workers have been found to experience a disproportionate level of physical and sexual violence compared to cisgender sex workers. Lyons et al. (2017) in their research on the experiences of trans sex workers in Vancouver, Canada, categorise this violence into three types – transphobic violence; gender identity discovery; and police inaction. *Transphobic violence* refers to violence from clients who initially seek out services from a worker advertising as trans but then regret the encounter afterwards, and this manifests in expressions of violence. As one of their participants described when recollecting an incident of a client threatening them with a knife: '*you have to be careful because a lot of people wanna try [sex with a trans sex worker]. And after they've tried it, they get the guilt and they can't deal with it . . . and that's when it becomes rage*' (Lyons et al. 2017: 185). Mai (2012) argues that this type of violence is commonplace for trans sex workers as clients sometimes buy the services of trans workers in order to explore their own sexuality; but then after the transaction sometimes have a negative or violent reaction. *Gender identity discovery* occurs as a result of clients misreading the gender identity of the trans sex worker during the initial negotiation of the terms and services. For example, one participant described a violent incident where a client discovered that she had a penis during a meeting in a public bathroom. On discovery that she was not a cis-female the client physically assaulted her and cracked her cheek bone. Some participants even feared being murdered if clients felt they might have been misled, or if they were not clear about the type of sexual encounter they had sought out. As a consequence, Lyons et al. (2017) identified that, amongst the participants in their study, it had become common practice for trans sex workers to be upfront and explicit about their gender and their bodies from the outset, so as to minimise risks of violence.

Despite their susceptibility to violence and victimisation, the evidence base indicates that trans sex workers experience violence, harassment and discrimination by the police, mainly because of the overlap between societal transphobia and the ongoing criminalisation and stigmatisation of sex work. One report found that this violence and harassment was experienced particularly by trans women of colour (Fitzgerald et al. 2015), thus suggesting that trans sex workers are simultaneously over-policed and under-protected by the state institutions formally responsible for ensuring their protection. For example, the aforementioned research by Lyons et al. (2017) identified a third typology of violence, *Police Inaction*, which describes how trans sex workers were unlikely to report client violence to the police because they felt that the police would not protect them and instead were more likely to arrest them for prostitution and suspected drug consumption. Examples of police corruption and bribery, sexual exploitation, and violence and harassment from the police towards trans sex workers are also found in the existing literature (Sausa 2007; Lyons et al. 2017).

As well as the risk of violence and institutional discrimination from the criminal justice system, the literature also highlights the heightened health risks trans sex workers can face in the course of their work (Jürgens et al. 2010; Poteat et al. 2015). Specifically, evidence suggests that in some studies trans sex workers are more likely to become victims of sexual violence compared to their cis-gendered counterparts, and as such, it is argued that they are more vulnerable to HIV infection and other sexually transmitted diseases. Indeed, Infante et al. (2009) uncovered that risk related to HIV is heightened due to the lack of dedicated sexual health services and support for trans sex workers.

Although these risks exist, sex work continues to be a viable occupation for some trans people, and as the literature suggests, sex workers individually and collectively develop strategies to minimise and manage risk. As such, Sausa et al. (2007) explored some of the benefits and motivations of selling sexual services amongst trans women of colour in San Francisco. The most common reason cited in Sausa et al. (2007) was that it provided a sense of community, and that entering sex work had opened doors and networks to other trans people (see also Ross 2015). This is pertinent given that the evidence suggests that trans sex workers can also be at risk from abuse and violence from their families and partners due to their gender identity and involvement in sex work. Sex work was also seen in Sausa et al. (2007) as a mechanism to overcome workplace and societal stigma and discrimination; providing a sense of independence where they could be their own boss, set their own terms/environment and work with people who are more likely to understand their trans identity. As one participant explained '*Because after a while I gave up, and prostitution was easy; it was easier than going and dealing with society; it was easier than going out looking for a job and getting fired, and I was my own boss*' (Sausa et al. 2007: 772). The same research notes that sex work also provided financial security and the ability to fund hormone therapy and other surgeries. Interestingly, Sausa et al. 2007 found that those trans women who 'passed' – i.e. '[b]eing perceived by others as a particular identity/ gender or cisgender regardless of how the individual in question identifies' (Trans student education network 2017: np) – were more likely to obtain mainstream jobs and be less likely to be reliant on sex work compared to those who didn't pass; thus, they experienced transphobia in society and/or in the workplace (Sausa et al. 2007).

Despite the valuable insight that these international projects provide, their applicability as a tool for evidence-informed policy in jurisdictions outside of their geographical focus is limited. Indeed, cultural context matters in the sale of sex as exchanges and transactions take on different meanings in different places, and can be shaped by legal frameworks, social sexual norms, constructions of gender and sexuality amongst other infrastructures (Agustin 2007). In addition, the context and sector in which individuals operate can shape experiences of violence, discrimination and safety. As Lyons et al. (2017) argue, the experiences of trans sex workers are shaped by socio-structural frameworks made up of social attitudes towards trans issues, legal inclusion and protection of trans people, the availability of specialist/tailored trans health provision and police/criminal justice recognition of/responses to trans communities. As such research/knowledge should exist that recognises these varying contexts. For example, in England and Wales the rights and protection of trans individuals are becoming increasingly strengthened as trans awareness/recognition is becoming a contemporary social issue. Further, the police have worked hard to strengthen relationships with the trans community and now have a National Trans Police Association to represent and protect those police officers who identify as transgender. However, these positive developments are being muddied by national variances related to the policing/ criminalisation of sex work (see Chapter 1 by Feis-Bryce in this collection).

Accordingly, comprehensive and robust research to inform policy and practice in England and Wales is needed to examine the contemporary experiences of trans sex workers to ensure that their aforementioned vulnerabilities to violence and physical/health risks are minimised, that they have access, without discrimination to public protection from criminal justice agencies, and appropriate tailored or mainstream services should individuals choose or need this. Research, designed by, with and for trans sex workers and supporting organisations/practitioners, could address gaps in knowledge including: motivations to enter sex work; client demographics; knowledge of rights and protections for trans people; advertising platforms and methods of advertising used by trans people who sell sex; experiences of the police and informal security/safety strategies (local and national experiences of responding to incidents involving trans sex workers); experiences of violence; relationships with other sex workers; health risks and the impact of sex work on wider trans identities.

Trans sex workers and access to services

Building on the academic overview, this section outlines some areas that services offering provision to trans sex workers might consider. Ensuring appropriate service provision (whether specialist or mainstream) is essential in the context of the safety and security of sex workers of all genders. From outreach (Pitcher et al. 2006; Whowell 2010), to the more formal patrolling of 'managed areas' (Sanders and Sehmbi 2015), services play a part not only in ensuring the safety and security of trans sex workers, but also in terms of ensuring access to criminal justice processes should this be required.

Meeting the service needs of trans sex workers

Front line projects hoping to encourage trans sex workers to use their services need to implement additional strategies other than just marketing themselves as 'gender neutral' or 'LGBTQ friendly'. Indeed, some trans people see the T in LGBTQ (normatively, lesbian, gay, bisexual, trans and queer or questioning) as standing for 'token' with many service providers not having a full or current understanding of diversity in the broad 'spectrum' of 'trans' or 'transgender'. Front line services wanting to offer provision to trans people who sell sex, or trans sex workers – noting that not all sex workers who advertise as trans will identify as trans in their everyday lives; and not all trans sex workers will advertise as trans, some advertise using a cisgender identity – will also need to show insight as to the reasons why trans people are involved in sex work. There needs to be a detailed understanding of what the sometimes specific physical, mental and sexual health needs might be relating to sex work, and in turn the barriers people might face in the context of accessing support services including the police and services within the criminal justice system. For services to demonstrate an in-depth understanding of these issues and also increase perceived accessibility to service users, it could be beneficial to have trans and/or non-binary people as part of the team.

A very common complaint for many trans people is being mis-pronounced, or support workers using the wrong pronoun, or switching pronouns mid-sentence. Project workers should feel comfortable asking questions like "how do you define or identify your gender?" Although it should be noted that such a question can appear confusing/irrelevant to migrant workers because English may not be their first language and such terminology can seem 'jargonistic'. Elaboration may be beneficial, for example asking something like 'do you live your life as male or female?' For sex workers an additional question could be asked 'Do you work as male, female, trans male or trans female?'

In some sex work projects, especially those in London (UK), around 80% of trans service users are migrant workers, typically from Latin America, South Asia and Eastern Europe as well as other parts of the EU. Therefore, resources provided by the service should reflect this and where possible materials translated into different languages should be available. In terms of data collection within services, it is often desirable to be able to record the gender of the service user as they self-identify, in as accurate a way as possible. However, some trans sex workers might identify as both male and female, and see no reason for their trans history to be recorded. A two-stage data collection process therefore offers an effective way of recording this information without forcing disclosure. So, for example, new service users could be asked to first identify their gender from a list which could look something like this: male; female; trans male; trans female; non-binary; other; prefer not to say; and then they would be asked what sex they were determined to be at birth and select from the following: male; female; intersex; prefer not to say.

One common thread in the literature, although further research needs to be completed to ascertain how prevalent this practice is, is the notion that trans sex workers sell sexual services in order to fund surgical or hormonal procedures (Jacques 2010). Front line services should have a working and up-to-date knowledge of what treatment is available on the National Health Service (NHS), alongside what is unavailable to them (for example feminising procedures); waiting times on the NHS (which could possibly be up to two years or more) and the potential risks in getting treatment/accessing hormones abroad or online. It is believed, although further research would be useful to clarify this, that most trans sex workers are male to female (Smith and Kingston 2015), and many may choose to not have lower surgery whilst working in the sex industry.

Some sex workers have reported to services that they often see clients who identify as heterosexual (and it is often perceived by workers that these clients are negotiating their sexuality through purchasing services) and pay well. Workers in organisations providing services to trans sex workers should be comfortable and willing to discuss issues such as this with trans sex workers. In addition, practitioners should also be prepared to speak with trans workers who have saved the money for surgical interventions about plans to either leave sex work or possibly continuing to sell sex under a different gender identity which may attract a different kind of client. Sex workers may also want to discuss concerns about gender history or sex assigned at birth.

Trans service users should also be able to access information from services to get a clear understanding of their rights in the UK. For example, information should be available about the Gender Recognition and Equality Acts. If they are migrant workers, as many are especially in larger urban centres such as London, having correct information about rights is essential and may be complex.

As is the case with other niche occupations, trans sex workers sometimes report to services that they can experience feelings of empowerment in the context of their work, precisely because of them being able to offer a specialised service to a niche market. The downside of this is that trans people have reported feeling 'commoditised' and they question whether their clients are interested in them as individuals or if they are just interested because of the type of services and experiences they can provide. In addition, some trans sex workers report feeling objectified by their clients, which could for some people potentially lead to mental health issues. Front line services wanting to engage trans sex workers could offer counselling and other complimentary therapies. Indeed, in some cases trans sex workers can disclose feeling highly stressed in the context of their work and may respond well to a varied range of well-being-centred interventions such as drama therapy, or group work which can act as a positive response to social isolation.

Some trans sex workers who have not had lower surgery have also reported to services that they have experienced demanding and occasionally violent and abusive clients who present as heterosexual at the time of the appointment. Although some sex workers have strategies and modalities of work to deal with such clients; for those that don't, being unable to manage and respond to difficult and potentially dangerous situations can mean there is an increased chance of risky sexual practices and transmission of HIV and STIs. Indeed, in terms of sexual health, it should not be assumed that all trans sex workers have a full understanding of the risks involved in the work they do. Many are highly organised and manage risk well, whilst others can feel pressurised into offering risky or bareback services. For example, some may offer oral sex without a condom and perhaps be unaware of the risk of sexually transmitted infections linked to this. Trans sex workers who have not had lower surgery are at risk of HIV in the same way that men who have sex with men are. Service providers should be willing to have discussions around regular (three month) testing, condom use and PREP (pre-exposure prophylaxis) and PEP (post-exposure prophylaxis)[2]; and information should be made available about where services can be accessed.

Lack of rights for trans people or sex workers in their country of origin often leads them to work in the UK where they are better protected by the law and have access to health care. In major cities they can also find themselves as being in high demand, often describing their clients as young straight men who want to be penetrated by an active female. Again, this can lead the trans sex worker to feel different types of emotions from feeling special and valued to at times also feeling used and commoditised.

Trans sex workers who want to leave sex work may also benefit from confidence building and life skill interventions from services, including access to workshops/ classes or information about interviewing skills, CV writing, volunteering and work placements which should – where appropriate – respond to concerns about gender disclosure. A trans person should be able to disclose their trans history if they want to, but should also be advised that they are at no obligation to do so; and if they have a gender recognition certificate, they should know that they are legally protected and asking for sight of their original birth certificate is unlawful. Learning new interview skills may be of use to many trans sex workers who might have faced transphobia whilst previously accessing mainstream employment. Trans sex workers by the very nature of their work and their gender often face multiple and layered stigma – sometimes even from their own community – who may see them through a stereotypical lens. However, trans sex workers often voice a desire in the context of service provision to meet positive role models and peers with whom they can discuss the specific issues they might face.

In the context of criminal justice, trans sex workers face many barriers in the context of accessing criminal justice processes and services and especially in the

---

2 See www.tht.org.uk/sexual-health for more on PREP and PEP.

context of reporting crime. This might be in terms of disclosing gender, which in the context of an incident involving sexual violence could necessitate describing/ revealing very personal information about genitalia and their body which could in and of itself be a very difficult experience and process to manage.

As NUM (2017) points out, and as will be discussed in the next section, practitioners and organisations working with male and trans sex workers have noted that sex workers can experience hate crime (homophobic, whorephobic and/or transphobic) when subject to other sorts of criminality including violent crime. This can especially affect individuals who are visibly undergoing transition, or who do not pass as cisgender; and those individuals who do not pass could potentially be more at risk of violence (NUM 2017). It has been found that trans sex workers are less likely to report crimes committed against them; this is because of concerns around being misunderstood or feeling uncomfortable discussing and disclosing information about their gender, their sex work and if they are migrants, their immigration status (NUM 2017). It has been reported by specialist organisations in London that many of the trans sex workers accessing their provision are on either student or tourist visas and therefore need help, information and support when reporting crimes committed against them (NUM 2017). One mechanism that can be accessed by services and sex workers themselves to report crime is National Ugly Mugs, and it is to this we now turn.

Trans sex workers and reporting practices: data from National Ugly Mugs

National Ugly Mugs is an organisation whose goal is to end violence against sex workers. Based in the UK, they seek to provide greater access to public protection, as well as social and criminal justice for sex workers by providing email and text alerts about potentially dangerous individuals posing as clients. The process which originated in Australia in the 1980s has historically been carried out by specialist services providing outreach provision to street-based sex workers, wherein after an incident sex workers would report to projects what happened to them. Following this, the project would then make this report and the information about the alleged offender available to other sex workers by word of mouth, via information boards, newsletters and other media. Although hugely valuable and important work in promoting sex worker safety, one of the drawbacks of this approach is that information is only gathered and shared locally and does not capture offenders who travel. For example, if a street-based sex worker is assaulted in Leeds; street-based sex workers in Leeds might get access to information about the alleged perpetrator, but the same perpetrator could then travel to Manchester, and sex workers there would have not seen the alert about the individual. In addition, those workers operating off-street in Leeds could miss out on the information if they do not access the sex work project sharing the information. These types of local 'Ugly Mugs' schemes are usually only, or better established amongst areas with specialist organisations who work with street sex workers; thus, their reach is limited to areas which have funded projects and usually to areas of street-based sex work.

Sex workers operating online and independently employ numerous strategies to manage safety and risk; and there are online spaces where sex workers not operating on the street can share information about alleged and potential offenders in a peer to peer format. However, National Ugly Mugs enables members – who can be sex workers, or front line organisations providing services to sex workers – to submit reports of incidents, which are then turned into data legal reports (and thus can be utilised in criminal justice processes) which can then be shared widely and nationally to NUM members.

The most recent impact report published by NUM notes that around 15,000 sex workers across the UK have access to NUM alerts; and that 46% of sex workers accessing the alerts had avoided appointments with specific individuals as a result of this (NUM 2016/2017). NUM members can select which regions they receive alerts for, and alerts can be received via text or email. NUM also have a number checker and email checker, wherein sex workers can enter the phone number or email address of their prospective client to see if the information has been associated with any reports previously made by NUM members. The impact report notes that 32% of sex workers who took part in a survey had avoided potentially violent individuals because their number came up as an 'ugly mug' via the number checker (NUM 2016/2017).

When an incident is reported to NUM, the person submitting the report has a choice: they can consent for information about the crime and offender to be shared with the police as anonymous intelligence; or they can make a formal report to the police which would involve sharing details about the individual sex worker and incident with the police (Feis-Bryce, this edition). Since its beginning in 2012, NUM has received almost 2000 separate reports (Feis-Bryce 2017). Around 60 incidents are reported to NUM every month, and from these 25% of victims are willing to make a formal report directly to the police, and more than 90% agree that the details of their report can be shared anonymously; this means that the police have access to intelligence to which they would not normally be party (NUM 2016/2017).

In terms of the membership, at the time of writing (April 2017), NUM have 13 members who identify as 'trans male', nine of whom work privately/independently and the other four put 'rather not say' for their work sector. Regionally these participants originate from a combination of London; East of England; the South East and South West, Scotland, Yorkshire and Humber and four did not specify a region. This does not mean these members only sell sex in these regions. In addition, there are 112 members who identify as 'trans female'. A majority of whom work privately/independently (N = 89), four escort through an agency, one operates from a sauna/parlour/brothel, three are street-based and 15 operate in other spaces which are not specified or the member would rather not say. Of the trans female membership, 110 members are individual members and there are two establishment members. It is not known why there are so many fewer 'trans male' members, although it could just be that there are fewer individuals identifying in this way providing sexual services. Smith and Kingston's 2015 analysis of 27,408 members of a large advertising platform found that of the membership, 33% advertised as male, 63% as female and 4% as trans – and of these 70% as female, 27% as male and 3% as non-binary.

As with the trans male members, the trans female membership is spread across the UK, with the highest number being in London (N = 36) and the only other region having more than 10 members being the Northwest (N = 14). There are however members in the following regions: Northern Ireland, Wales, Scotland, Northeast, Yorkshire and Humber, Midlands, East of England, South east and South west. For 13 members, the region was either not specified or they selected 'rather not say'.

At the time of writing (April 2017), NUM had 33 reports submitted by members recording incidents committed against trans sex workers, the first of which was reported in November 2012. All of the reports concerned incidents committed against trans female sex workers. Of these, 17 reports came from individuals; three came from police services; one was made anonymously; one came from an establishment ('establishment' is as defined by the person making the report but it could include an escort agency, a brothel or even an online space); and 12 came from projects offering support to sex workers which could either be specialist sex worker services or generic support services, for example sexual health clinics and drug and alcohol services. Of the victims identified in the reports, a majority (N = 23) were working privately or independently at the time of the incident; one was operating through an escort agency, five were street-based and the other five were either not specified or working in an 'other' space of work

The type of offence recorded in the reports was varied and in some reports, multiple offences were recorded. Across the data however there were four reports of rape, in two cases the victims were street-based sex workers, in the other two cases space of work was not specified; five of sexual assault other than rape, in one of the cases the victim was street-based, in three private/independent and in one case sector was not specified. There were nine cases of robbery or attempted robbery, six of which were private/independent workers, two were street-based and one was unspecified. There were 13 incidents of violence, nine of which were committed against private/independent workers, three were street-based and one was not specified; one offender tried to remove a condom, another refused the use of a condom. There were two reports of fraud and nine of stalking or harassment, which were largely committed against private/independent workers.

In this edited collection, Campbell discusses the 'Merseyside approach' wherein crimes committed against sex workers in the Merseyside police area are designated as hate crimes. In around a third of reports (N = 12) there was evidence that the incident should be classified as a hate crime as hateful language was used by the perpetrator. Of the 12, eight offenders used 'whorephobic' language (Schaffauser 2010), three used transphobic language and one used both whorephobic and transphobic language.

In terms of reporting, eight people gave consent to make a 'full report' which means that the victim gave consent for their personal information to be shared with the local police and the Serious Crime Analysis Section (SCAS) of the National Crime Agency (NCA). SCAS holds data from police services nationally about serious violent crime, sexual crime and murder. It was set up after a review of the Yorkshire Ripper case and is analysed for evidence of serial or repeat offending (NCA no date). A majority of people (N = 29) gave consent to share their report anonymously with the police and SCAS and for it to be used as intelligence. In one of the cases, the sex worker gave consent to share information about the incident with the police anonymously, and the police came back to

NUM and requested that the victim make a full report which they went to do. In 19 of 33 possible reports, NUM were able to add the alleged offenders' mobile number to their online number checker. In three reports weapons were identified as being used by offenders; these included knives and guns.

In terms of the geography of the reports and where the incidents took place: one originated each from Scotland and Northern Ireland; six were from the North-west; four were from Yorkshire and Humber; three were in the West Midlands; one was from the East of England and nine were recorded as happening in London (Central (N = 4) and boroughs (N = 5). In most reports (N = 30), just one perpetrator was identified by victims; however across four reports there was more than one offender identified with a 'group' plus two, four and five perpetrators identified respectively.

More broadly, NUM have expressed that they would be keen to grow their trans membership, knowing that there are many more trans sex workers in the UK than the 125 members. As Smith and Kingston's 2015 analysis of 27,408 profiles shows, 4% as of these members identified as trans which equates to 1096 people, and their analysis related to just one advertising platform. As an organisation, NUM perceive that there is an apprehension from trans people to join as members because of previous experiences of judgement from services, society and the police. One of the key issues NUM have faced when working with trans sex workers is the lack of knowledgeable trans friendly services to which to signpost, especially outside of London, with many of the generic services not knowing what language to use when speaking to a trans sex worker. As highlighted in the previous section, any service wanting to engage trans people in a meaningful and practical way must be able to communicate appropriately with this group (Swindells 2017).

Discussion and conclusion

This chapter has sought to outline the extant knowledge on trans sex work in the UK. It is one of the very few contributions to the literature which explicitly seeks to discuss the experiences of trans sex workers in the UK (see also Mai 2012; Barton 2017). From this chapter it is evident that much more work with trans sex workers is needed. By with, we mean not just research 'on' trans sex work or 'on trans sex workers' but actually 'with' and 'alongside' or simply 'by' sex workers themselves. Indeed, for many sex workers – including trans sex workers – sex work is an additional or secondary form of income (Bowen 2016), and many individuals operating in the sex industry have varied skill sets, including those relevant to research. Therefore, where possible sex worker-led, or sex worker-centred research should be facilitated and supported through enabling collaborative approaches. Research produced by sex workers and collectives should be centred in academic and policy discussions.

The literature review citing evidence from around the world evidences the specific vulnerabilities some trans sex workers face in the context of their work, especially around embodied disclosure of their gender in commercial sex. As highlighted, trans sex workers are potentially vulnerable to multiple types of violence, including physical and verbal attacks as well as sexual assault and rape. This is also reflected in the discussion of services and NUM data which demonstrates the plethora of offences reported, and this is very likely to be a very limited picture of experiences given the comparatively small number of trans members in the context of NUM as a whole. The types of criminality perpetrated against trans sex workers reveals the multiple stigmas faced by the group; evidently, crimes committed against trans sex workers have the potential to not only be transphobic but also whorephobic. Violence from individuals posing as clients is compounded by what could either be construed as police action (and essentially a poor or inappropriate response) or inaction and failure to respond in a proactive, appropriate and positive way. Although in some areas of the UK, the policing of sex work is more progressive than others, with some services adhering to the National Police College guidelines on sex work (NPCC 2016) and working alongside sex workers to ensure their safety and public protection, in other areas sex workers remain fearful of going to the police to seek social and criminal justice. This might be because of their status as a trans person, as a sex worker or it could be because of migration status, or not being aware of their rights and protections in the UK.

However, this is not to say that sex work is not a flexible and viable occupation for some trans people; indeed, not all trans sex workers experience violence or perceive their engagement with sex work as a negative, problematic or as being a difficult thing. Equally, others may experience it as anyone experiences many types of paid employment – as something which has positive and negative connotations but which suits them at that point in their lives. The sex workers' rights movement in the UK is gender diverse, and within this there are emerging, dynamic and powerful spaces for trans sex workers to engage and support each other.

In sum then, we argue that future research and engagement with trans sex workers and trans people who identify somewhere within the broad umbrella definition of trans should be completed alongside, with and by the community. Given the real paucity of research and accessible knowledge on the experiences of trans sex workers in the UK, this should be recognised as a lacuna amongst the real breadth and depth of extant knowledge on the sex industry. Further research could contribute usefully to three key areas: (i) as an evidence base useful for advocacy by and for sex workers; (ii) as a body of work useful for informing policy and law and finally (iii) to inform service provision, so those trans people who need to access services in relation to their sex work can have a positive experience with knowledgeable and confident service providers.

Acknowledgements

Thanks to National Ugly Mugs for providing the report data which is discussed here. Although National Ugly Mugs provided the data for analysis, the discussion presented here is based on the research and opinions of the authors, and does not necessarily reflect the views of National Ugly Mugs.

References

Agustin, L. (2007) *Sex at the margins*. London: Zed Books.
Barton, L. (2017) 'Compound harms: What the literature says about UK and US trans young people in survival sex', in Nuttbrock, L. (Ed.) *Transgender sex work and society*. New York: Harrington Park Press.

Bowen, R. (2016) 'Squaring up: Experiences of transition from off-street sex work to square work and duality – concurrent involvement in both – in Vancouver BC', *Canadian Review of Sociology*, 52 (4), 429–449.

Browne, K. (2004) 'Genderism and the bathroom problem: (Re)materialising sexed sites, (re)creating sexed bodies', *Gender, Place & Culture*, 11 (3), 331–346.

Feis-Bryce, A. (2017) *'Ugly mugs': The technology saving the lives of sex workers*. Available at: www.theguardian.com/voluntary-sector-network/2017/may/10/national-ugly-mugs-the-technology-saving-the-lives-of-sex-workers Accessed 17/05/17 (Accessed 11 July 2017).

Fitzgerald, E., Patterson, S. E., Hickey, D., with Biko, C. (2015) *Meaningful work: Transgender experiences in the sex trade*. Available at: file:///C:/Users/QWYH7/Dropbox/UK%20Trans%20Sex%20Workers%20Project/Reading/Meaningful%20Work-Full%20Report_FINAL_3.pdf (Accessed 18 May 2017).

Gregory, K. (2010) 'Transgendering in an urban Dutch streetwalking zone', in Hines, S., and Sander, T. (Eds.) *Transgender identities: Towards a social analysis of gender diversity*. London: Routledge, pp. 169–186.

Hines, S. (2010) 'Queerly situated? Exploring negotiations of trans queer subjectivities at work and within community spaces in the UK', *Gender, Place and Culture*, 17 (5), 597–613.

Hines, S., and Sanger, T. (Eds.) (2010) *Transgender identities: Towards a social analysis of gender diversity*. London: Routledge.

Infante, C., Sosa-Rubi, S., and Cuadra, S. M. (2009) 'Sex work in Mexico: Vulnerability of male, travesty, transgender and transsexual sex workers', *Culture, Health & Sexuality*, 11 (2), 125–137.

Jacques, J. (2010) *No wonder many transsexual people end up in sex work*. Available at: www.theguardian.com/lifeandstyle/2010/aug/25/transsexual-people-sex-work (Accessed 17 May 2017).

Jürgens, R., Csete, J., Amon, J. J., Baral, S., and Beyrer, C. (2010) 'People who use drugs, HIV, and human rights', *The Lancet*, 376 (9739), 475–485.

Kingston, S., Hammond, N., and Redman, S. (2018) *Women who buy sex*. London: Routledge.

Laing, M., Pilcher, K., and Smith, N. (Eds.) (2015) *Queer sex work*. London: Routledge.

Lyons, T., Krusi, A., Pierre, L., Kerr, T., Small, W., and Shannon, K. (2017) 'Negotiating violence in the context of transphobia and criminalization: The experiences of trans sex workers in Vancouver, Canada', *Qualitative Health Research*, 27 (2), 182–190.

Mai, N. (2012) 'The fractal queerness of non-heteronormative migrants working in the UK sex industry', *Sexualities*, 15 (5), 570–585.

Minichiello, V., and Scott, J. (2014) *Male sex work and society*. New York: Harrington Park Press.

NCA. (no date) *Serious crime analysis sections*. Available at: www.nationalcrimeagency.gov.uk/about-us/what-we-do/specialist-capabilities/serious-crime-analysis-section (Accessed 18 May 2017).

NPCC. (2016) *National policing sex work guidance*. London: National Police Chiefs Council.

NUM. (2016/2017) *Impact report*. Manchester: National Ugly Mugs.

NUM. (2017) *Trans* sex workers*. Available at: https://uknswp.org/um/safety/transgender-sex-workers/ (Accessed 17 May 2017).

Nuttbrock, L. (2017) *Transgender sex work and society*. New York: Harrington Park Press.

Pitcher, J., Campbell, R., Hubbard, P., O'Neill, M., and Scoular, J. (2006) *Living and working in areas of street based sex work*. Available at: www.jrf.org.uk/report/living-and-working-areas-street-sex-work (Accessed 17 May 2017).

Poteat, T., Wirtz, A. L., Radix, A., Borquez, A., Silva-Santisteban, A., Deutsch, M. B., and Operario, D. (2015) 'HIV risk and preventive interventions in transgender women sex workers', *The Lancet*, 385 (9964), 274–286.

Ross, B. (2015) 'Outdoor brothel culture: The un/making of a trans stroll in Vancouver's West End 1975–84', in Laing, M., Pilcher, K., and Smith, N. (Eds.) *Queer sex work*. London: Routledge, pp. 189–199.

Sanders, T., and Sehmbi, V. (2015) *Evaluation of the Leeds managed area pilot project*. Available at: www.nswp.org/sites/nswp.org/files/Executive%20Summary%20Leeds,%20 U%20of%20Leeds%20-%20Sept%202015.pdf (Accessed 5 April 2017).

Sausa, L. A., Keatley, J., and Operario, D. (2007) 'Perceived risks and benefits of sex work amongst transgender women of color in San Francisco', *Arch Sex Behaviour*, 36, 768–777.

Schaffauser, T. (2010) *Whorephobia affects all women*. Available at: www.theguardian. com/commentisfree/2010/jun/23/sex-workers-whorephobia (Accessed 17 May 2017).

Smith, N. (2012) 'Body issues: The political economy of male sex work', *Sexualities*, 15 (5–6), 586–603.

Smith, N., and Kingston, S. (2015) *Policy-relevant report: Statistics on sex work in the UK*. University of Birmingham and Lancaster University.

Stryker, S., and Aizura, A. (Eds.) (2013) *The transgender studies reader: 2*. London: Routledge.

Stryker, S., and Whittle, S. (Eds.) (2006) *The transgender studies reader*. London: Routledge.

Swindells, K. (2017) *Personal conversation about trans sex workers and access to National Ugly Mugs*.

Trans Student Education Network. (2017) *LGBTQ+ definitions*. Available at: www.trans student.org/definitions (Accessed 17 May 2017).

Whowell, M. (2010) 'Walking the beat: Doing outreach with male sex workers', in Hardy, K., Kingston, S., and Sanders, T. (Eds.) *New sociologies of sex work*. London: Routledge, pp. 75–90.

Wolkowitz, C., Cohen, R., Sanders, T., and Hardy, K. (Eds.) (2013) *Body/sex/work – Intimate, embodied and sexualised labour*. Basingstoke: Palgrave.

3   Beyond hate

Policing sex work, protection and hate crime

Rosie Campbell

Introduction

Building on existing definitions of hate crime to support a widening of hate crime groups and an intersectional approach to hate crime, I have begun to develop a conceptual framework for understanding crimes and targeted harassment against sex workers as hate crime (see Campbell 2014, 2016). This has been influenced not only by research but my involvement as a practitioner coordinating Armistead Street and Portside sex work projects in Liverpool,[1] when Merseyside Police Force were the first force to introduce the policy of treating crimes against sex workers as hate crime, heralding a distinctively different policing approach and relationship between sex workers and the police. The approach received considerable policy and media attention because of the increase in cases of crimes against sex workers being reported to the police, investigated and successfully prosecuted.

My PhD thesis documented the development of the approach describing the varying policy drivers and events, local and national which shaped the approach. This included a historical legacy of multi-agency partnership approaches to sex work which had improved the safety and welfare of sex workers as a key objective (Kilvington et al. 2001), being open to innovation (including in the harm reduction field) and a willingness to advocate for changes in national law and policy. It identified tragic murders of sex workers as key catalytic events in the formal adoption of the hate crime approach in Merseyside. On 15th September 2005, three months after the Armistead Street outreach and support project was established, Anne Marie Foy was murdered, creating local political and public media debate about the safety of sex workers. A review of police policy on sex work was launched producing, 'Sex Workers in Merseyside – Review of Process' (2006), which amongst other things recommended including crimes against sex workers in police hate crime procedures. This was already going through channels for authorisation when, in early December 2006, the horrifying murders of five women in Ipswich took place; the policy was signed off on 15th December 2006.

---

1 Armistead Street was the outreach and support project for street sex workers in Liverpool and Portside the sexual health outreach project for indoor sex workers in Liverpool and Sefton, at the time the approach was adopted. Both were NHS services managed within North Liverpool Community Health Trust.

I have described the Merseyside hate crime approach to sex work as 'an umbrella term for a number of initiatives' (Campbell 2014: 61) including, but not exclusively, the inclusion of sex workers in Merseyside's wider hate crime policy itself. In the more recent 'Merseyside Police Hate Crime: Policy and Procedure' (2015: 2), it is stated that any crime can be motivated by hate based on 'any identifying factor, including, but not exclusively, the following strands of equality: Disability, Race, Religion/Belief, Sexual Orientation, or Gender Identity' and it makes direct reference to the inclusion of sex workers:

> Merseyside Police has adopted the approach that crimes committed against Sex Workers would be treated as Hate Crime. This recognises the fact that violence against sex workers is often shaped by discrimination, attitudes of hostility and prejudice. As such, it required an approach that encouraged sex workers to come forward and report crimes in the knowledge that Merseyside Police would take their report seriously.
>
> (Merseyside Police 2015: 2)

Researchers have identified a range of aspects of hate-crime-policing models from which victim groups can benefit (Hall 2005, 2014), such as training for officers, intelligence initiatives to support prevention, monitoring and detection, specialist hate crime units to offer support and protect victims, and investigation of crimes in line with specific quality standards. My research found the hate crime policy model increased the status of crimes against sex workers, improved victim care, signalled that reports of crime should be taken seriously and responded to professionally, provided a focused team (SIGMA North)[2] with a monitoring and coordinating role for crimes against sex workers, which liaised closely with the project and sex workers, monitored investigations and directly investigated some crimes (Campbell 2016).

Other key elements making up the approach included: close partnership work between the police and sex work project; championing by senior police officers; policing initiatives to proactively built trust and confidence in order to encourage reporting from sex workers; appointing police sex work liaison officers; enhancing the local ugly mugs scheme and promoting a National Ugly Mugs scheme.[3] The introduction of the first specialist Independent Sexual Violence Advisor (ISVA) for sex workers was a vital element in improving victim support for sex workers, recognised as effective practice for supporting sex worker victims of sexual offences (Blair 2011; Home Office 2011), as were the buy-in of both a new sex

2 SIGMA units were the specialist hate crime units set up in each basic command area of Merseyside Police force, with the North area taking a lead re sex worker hate crime.
3 'Ugly Mugs' schemes are third-party reporting schemes, usually run by local sex work support projects, to which sex workers can report individuals who are a danger to sex workers. Legally sanitised alerts can be shared with other sex workers and details about perpetrators can be shared anonymously with the police should sex workers consent. (Sex workers can also be supported in reporting crimes to the police.) 'National Ugly Mugs' (NUM) was set up to link local projects and enable the more effective identification of perpetrators of crimes against sex workers in the UK. Projects and sex workers can join as members submit reports and receive alerts. Alerts are circulated nationally, and report data can be shared into police intelligence systems.

worker friendly specialist rape and sexual offences unit – the Unity Team – and a sexual assault referral centre (Safeplace Merseyside), which contributed to an improved victim care responses for sex worker victims of sex offences, as well as improved investigation and prosecution. Finally, a critical element, which I will return to later in this chapter, was broader changes in the relationship between sex workers and the police which evolved from the police adoption of 'strategic enforcement' and a move towards protection-focused policing.

Drawing on research studying the Merseyside approach (Campbell 2016), this chapter highlights improved relationships between sex workers and the police, locates the hate crime approach on the protection axis of a continuum of policing approaches to sex work in the UK (ranging from enforcement-focused to protection-focused policing) (Campbell 2011) and explores sex worker and police perspectives on treating crimes against sex workers as hate crime. I argue the hate crime approach is progressive and protection-focused; it is influential and cited as good practice in national debates on policing sex work and hate crime (College of Policing 2014; NPCC 2016). It has the potential to be a rights-based approach to addressing crimes against sex workers as it is not limited to notions of victimhood or pathologising notions of vulnerability (Sanders and Brown 2017), particularly at a time when policing 'vulnerability' is to the fore. Yet the hate crime approach has its limits within a framework of quasi-criminalisation of sex work in the UK; hence, it should not be understood as an alternative to decriminalisation, but as an approach which can complement advocacy for decriminalisation.

Methodology

This chapter draws on PhD research carried out between 2010 and 2012 exploring the Merseyside approach. Prior to this, no research/evaluation had been undertaken on the approach or specifically addressing violence against sex workers as hate crime. The methodology constituted one-to-one, semi-structured interviews with 22 current and former sex workers, 38 Merseyside police officers, one police community support officer, two police officers from other forces involved in national policing portfolios, one Crown Prosecution Service representative and 14 service providers or commissioners. In total, 78 one-to-one interviews were carried out. The majority of sex worker participants had been involved in street sex work, two participants were working as independent escorts at the time of interview; all were cis-female, except one transgender woman. A focus group was also completed with seven police officers. A comprehensive thematic analysis of the data was carried out using NVIVO 9; this chapter draws on the Merseyside police and sex worker findings.

Literature review: violence against sex workers and hate crime

A considerable UK and international research literature illustrates levels, types and patterns of victimisation of sex workers, evidencing the disproportionate levels of violent (Deering et al. 2014) and other crimes, including targeted harassment committed against sex workers, with risks varying according to market/sector (Doherty

2011; Sanders and Campbell 2007). Academics examining the regulation of sex work have theorised the causes of violent and other crime against sex workers. Literature has identified stigmatisation, 'othering' and prejudice towards sex workers as leading to social marginalisation, hostility, violence, a denial of rights and a lack of protection, and directly contributing to sex worker victimisation (O'Neill 1997, 2007). A range of discourses have been identified as playing a role in this 'othering' of sex workers, creating and fostering the cultural attitudes that contribute to conditions for violence against sex workers (Kinnell 2008; Lowman 2000).

Research on the policing of sex work in the UK shows that criminalization alongside national and local government policies often foreground public order, the removal of nuisance and trafficking, with the police role enforcing law. Enforcement approaches have been widely critiqued for creating dispersal and displacement, being ineffective, undermining safety of sex workers, hindering access to services and creating poor relationships between sex workers and the police (Brooks-Gordon 2006; Kinnell 2006, 2008; Shannon et al. 2009). Studies highlight that whilst, at a local level, unwritten 'rules of engagement' develop (Brooks-Gordon 2006; Hubbard and Sanders 2003; Sharpe 1998), there remains a difficult relationship between sex workers and the police with limited confidence and trust evident (Kinnell 2006; Sharpe 1998). This and a range of other factors deters the reporting of crime by sex workers who believe they will not be taken seriously and fear judgemental attitudes, arrest or closure of premises (Benson 1998; Boff 2012; Kinnell 2006; Sherman 2015) and heightening vulnerability to violent and other crime. At the crux of the problematic relationship is the dual role of the police in the context of enforcement and protection (Campbell 2016); as Lowman (2000: 1007–1008) argued: the quasi-criminalisation of sex work perpetuates violence against sex workers by alienating them from the protective potential of the police, and creates an 'adversarial relationship' between parties.

Sanders and Campbell (2014: 542) note that in some countries with criminalisation there have been 'some policy initiatives at a local level that indicate a shift towards more protection rather than enforcement-based approaches'. The policing of sex work is not monolithic across the UK and it takes 'complex and spatially varied forms where the morality of individual officers coalesce with wider understandings of vice laws' (Hubbard 2006: 122). The extent to which prostitution laws are enforced or initiatives to address sex worker safety developed, vary across police forces and multi-agency partnership areas (Hubbard 2006; Pitcher et al. 2006).

The most recent guidance for policing comes from the National Police Chiefs Council (NPCC) 'National Policing Sex Work Guidance' (2016), emphasising sex worker safety as a key priority and criticising enforcement stating that: 'enforcement does not resolve the issue, but rather displaces it, making sex workers more vulnerable' (NPCC 2016: 10). Some researchers have described police forces working in partnership to develop alternatives to enforcement and build trust and reporting amongst sex workers (Pitcher et al. 2006). Hester and Westmarland (2004) assessed community mediation approaches to street sex work (adopted as part of the Home Office Funded Crime Reduction Program 'Tackling Prostitution What Works?'), as more effective than the enforcement models adopted in other areas. Some have identified the appointment of non-arresting police sex work liaison officers as contributing to the development of more positive relationships

(O'Neill and Campbell 2002). Police participation in local and national 'Ugly Mugs' schemes, identifying the value of such third-party schemes for encouraging reporting to the police and supporting convictions have also been identified (Laing et al. 2013; Penfold et al. 2004). Others have examined the designation of spaces for street sex work (Campbell and Van Doorninck 2006; Hubbard 1997, 1999). Sanders and Sehmbi (2015); evaluating the pilot of a managed area for street sex work in Leeds, West Yorkshire, found that a move away from criminalisation and the introduction of a police sex work liaison officer had led to improved trust and an increase in reporting. Cooper's (2016) study highlighted a considerable degree of toleration and local legal regulation of parlour sex work in one area of Lancashire. Such studies capture 'alternative' approaches to the regulation and policing of sex work in the UK; they describe more 'public- protection-focused policing' initiatives (Campbell 2011) in which sex worker safety is considered, of which the Merseyside hate crime approach has proved an innovative example.

Towards a protection-focused approach: changing relationships between sex workers and the police in Merseyside

Researchers have documented how the policing of sex work in many areas of the UK has been characterised by the enforcement of soliciting, brothel keeping and other legislation which has been problematic in terms of sex worker safety and community relations between sex workers and the police (Brooks-Gordon 2006; Hubbard 2006). Consequences include low levels of trust amongst sex workers towards the police, sometimes an adversarial relationship with law enforcers and significant under-reporting of crimes committed against sex workers, with sex workers not getting the protections to which they are entitled (Campbell 2016; Kinnell 2008; Lowman 2000). Hate crime theorists have argued that, historically, hate crimes have not been treated seriously (Sibbit 1997); the distrust of and dissatisfaction with police amongst minority groups vulnerable to hate crime leading to a disinclination to report incidences is well-documented (Hall 2005, 2014; Hall et al. 2011). My research found that sex workers in Merseyside share with established hate crime groups (such as BME groups and the LGBTQ community), a past history of poor relationships with the police and an experience of policing in which officer responses and attitudes were frequently shaped by prejudice, as highlighted by the comment of one sex worker participant;

> They were bastards. . . . They didn't like us, they hated dealing with us, like they could catch something off us . . . it was obvious.
>
> (Participant 4)

A key theme amongst longer serving officers was that there had in the past been a greater prevalence of negative attitudes amongst some officers;

> I think, for a variety reasons, sex workers were viewed as an annoyance, in the food chain of life, they were right down there. . . . I'm pigeonholing, you know because there was a broad spectrum of views.
>
> (Police 666)

In my study, sex workers who had worked prior to the 2000s reported that whilst there was a minority of officers who asked about their safety and welfare, generally policing had focused on enforcing the laws on sex work and criminalising sex workers. Reports of crimes against sex workers were perceived by sex workers as not being taken seriously and were severely under-reported. As one sex worker explained;

> Never in a million years did we report! Who could we report it to? The bizzes that were coming round being bastards anyway? Arresting us. 'Who's going to listen to you? You're just a prostitute'.
>
> (Participant 1)

Hence the description, by Chakraborti and Garland (2009), of hate crime victim groups as historically over-policed (subject to police attention and harassment as offenders) and under-protected (crimes against them not taken seriously) matches the past experiences of sex workers in Merseyside – and is still the experience of sex workers in many other areas of the UK (Feis-Bryce 2017).

This history has required a radical shift in local policing in an effort to gain trust and confidence amongst sex workers and begin to put in place the protections they have previously not received; a key aim of the Merseyside approach was to build trust and encourage reporting. My research found a significantly changed and improved relationship between these groups. This was linked to a policing model which moved away from enforcement and the adoption of what was referred to by Merseyside police as 'strategic enforcement'. Describing only utilising prostitution laws in a strategic manner, in order to create spaces sex workers could work without fear of arrest or disruption and to address violence and exploitation, this was a critical part of the hate crime approach. For example, an 'area of lesser chance of arrest' was negotiated in 2005 providing a predominantly non-residential area on the existing street beat where street sex workers could work, between certain times, without fear of arrest; also 'brothels' were not routinely raided or closed but assessment made about risk and exploitations.

When my fieldwork was carried out in 2011, there had been an important shift in the official approach towards policing sex work in Merseyside. There had been a reduction in enforcement which had contributed to a consequent shift in the relationship between sex workers and the police; including progressive changes in officer attitudes towards sex workers generally and in relation to crimes committed against sex workers. Sex workers experienced a less judgemental, more respectful, professional attitude with accompanying concerns about welfare. Incivility and misconduct exhibited by police officers was reduced and police officers characterised as more focused on enquiring about sex worker safety and welfare. The majority of participants reported having greater trust and confidence in the police, and would now be more likely to report crimes against them:

> I would report . . . when I've reported two robberies, the police have been sound. I didn't report getting strangled, 'cause it's five years ago now. But now I would, so that's the difference between five years and now.
>
> (Participant 13)

Yes, too right I would, and I've told other people on the forums too. Girls who have posted (For example) "I've got this guy and he's stalking me". I say, "Go to the police". . . . With recent attacks that have gone on in Liverpool, the police seem to be spot on now. They are taking it really seriously.

(Participant 6)

Such changes were experienced as a particularly dramatic for some women, especially those who had worked during 'enforcement' approaches, and they talked about this comparatively:

When I went back out again . . . Every time I saw the police, I was hiding in the bushes and one of the girls was just standing there. . . . She said, "No, they don't nick you now". . . . They stop and have a chat and see how you are. . . . You could talk to them . . . with the rape case it was so different than before – they were so nice to me, no matter what was going on. . . . I don't know what the hell had happened to them in that space of time. You know it's like someone has waved a magic wand or something and they have gone from bad to good.

(Participant 4)

When I started sex working, the police were a bit more politically incorrect, can I put it? . . . Comparing that to me coming working out. . . . They are more this time round, "Are you alright, are you keeping yourself safe? More professional. They wouldn't get away with talking to you like they did then now. You see it in the way they talk to you now – they are really sound."

(Participant 20)

The dominant discourse amongst police interviews was public-protection policing, and promoting sex worker safety and reducing harms. Policing moved away from prohibition and criminalisation, to active 'management' of sex work, with enforcement used strategically and proportionately. Policing resources were realigned to focus on building confidence amongst sex workers, encouraging reporting and investigating/prosecuting crimes committed against them. A police officer with a lead role in sex work policy development stressed this public protection led approach:

Even (in) the mid-2000s, I think there were still officers who acted in isolation and still had a historical attitude to enforcement . . . it is much more the case now that people realise that it is much more important that we are protective to women who are involved.

(Police 499)

A detective sergeant noted a move away from enforcement to a more balanced approach:

When I went back I never saw anyone being arrested for it. . . . All I had was a very willing section of people saying, "Teach me, educate me, let me know what I need to be thinking". So a completely different ball game and people very open to the new way with safety, building communication (and) trust. . . . I have to say I feel really quite proud of what Merseyside Police have done.

(Police 512)

Most police respondents were of the view sex workers were more confident to report:

Historically . . . it was regarded by some people as an occupational hazard and that sort of attitude has been overcome, wholly. The whole mind set is different now, the whole policy. It's this is crime on a member of the public which must be taken very seriously and investigated in a professional manner.

(Police 848)

Data showed increased reporting and prosecutions; between April 2005 and March 2008 there was a year-on-year increase in sex workers reporting to the local ugly mugs scheme from 12% in 2005–06, to 39% in 2006–07 and 49% in 2007–08 (Campbell and Stoops 2008). Between 2005–13, Merseyside brought more offenders who target sex workers before the courts than the majority of other UK forces, and secured high conviction rates which were: 83% for June 2007 to June 2011 and 75% for cases involving rape and sexual offences. The national 'generic' rate was at the time 58% (Stoops and Jones 2011).

Enforcement-focused policing seeks to eradicate, reduce or disrupt sex work, and focuses on implementing relevant prostitution laws and associated orders. Evidence suggests that enforcement-focused policing contributes to social marginalisation and under-reporting (Kinnell 2008). Bowen (2015: 431) in the context of sex worker murders in Canada sees these murders as the outcome of the criminalisation and dehumanisation of sex workers 'to the extent that they are excluded from social and legal protections', including those which police protection can afford. Police failing to prioritise sex worker safety contributes to the conditions which lead to the targeting of sex workers by predatory offenders. In the protection-focused models of policing the safety of sex workers is a priority, and the predominant ethos is one of improving safety and reducing harm. A range of proactive initiatives are often put in place to encourage the reporting of crimes and improve safety for example police sex work liaison officers. Enforcement of the prostitution laws is avoided, applied strategically and as a last option, following mediation and diversion approaches. The objective is for relationships between sex workers, the police and support projects to be improved, and trust and confidence increased. Merseyside's approach is protection-focused, and one where evidently relationships between sex workers and the police have improved which has resulted in high rates of reporting and convictions.

Sherman et al. (2015: 478) evidenced that sex workers in the United States experienced a policing approach that was enforcement-focused and called for research to find 'points for leverage in preconceiving (the) police's role, identifying a guardianship framework that includes rather than excludes' sex workers'. In this, they postulate that police would be an access point for services rather than a deterrent to health and support services. The Merseyside hate crime approach can contribute to contribute identifying elements of a 'guardianship framework' for sex workers.

Crimes against sex workers through the lens of hate: police and sex worker conceptualisations, hostility, easy targets and perceived vulnerability

There is discussion about the widening of hate crime victim groups beyond those which are established and formally monitored, as well as the conceptual and policy-based implications of this (Chakraborti and Garland 2009; Garland 2010; Mason-Bish 2010). Some have cautioned against over-zealous restriction of hate crime status to certain social groups, which risks the creation of victim hierarchies (Chakraborti and Garland 2009, 2012; Mason-Bish 2010). The experiences of a number of groups, such as members of alternative sub cultures (e.g. Goths) (Garland 2010), are increasingly being recognised through the lens of hate crime. In this context, I wanted to explore whether sex workers are one group who may benefit from inclusion and the 'special protection afforded to the officially recognised minority groups' (Chakraborti and Garland 2009: 16). Since first looking at violence against sex workers as hate crime (Campbell 2014), some hate crime theorists have recognised sex workers in the debate (Chakraborti and Garland 2015) and other scholars of sex work have begun to consider sex workers experiences through the lens of hate (Ellison and Smith 2017).

I argue (Campbell 2014) that sex workers experiences fit established definitions foregrounding 'othering' and social hierarchies, defining hate crimes as expressions of prejudice, discrimination and power (Hall 2005; Perry 2001; Sheffield 1995) 'against those without rights, privilege and prestige' (Chakraborti and Garland 2009: 5). Perry's (2001) emphasis on groups who experience historical social marginalisation and acts of violence and intimidation which 'put them in their place' connects directly with the literature on the enduring stigmatisation, social marginalisation and othering of sex workers (Kinnell 2008; Lowman 2000). These processes have long been identified as central to creating hostility and prejudice towards sex workers, leading to a denial of rights, lack of protection and victimisation, and highlighting what some theorists have argued is the lack of full citizenship (O'Neill 2007). Treating crimes against sex workers can be a recognition of this discrimination and 'othering'.

Another useful conceptualisation (see Campbell 2014, 2016) proposed by Chakraborti and Garland (2012: 507), argues for a more inclusive conceptualisation of hate crime, including definitions of hate crime as violence, hostility and intimidation perpetrated because of 'perceived difference' – a concept which describes perpetrators seeing 'their target: as weak, defenceless, powerless, with a limited capacity to resist'. They also argued that hate crime can manifest through 'a complex interplay of factors' (2012: 506) which guards against 'homogenized generalisations' (2012: 510) about hate crime. Kidd and Witten (2008) noted transphobic hate crime was fuelled not just by prejudice but because trans people can be perceived stereotypically by offenders as easy targets.

Sixty-two percent of sex worker participants had heard of hate crime; understood as crimes committed out of prejudice against groups such as black, migrant, ethnic minority groups and gay people. The majority of participants had not been aware of the inclusion of sex workers in the hate crime policy until it was discussed at interview. The reaction from a majority of women was positive. The majority of sex workers felt that sex workers could be victims of hate crime, with targeted victimisation being a lived reality. Hate crime was understood by sex workers in two ways: that offenders held hostile and prejudicial attitudes towards sex workers linked to wider 'othering' discourses; and/or they took advantage of the perceived vulnerabilities of sex workers which they believed made sex workers 'easy targets', increasing their own chance of 'getting away with' their crimes.

The majority of police officers interviewed said hate crime policy made sense and they supported it. The elements of *vulnerability*, *targeting* and *membership of a minority or identifiable minority group* were recurrent in the narratives of police officers.

Reflecting definitions which emphasise 'othering' and social hierarchies and understand hate crime as an expression of power and prejudice (Perry 2001) in their narratives, the majority of sex workers directly connected violent, harassment and other crimes, including incidents they had experienced, with hate crime, seeing these as motivated by hostile, derogatory and prejudicial attitudes to sex workers as 'lesser'.

> I think it's good. Because the amount of stick and stones you get. And people think because you do what you do, they can do what they want to you because you're lower than the low in some people's eyes.
>
> (Participant 19)

> Yeah, I have. . . . Because I'm a sex worker. The kids calling me names and chasing me down the street and throwing stuff at me, even men beating me up. . . . In their little heads, they thought, "It's ok if I do that to her because she's a prostitute!"
>
> (Participant 17)

Participants felt sex workers were objectified, demonised and vilified; the 'dregs of society', 'scum', 'lowlifes' were phrases used, these attitudes they saw as leading to hate crime. They referred to how offenders expressed anger and hostility towards sex workers, humiliated them and 'put people in their place', which is a core element of hate crime for Perry (2001).

In parallel sex workers' narratives revealed they felt had been targeted and crimes had been committed against them because they were perceived as *vulnerable*. Chakraborti and Garland's (2012) concept of 'perceived vulnerability' is relevant here, with hate crime offenders targeting groups who they perceive for a range of reasons as vulnerable, whom they can harass, commit crimes against and get away with it; this concept does not see these vulnerabilities as inherent and automatically putting people at risk. First, they described offenders who perceive sex workers as easy targets specifically because they 'think' they will not report to the police, if they do they will not be taken seriously, increasing their chance of getting away with crimes;

> I've even had ones who have said like, "What you going to do about it? You're not going to the police, they won't do anything you're a prozzie".
>
> (Participant 2)

Sex workers are also perceived as 'situationally vulnerable' – targeted because of their (often isolated) presence in public space. Participants described the particular visibility and easy access to people working on the street, 'situational vulnerability' linked to the organisation of street sex work;

> When you're on the street, everyone can see you. Them attacking working girls it's easy for them – they know where they'll find us. They can come up to us, pretend they want business or just throw things.
>
> (Participant 1)

> They want the money, you going somewhere secluded and quiet so obviously for some people it's perfect.
>
> (Participant 19)

Some participants referred to other vulnerabilities for some sex workers, such as drug use and estrangement from families, which perpetrators exploited:

> Yeah definitely!! Because they think, because they're out there doing what they do the police aren't going to take them seriously for one . . . people just think, "Oh, it's just another junkie on the street and a lot of them have cut ties with the family, they're homeless so if they go missing, who's going to notice they've gone missing??" They are taking advantage of all that.
>
> (Participant 18)

In such ways sex workers described vulnerability as one of the reasons they were victims of hate crime; discourses of vulnerability were linked to issues of prejudice, injustice and beliefs that sex workers had limited protections and were easy targets.

Discourses of vulnerability were to the fore in police narratives about why sex workers were victims of hate crime. As a group, they were specifically targeted because they were members of a minority and vulnerable group, who offenders perceived as easy targets; police officers talked about vulnerability in a number of ways. Sanders and Brown (2017) examined a number of discourses of vulnerability employed by practitioners, including police officers, involved in the management of street sex work in Leeds, identifying multiple and overlapping discourses ranging from essentialist discourses focusing on individual factors resulting in pathologisation to constructive situational discourses focusing on environmental spaces and working conditions, which could accommodate an understanding of the structural factors that contribute to violence against sex workers. The latter were more common in the narratives of Merseyside police officers. The strategic lead for sex work in Merseyside Police identified vulnerability within an understanding of crimes against sex workers, reflecting a rights framework:

> Given their vulnerabilities, they need an enhanced service . . . especially the way they were treated up to 2006. After Stephen Lawrence, there was a sea change in policing minority groups as victims . . . under Article 2 of the European convention, we have to protect the lives of all. In Merseyside, we approach investigation of crimes against sex workers as hate crime and from the viewpoint that safety of sex workers must be prioritised above all else.
>
> (Police 499)

Grieve (2004), outlining key success factors for hate crime policing, notes policing should be guided by human rights. Situational narratives pointing to adverse environmental factors, injustices and inequalities featured in police narratives. A female detective constable, who had supported sex worker victims of crime, pointed to motivations and beliefs which she felt shaped the actions of perpetrators targeting sex workers:

> I think it is hate crime . . . they are targeted . . . getting raped because of what they do, because of who they are and that is a hate crime. . . . They think, "Nobody's going to believe a sex worker and the police are just gonna go, 'Well that's what you do for a living don't be reporting it to us'" . . . think they've got a better chance of getting away with it . . . if you're gonna go and rape somebody, sex workers (are an) easy target for them. That makes them vulnerable from these offenders.
>
> (Police 963)

A discourse of vulnerability through which a minority of police constructed sex workers was the identification of individual 'lifestyle' or 'risk' taking factors, or notions of sex work as inherently dangerous;

> They do put themselves in that danger but they shouldn't have to be targeted because they are sex workers. . . . So they should be allowed that protection and it should be viewed as a serious crime.
>
> (Police 727)

Terms such as 'putting themselves at risk' were present in only a small section of police narratives; these risk lapsing into 'victim blaming' or a construct of sex worker vulnerability which ignores or minimises structural factors and can be an essentialising discourse (Sanders and Brown 2017). Yet as demonstrated in the previous quote, in the wider narratives of participants who expressed these, there was evidence of a commitment to the view that sex workers deserved to work free from violence. Sanders and Brown (2017) note essentialist discourses around sex work, offer a more problematic conceptualisation of sex work and vulnerability. More prevalent in Merseyside police narratives were situational narratives, including those which recognised the cultural and structural factors that lead to targeted violence and other hate crime against sex workers. Police officers' conceptualisations of hate crime which deploy vulnerability in this way, can be understood as describing how 'perceived vulnerability' (Chakraborti and Garland 2012) operates in contributing to hate crime against sex workers. 'Perceived vulnerability' as a factor in motivating hate crime is useful to make sense of sex worker and police conceptualisations of hate crimes against sex workers; it does not posit vulnerability as something inherent to hate crime groups, nor accept that hate crime against any particular group is inevitable or that they are passive victims. As Sanders and Brown (2017) acknowledge, the 'vulnerability' framework for policing sex work is a progressive shift, but the concept of vulnerability also can be limited in terms of dealing with wider inequalities and problematic social policy. It is vital to ensure that hate crime targeted at sex workers is not conceptualised in a way which draws on discourses of vulnerability which remove agency (Sanders and Brown 2017) and resistance from sex workers, or which essentialise sex work as inherently violent, and sex workers themselves as inevitable victims of violence. When considering vulnerability, it is important to recognise the perceived vulnerability that motivates some perpetrators is in fact structurally generated (Campbell 2016), as part of the 'structural violence' that sex workers face globally (International Committee for the Rights of Sex Workers in Europe 2014), including the laws which criminalise sex workers and policies which deny sex worker rights to protection and justice.

Progress but challenges: towards protection-focused policing and decriminalisation

The hate crime approach received a great deal of support amongst sex workers and the police, and contributed to an improved relationship between sex workers and a shift to protection-focused policing. It has made an innovative contribution to public-protection-focused approaches by its inclusion of sex workers in force hate crime policy and to reshaping national policing guidance on sex work. New guidance policing sex work (National Police Chief's Council 2016: 12) produced under the auspices of a national policing lead from Merseyside Police, advocates for treating crimes against sex workers as a priority and specifies 'Crimes against sex workers to be dealt with as hate crimes'. The 'Hate Crime Operational Guidance' (College of Policing 2014) reinforced the message that forces locally have the discretion to include victim groups outside the monitored strands if it will achieve community safety goals; Merseyside's inclusion of sex workers was used as an example of this. Whilst both these sets of guidance are not compulsory for forces, they do exert influence; it has also been recognised at a national level as good practice (Crown Prosecution Service 2012; Home Office 2011). Whilst important to stress this legacy of innovation, my data also found the approach was not without challenges and limitations.

Some officers raised concerns that awareness about the policy and its proactive implementation could wane – that, whilst treating sex workers as victims of hate crime was included in policy on paper, it was not always implemented systematically. Some officers felt there could not be complacency and the hate crime policy needed to be championed at a high level consistently so all officers were aware, especially in the context of austerity. The issue of threats to resourcing key partnership elements to the approach was also raised by officers, with concerns that funding for the specialist ISVA, and the level of wider sex work support service interventions which had supported the approach were being eroded. Research has found sustaining change in hate crime policing across all ranks on the ground is challenging (Chakraborti and Garland 2009).

My research carried out in 2011 found limited awareness of the policy of treating crimes against sex workers as hate crime and also that it had not become fully integrated cross force (including in specialist SIGMA hate crime units) nor into multi-agency hate crime practice and procedure in Merseyside. This was evidenced by the lack of awareness of the policy by some officers including in SIGMA hate crime units (including in the area which had lead on introducing the policy). SIGMA had a less active role in coordinating, monitoring and investigating sex worker hate crimes than when the policy was introduced in 2006. An officer responsible for centralised monitoring of hate crime in the area based unit which had previously taken a lead, had not heard of the policy and had not been involved in a case with a sex worker victim whilst with the unit:

> As far as I was aware it was just the LGBT, the ethnic minorities and now the disability hate crime that comes under a separate category of hate crime. . . . Just speaking from my own experience, I dealt with a few jobs which were robberies and assault against sex workers and I didn't refer those to the SIGMA team and nobody ever suggested to me that I ought to refer it to the SIGMA team because as I say I wasn't aware that came under the hate crime policy.
>
> (Police 444)

He felt that sex-worker- motivated hate crime could be easily recorded within the system but lack of knowledge amongst officers across the force about the policy would contribute to crimes not being recorded as hate crime. A representative from the local authority who had a lead role in hate crime strategically and operationally was not aware of the policy and hate crime against sex workers was not considered by the multi-agency Hate Crime Joint Action Group (JAG), who had the role of considering hate crime cases and agreeing packages of intervention and support from agencies to ensure an optimum and joined up response. Many sex workers interviewed, before taking part in the interview, were aware that the police were making an effort to take crime against sex work seriously but were unaware that Merseyside Police officially treated sex workers as a hate crime group. This meant sex workers were not aware of the process: i.e. that if a sex worker is treated as a victim of hate crime, a set of procedures should be triggered and they can have certain expectations about the treatment they should receive from the police. Indeed, all stakeholders were not resistant to the inclusion of sex workers in hate crime policy and were keen for the policy to be maintained and developed. Hall (2005: 207) has noted the difference between having a proscriptive police hate crime policy and its implementation and success in the 'real world', noting that 'the transformation of police policy into effective practice is a complex and vulnerable process'. My research showed refreshed action was needed in Merseyside Police to promote the policy and raise awareness across groups.

Whist the hate crime policy has not yet led to the full integration of sex workers into hate crime procedures in the Merseyside force, it has had some important and progressive effects that could be lost if the policy was discontinued, for example increased confidence and trust in the police amongst sex workers, levels of reporting increasing and improvement in the quality of investigations of crimes against sex workers. Also, the support demonstrated amongst police officers, and sex workers who took part in this research, gives the sex work and hate crime policy a level of legitimacy not generally found in studies that have examined police and sex worker attitudes to policing sex work in the UK (Brooks-Gordon 2006), which are much more contested and often divisive. These things may be lost if the approach was abandoned and indeed I would argue the impact of the 'hate crime approach' could be much greater if there was greater integration of sex workers within hate crime practices (for example in the Merseyside context the same levels of rigour applied to sex worker hate crime recording and monitoring as to other forms and sex worker cases considered at hate crime JAG). There is further potential to develop the approach in Merseyside both locally and nationally. Such efforts could more proactively include people working in off-street, internet-based sex workers, male and transgender sex workers. A fully-fledged hate crime approach, in which crimes against sex workers were monitored, investigated and prosecuted in the same way as other established other hate crimes, with the same multi-agency partnership capacity and oversight, could have further benefits for sex workers and enhance response to crimes against them – with improved support, monitoring information and preventative strategies. The hate crime policy element of the Merseyside approach is one way of indicating to officers these crimes cannot be dismissed and should be treated seriously within the same procedures as other hate crimes, and it enables senior officers to give a strong message to officers, the public and sex workers in this vein. It also suggests an understanding of the roots of violence against sex workers, that sex worker victimisation is not a random act or a result of 'risky behaviour' but a result of discrimination, hostility, prejudice and the targeting of 'perceived vulnerability'.

There is a need for further comparative research to examine contemporary policing approaches across a range of forces in the UK, to further develop models for understanding the policing of sex work nationally, to capture other models of protection-focused policing and policing informed by 'vulnerability' (Sanders and Brown 2017; Sanders and Sehmbi 2015) and which assess the extent to which forces in England and Wales have responded to new national guidance which specified sex worker safety as a priority objective for police forces (as discussed earlier in this chapter).

Hate crime approach: a step towards decriminalisation?

I have identified a continuum of policing along which police forces can be positioned, ranging from enforcement-focused policing at one end to protection-focused policing at the other (Campbell 2011, 2014). The hate crime approach sits at the protection end and brought real pragmatic and progressive improvements in the policing of crimes against sex workers in Liverpool. Taking all its constituent parts, I would argue it is a progressive approach to addressing violence, harassment and other crimes against sex workers which accepts the personhood, citizenship and human rights of sex workers, including the right to equality and non- discrimination, the right to liberty and security of the person, and the right to access to justice. But the approach can only achieve so much, if the national framework of criminalisation, which contributes to violence against sex workers, is left intact. Hence, it is important that the hate crime approach should not be seen as the end goal in itself for the regulation of sex work at local and national level in the UK. The weight of international research evidence demonstrates that decriminalisation is the most conducive regulatory framework in which to reduce violence against sex workers and improve safety, and ensure sex workers receive adequate health care, legal assistance and other support as needed and promote sex worker rights (Beyer et al. 2015; Deering et al. 2014). Support is growing from major international human rights and health organisations which have adopted formal policies in support of decriminalisation of consensual sex work (World Health Organisation 2014; Amnesty International 2016). Decriminalisation is the regulatory framework required to enable a radical transformation of the relationship between sex workers and the police across the UK, and make significant impacts on reducing violence and targeted hate crime against sex workers. It would remove the current structural framework which has many detrimental effects, including the creation of a problematic adversarial relationship between sex workers and the police and would remove many of the social, legal and cultural conditions which create structurally generated violence against sex workers. It would enable employment rights, health and safety, and other appropriate regulatory frameworks to be focused on creating safer work spaces and conditions for sex workers, and for scarce policing resources to be focused on those who continue to commit any crimes against sex workers. In a framework in which policing focuses on improving the safety of sex workers: public protection policing would be the norm.

This does not mean there is no role for a hate crime policing approach in addressing crimes against sex workers in a decriminalised context. Research in New Zealand where the Prostitution Reform Act 2003 introduced decriminalisation (Abel and Fitzgerald 2010a), has found that whilst decriminalisation has not eliminated violence against sex workers, it has improved the relationship between sex workers and the police, and has provided sex workers with legitimacy through the 'realisation of employment, legal, health and safety rights' (Abel and Fitzgerald 2010b: 256). Armstrong (2016a: 1) found decriminalisation enabled 'a dramatic shift in the approach to policing sex work', with much greater trust amongst street sex workers in the police and a sense of responsibility amongst the police for sex worker safety. But her research also flags that violence against sex workers is also tied up with embedded cultural and social discourses around violence against women and sex workers which will take concerted efforts to erode. Protection-based models of policing such as the hate crime approach may have something to offer, providing a model for delivering a police service to people in sex worker communities who still face discrimination, prejudice and violence generated by stigmatisation and 'othering' – in the same way that hate crime policing has been an important way of improving relations between LGBTQ communities and the police in a number of international jurisdictions.

The hate crime approach has not eliminated violence against sex workers in Merseyside, but it goes further than many other local regulatory approaches in the UK to prioritise sex worker safety, ensure justice and assert sex workers' equal right to protection. I suggest it should not be a case of the hate crime approach *or* decriminalisation and whilst there is a need to look beyond the hate crime approach, it should not be overlooked; it can be adopted within the current legislative framework to move towards a policy and legislative context which does not contribute to the conditions generating targeted crimes against sex workers.

References

Abel, G., and Fitzgerald, S. (2010a) 'Introduction', in Abel, G., Fitzgerald, L., Healy, C., and Taylor, A. (Eds.) *Taking the crime out of sex work: New Zealand sex workers fight for decriminalisation.* Bristol: Policy Press, pp. 1–21.

Abel, G., and Fitzgerald, L. (2010b) 'Decriminalisation and stigma', in Abel, G., Fitzgerald, L., Healy, C., and Taylor, A. (Eds.) *Taking the crime out of sex work: New Zealand sex workers fight for decriminalisation.* Bristol: Policy Press, pp. 239–258.

Amnesty International. (2016) *Amnesty International publishes policy and research on protection of sex workers' rights, 25th May.* Available at: www.amnestyusa.org/news/press-releases/amnesty-international-publishes-policy-and-research-on-protection-of-sex-workers-rights (Accessed 27 May 2016).

Armstrong, L. (2016a) 'From law enforcement to protection? Interactions between sex workers and police in decriminalized street-based sex industry?', *British Journal of Criminology*, 18, 1–19.

Benson, C. (1998) *Violence against female prostitutes.* Department of Social Sciences: Loughborough University.

Blair, E. (2011) *'I am not a victim': A preliminary evaluation of the first Independent Sexual Violence Advisor (ISVA) service for men and women selling sex in East London.* London: Homerton Hospital Trust.

Boff, A. (2012) *Silence on violence: Improving the safety of women – the policing of off street sex work and sex trafficking in London.* Available at: http://glaconservatives.co.uk/wp-content/uploads/downloads/2012/03/Report-on-the-Safety-of-Sex-Workers-Silence-on-Violence.pdf (Accessed 4 May 2015).

Bowen, R. (2015) 'Squaring up: Experiences of transition from off-street sex work to square work and duality – concurrent involvement in both – in Vancouver, BC', *Canadian Sociological Association*, 52 (4), 429–499.

Brooks-Gordon, B. (2006) *The price of sex: Prostitution, policy and society.* Cullompton, Devon: Willan Publishing.

Brown, K., and Sanders, T. L. M. (2017) 'Pragmatic, progressive, problematic: Addressing vulnerability through a local street sex work partnership initiative', *Social Policy and Society*, 16 (3), 429–441.

Campbell, R. (2011) 'A case of hate: Approaching crimes against sex workers as hate crime in Merseyside'. Presented at: *British Society of Criminology Annual Conference*

2011: economies and insecurities of crime and justice, 3rd – 6th July 2011, Northumbria University.

Campbell, R. (2014) 'Not getting away with it: Linking sex work and hate crime in Merseyside', in Chakraborti, N., and Garland, J. (Eds.) *Responding to hate crime: The case for connecting policy and research*. Bristol: Policy Press, pp. 55–78.

Campbell, R. (2016) *Not getting away with it: Addressing violence against sex workers as hate crime in Merseyside*. Ph.D. thesis. University of Durham.

Campbell, R., and Stoops, S. (2008) *Responding to violence against sex workers in Liverpool: An analysis of the Armistead Street Ugly Mugs scheme data and an overview of the Independent Sexual Violence Advisor role*. Liverpool: Liverpool Primary Care Trust.

Campbell, R., and Van Doorninck, M. (2006) ' "Zoning" street sex work: The way forward?', in Campbell, R., and O'Neill, M. (Eds.) *Sex work now*. Cullompton, Devon: Willan Publishing, pp. 1–32.

Chakraborti, N., and Garland, J. (Eds.) (2009) *Hate crime: Impact, causes and responses*. London: Sage.

Chakraborti, N., and Garland, J. (2012) 'Reconceptualizing hate crime victimization through the lens of vulnerability and difference', *Theoretical Criminology*, 16 (4), 499–514.

Chakraborti, N., and Garland, J. (2015) *Hate crime: Impact, causes and responses* (2nd edn). London: Sage.

College of Policing. (2014) *Hate crime operational guidance*. Coventry: College of Policing Limited.

Cooper, E. (2016) ' "It's better than daytime television": Questioning the socio-spatial impacts of massage parlours on residential communities', *Sexualities*, 19 (5–6), 547–566.

Crown Prosecution Service. (2012) *Violence against women and girls crime report 2011–2012*. London: CPS, Equality and Diversity Unit.

Deering, K., Amin, A., Shoveller, J., Nesbitt, A., Garcia-Moreno, C., Duff, P., Argento, A., and Shannon, K. (2014) 'A systematic review of the correlates of violence against sex workers', *American Journal of Public Health*, 104 (5), e42-e54.

Doherty, T. (2011) 'Victimization in off-street sex industry work', *Violence Against Women*, 17 (7), 1–20.

Ellison, G., and Smith, L. (2017) 'Hate crime legislation and violence against sex workers in Ireland: Lessons in policy and practice', in Haynes, A., Schweppe, J., and Taylor, S. (Eds.) *Critical perspectives on hate crime contributions from the island of Ireland*. Belfast: Palgrave Macmillan, pp. 179–207.

Feis-Bryce, A. (2017) 'Policing sex work in the UK: a patchwork approach', in Sanders, T., and Lang, M. (Eds.) *Policing the sex industry: Protection, paternalism and politics*. London: Routledge, pp. 49–82.

Garland, J. (2010) 'The victimisation of goths and the boundaries of hate crime', in Chakraborti, N. (Ed.) *Hate Crime: Concepts, Policy, Future Directions*. Cullompton, Devon: Willan Publishing, pp. 40–57.

Grieve, J. (2004) 'The investigation of hate crimes: Art, science or philosophy?', in Hall, N. J. R., Abdullah-Kahn, N., Blackbourn, D., Fletcher, R., and Grieve, J. (Eds.) *Hate crime*. Portsmouth: Institute of Criminal Justice Studies.

Hall, N. (2005) *Hate crime*. Cullompton, Devon: Willan Publishing.

Hall, N. (2014) *Hate Crime* (2nd edn). London: Routledge.

Hall, N., Grieve, J., and Savage, S. P. (2011) 'Introduction: The legacies of Lawrence', in Hall, N., Grieve, J., and Savage, S. P. (Eds.) *Policing and the legacy of Stephen Lawrence*. London: Taylor and Francis, pp. 1–21.

Hester, M., and Westmarland, N. (2004) 'Tackling street prostitution: Towards an holistic approach', in *Home Office Research Study 279*. London: Development and Statistics Directorate, Home Office.

Home Office. (2011) *A review of effective practice in responding to prostitution*. London: Home Office.

Hubbard, P. (1997) 'Red light districts and toleration zones; changing geographies of female prostitution in England and Wales', *Area* 29 (2), 129–140.

Hubbard, P. (1999) *Sex and the city: Geographies of prostitution in the urban West*. Aldershot: Ashgate.

Hubbard, P. (2006) 'Out of touch and out of time? The contemporary policing of sex work', in Campbell, R., and O'Neill, M. (Eds.) *Sex work now*. Cullompton, Devon: Willan Publishing, pp. 1–32.

Hubbard, P., and Sanders, T. (2003) 'Making space for sex work', *International Journal of Urban and Regional Research*, 27, 75–89.

International Committee on the Rights of Sex Workers in Europe. (2014) *Structural violence: Social and institutional oppression experienced by sex workers in Europe*. Amsterdam, Netherlands: ICRSE.

Kidd, J., and Witten, T. (2008) 'Transgender and transsexual identities: The next strange fruit – hate crimes, violence and genocide against the global trans-communities', *Journal of Hate Studies*, 6 (1), 31–63.

Kilvington, J., Day, S., and Ward, H. (2001) 'Prostitution policy in Europe: A time of change?' *Feminist Review*, 67 (1), 78–93.

Kinnell, H. (2006) 'Murder made easy', in Campbell, R., and O'Neill, M. (Eds.) *Sex work now*. Cullompton, Devon: Willan Publishing, pp. 212–234.

Kinnell, H. (2008) *Violence and sex work in Britain*. Cullompton, Devon: Willan Publishing.

Laing, M., Pitcher, J., and Irving, A. (2013) *National Ugly Mugs pilot scheme: Evaluation*. Manchester: UK Network of Sex Work Projects.

Lowman, J. (2000) 'Violence and outlaw status of street prostitution in Canada', *Violence Against Women*, 6 (9), 987–1011.

Mason-Bish, H. (2010) 'Future challenges for hate crime policy: Lessons from the past', in Chakraborti, N. (Ed.) *Hate crime: Concepts, policy, future directions*. Cullompton, Devon: Willan Publishing, pp. 58–77.

Merseyside Police. (2006) *Sex workers in Merseyside: Review of process – Liverpool North memorandum, 15th December 2006*. Liverpool: Merseyside Police.

Merseyside Police. (2015) *Hate crime policy and procedure*. Liverpool: Merseyside Police.

National Police Chief's Council. (2016) *National policing sex work strategy*. London: NPCC.

O'Neill, M. (1997) 'Prostitute women now', in Scambler, G., and Scambler, A. (Eds.) *Rethinking prostitution*. London: Routledge, pp. 3–28.

O'Neill, M. (2007) 'Community safety, rights and recognition: Towards a coordinated prostitution strategy?', *Community Safety Journal*, 6 (1), 45–52.

O'Neill, M., and Campbell, R. (2002) *Working together to create change: Walsall prostitution consultation research*. Walsall: Walsall South Health Action Zone/Staffordshire University/Liverpool Hope University.

Penfold, C., Hunter, G., Barham, L., and Campbell, R. (2004) 'Tackling client violence in female street prostitution: Inter-agency working between outreach agencies and the police', *Policing and Society*, 14 (4), 365–379.

Perry, B. (2001) *In the name of hate: Understanding hate crimes*. London: Routledge.

Pitcher, J., Campbell, R., Hubbard, P., O'Neill, M., and Scoular, J. (2006) *Living and working in areas of street sex work: From conflict to coexistence*. Bristol: Policy Press.

Sanders, T., and Campbell, R. (2007) 'Designing out vulnerability, building in respect: Violence, safety and sex work policy', *British Journal of Sociology*, 58 (1), 1–18.

Sanders, T., and Campbell, R. (2014) 'Editorial: The governance of commercial sex: Global trends of criminalisation, punitive enforcement, protection and rights', *Criminology and Criminal Justice* (Special edition), 14 (5), 535–548.

Sanders, T., and Sehmbi, V. (2015) *Evaluation of the Leeds managed area pilot project*. Available at: www.nswp.org/sites/nswp.org/files/Executive%20Summary%20Leeds,%20 U%20of%20Leeds%20-%20Sept%202015.pdf (Accessed 5 April 2017).

Shannon, K., Kerr, T., Strathdee, S. A., Shoveller, J., Montaner, J. S., and Tyndall, M. W. (2009) 'Prevalence and structural correlates of gender based violence among a prospective cohort of female sex workers', *British Medical Journal*, 339, 442–445.

Sharpe, K. (1998) *Red light, blue light: Prostitutes, punters and the police*. Aldershot, Hants: Ashgate.

Sheffield, C. (1995) 'Hate violence', in Rothenberg, P. (Ed.) *Race, class and gender in the United States*, 3rd edition. New York: St. Martin's, pp. 432–441.

Sherman, S. G., Footer, K., Illangasekare, S., Clark, E., Pearson, E., and Decker, M. R. (2015) '"What makes you think you have special privileges because you are a police officer?" A qualitative exploration of police's role in the risk environment of female sex workers', *AIDS care: Psychological and socio-medical aspects of AIDS/HIV*, 27 (4), 473–480.

Sibbit, R. (1997) *The perpetrators of racial harassment and racial violence*. Home Office Research Study No 176. London: Home Office.

Stoops, S., and Jones, J. (2011) 'Not an occupational hazard: sex work and sexual violence'. Presented at: *Sexual Violence Conference*. Department of Forensic Services, Middlesex University, 8th September 2011.

World Health Organisation. (2014) *Consolidated guidelines on HIV prevention, diagnosis, treatment and care for key populations*. Geneva: World Health Organisation Press. Available at: www.who.int/hiv/pub/guidelines/keypopulations/en/ (Accessed 15 May 2016).

4 Decriminalisation, policing and sex work in New Zealand

Lynzi Armstrong

Introduction

Sex work is commonly constructed as a risky occupation, particularly in relation to the risk of violence. Laws and policies relating to the sex industry impact the management of risks of violence, and also influence justice system responses when violence occurs (Kinnell 2006; Sanders 2004a; Shannon et al. 2009). In contexts in which sex workers are criminalised, the risk of arrest creates high levels of distrust in police, which creates a significant barrier to sex workers reporting violence.

The sale and purchase of sexual services is decriminalised in New Zealand, since the passing of the Prostitution Reform Act (PRA) in 2003. New Zealand was the first country in the world to decriminalise sex work, and this framework continues to be particularly unique. Despite years of campaigning by sex worker-led organisations, the recommendations of many academics, and several international organisations such as Amnesty International endorsing decriminalisation as best practice from a human rights perspective, various forms of criminalisation remain the dominant legislative framework globally.

In the context of ongoing risks of violence, and the difficulties sex workers face reporting violence in criminalised contexts, it is important to continue to explore what alternative legislative models can offer. This chapter explores the impacts of decriminalising sex work in New Zealand, with a focus on how the change in law has shifted the police role in relation to the sex industry, and the significance of this for sex worker safety. This chapter begins with an overview of the sex industry in New Zealand, outlining the process of decriminalisation and the impacts on sex workers, before discussing the legacy of criminalisation and the changing role of the police in relation to the indoor and outdoor sex industries. The chapter concludes by highlighting research gaps and offering suggestions for further research in this area.

The sex industry in New Zealand

The sex industry exists throughout New Zealand but is mainly located in the three major urban centres of Auckland, Wellington and Christchurch. Estimating the true population of sex workers is a challenging task due to stigma presenting a barrier to disclosure, and the fact that people regularly move in and out of the sex industry. The most robust study estimating the size of the sex industry in New Zealand was conducted in 2006 and focused on the three major cities of Auckland, Wellington and Christchurch, along with two smaller cities. The research utilised several methods, including NZPC outreach workers collecting data during visits to brothels, requesting information from brothels, counting advertisements and street outreach workers conducting headcounts on the street. The findings of this research estimated the total population of sex workers as 2,396. The researchers therefore concluded that previous estimates of the size of the sex industry, which were far higher, were likely to be over-estimates (Abel et al. 2009). While there has been speculation regarding increases in the sex worker population, there is no evidence to suggest that there has been an increase in the overall number of sex workers in New Zealand in recent years

Sex workers in New Zealand work in four main types of setting, with 'managed' workers working in brothels, private workers working from their own homes or other premises (often with other sex workers in small owner-operated brothels), and street-based sex workers. It has been estimated that over half of all sex workers in New Zealand work in the managed sector, while over a third work privately and around a tenth work on the street (Abel et al. 2007). While indoor sex work occurs throughout New Zealand, street-based sex work predominantly occurs in the three main cities of Auckland, Christchurch and Wellington.

Sex workers in New Zealand comprise a diverse population. While most sex workers are cisgender women, men and transgender people also work in the sex industry. While most sex workers in New Zealand are permanent New Zealand residents, there is also a small population of migrant sex workers visiting temporarily from a range of geographic regions, including China, South East Asia, Latin America, the United States and the United Kingdom (Roguski 2013). A common myth that permeates globally is that only certain women do sex work. Research conducted in New Zealand in 2006 refutes this myth, highlighting the diversity of the sex worker population in New Zealand, with sex workers reporting diverse backgrounds, experiences and motivations for working in the sex industry (Abel et al. 2007).

The decriminalisation of sex work: a brief overview

There are four main approaches to regulating the sex industry globally: criminalisation of sex workers and/or third parties, legalisation, criminalisation of clients and full decriminalisation. The most common approach throughout the world is full or partial criminalisation – of sex workers, their clients and/or those who facilitate or profit from sex work. In 2003, New Zealand became the first country in the world to completely decriminalise sex work, with the passing of the Prostitution Reform Act (PRA). Prior to the passing of the PRA, the approach to regulating the sex industry was modelled on the UK approach, with the selling of sexual services not technically illegal, but many activities associated with it against the law. The PRA was passed following several years of work led by the New Zealand Prostitutes Collective (NZPC), New Zealand's sex worker organisation, which had direct involvement in the drafting of the law. As such, the PRA represented a particularly unique approach to policy making since the law was directly informed by sex workers, centring on their health, safety and human rights. The PRA is considered to represent an approach that is grounded in human rights, while also intending to minimise harm in the sex industry (Abel and Fitzgerald 2010).

As stated in part one (section three) of the Act, the purpose of the PRA was to decriminalise prostitution (while not endorsing or morally sanctioning prostitution or its use) and to create a framework that:

a) safeguards the human rights of sex workers and protects them from exploitation;
b) promotes the welfare and occupational health and safety of sex workers;
c) is conducive to public health;
d) prohibits the use in prostitution of persons under 18 years of age;
e) implements certain other related reforms (PRA 2003).

A fundamental aim of the PRA was to better equip and support sex workers to challenge exploitation in their work. The PRA therefore includes specific clauses to address exploitative working practices. The PRA prohibits inducing or compelling another individual to provide commercial sexual services, for instance through threats of blackmail (Abel et al. 2010). The Act also intends to empower sex workers in interactions with clients, through specific rights to withdraw consent to sexual acts or refuse, for any reason, to provide sexual services (Abel et al. 2010). Furthermore, the PRA afforded greater flexibility to sex workers on where they work, by permitting up to four sex workers to work together privately without someone in a management role, or on the street, in addition to the option of working in a managed 'brothel' setting (Abel et al. 2010).

It is important to emphasise that the PRA decriminalised all forms of adult, consensual sex work. Importantly, the PRA safeguards the right of individuals under the age of 18 to not be used in sex work, by making it an offence to arrange for, receive, facilitate or receive payment for commercial sexual services from an individual under the age of the 18. The PRA therefore recognises the vulnerability of young people under the age of 18, and the difference between commercial sex and other sexual activity (PLRC 2008). Importantly, young people themselves are not criminalised for engaging in commercial sexual activity, while those who facilitate, enable, profit from or arrange this can be held to account by the law.

One weakness of the PRA is that only sex workers who are permanent New Zealand residents and citizens are officially protected by the PRA. Section 19 of the Prostitution Reform Act relates to the Immigration Act 2009 and states that no person may be granted a visa if they have provided or intend to provide commercial sexual services, has acted or intends to act in a business of prostitution or has invested or intends to invest in a business of prostitution. If a person who has been granted a visa engages in commercial sex, then they can be deported. This aspect of the legislation was included to appease concerns about trafficking into the sex industry post-decriminalisation, though it is unclear just how this clause could help to prevent trafficking. The potential implications of this clause on migrant sex workers and their access to assistance from police will be discussed in more detail later in this chapter.

It is important to note that the PRA required the establishment of a Prostitution Law Review Committee (PLRC) to undertake a comprehensive review of the law change five years after its enactment, and to consider whether any future amendments may be required. The PLRC comprised 11 members with very diverse backgrounds, including a brothel operator, a former police commissioner, an academic and a nun (Abel 2010). Robust research has therefore followed the implementation of the Prostitution Reform Act to document its impacts. These impacts will be explored broadly in the next section, before considering the specific impacts on policing practices in relation to the sex industry.

The impacts of decriminalisation

One of the key strengths of New Zealand's approach to decriminalisation was a commitment to research in order to evaluate the impacts of decriminalisation in the five-year period following the passing of the PRA in 2003. Research conducted to evaluate the broad impacts of the PRA was conducted by researchers from the University of Otago's Christchurch School of Medicine in 2006 (Abel et al. 2007) and was also overseen by the Prostitution Law Review Committee, which reported on the impacts of the Act in 2008 (PLRC 2008). This research highlighted the diverse ways in which decriminalisation had benefitted sex workers, in relation to their health, human rights and safety.

Health

One key strength of the decriminalisation in New Zealand is that the sex industry is not heavily regulated through requiring mandatory health checks, which are required in many countries throughout the world, and are thought to have a negative impact on STI and HIV prevention (Jeffreys et al. 2014). Instead, the PRA allows sex workers full control over their sexual health but requires that sex workers and clients proactively protect themselves through the use of condoms and dental dams. This recognises that protecting their sexual health is in sex workers' own best interests, and that sex workers can be trusted to put in place these measures. In research conducted following the passing of the PRA only 3.7% of sex workers said that they did not get regular health checks (Abel 2014a). Since the PRA has been passed, it has been reported that this has shifted the balance of power in favour of sex workers in their negotiations with clients regarding condom use (Abel and Fitzgerald 2010). Sex workers can now use the law to enforce condom use with clients, and do make use of this law when necessary to seek justice when clients do not comply. While this aspect of the law has only been used a handful of times, with sex workers favouring earlier compliance, at the time of writing this chapter the most recent charges were brought against a client in early 2015 (Shadwell 2015). While an ideal situation would be for clients to comply with sex workers without difficulties, these cases demonstrate a willingness among sex workers to involve formal agencies such as police in situations in which clients threaten their health and well-being, thus exercising their rights under the PRA.

Sex worker rights

A key purpose of the PRA was to enhance the rights of sex workers through empowering them to challenge exploitative working practices. Research conducted following the passing of the PRA indicated that 95% of sex worker respondents felt that they had rights in the decriminalised context (Abel et al. 2007). Furthermore, this research also found that 60% of sex workers felt more able to refuse to see clients since the law had changed (Abel et al. 2007). In 2014 a sex worker raised a case of sexual harassment by a brothel operator, which was heard by the Human Rights Review Tribunal, and was awarded $25,000 in compensation (Duff 2014). This case demonstrates the powerful impact of decriminalisation in strengthening sex worker rights and ensuring that exploitative and abusive management practices can be challenged.

Safety

Research conducted since the PRA was passed also indicates a number of positive impacts for sex worker safety post-decriminalisation. The absence of data collected prior to the law change means that it is not possible to conclude statistically whether violence has decreased since sex work was decriminalised. It is important to stress that no law can prevent violence entirely, since perpetrators often make choices to offend regardless of the law in place. However, the evidence available does suggest that decriminalisation has had a positive impact in providing a safer environment which better supports risk management strategies. Street-based sex workers, for instance, can now stand on the street for as long as they wish before deciding whether or not to see a client because there is no risk of being arrested as there is in criminalised contexts (Armstrong 2014a). This means that street-based sex workers have more time to screen clients and make decisions about whether or not the potential client is trustworthy. Indoor sex workers also have an enhanced ability to screen clients in a decriminalised context. In contexts in which sex workers are criminalised, asking specific questions about clients and their service requirements could lead to arrest for soliciting. Similarly, when clients are criminalised they are less likely to be willing to provide personal, identifying information about themselves over the phone or in person. These processes are simplified in the New Zealand context since neither party is criminalised. However, sex workers do still experience violence in the decriminalised context, more commonly in the street sector. Research conducted following the passing of the PRA found that 39.5% of street-based sex worker participants had been threatened with violence in the previous 12 months compared to 16.3% of private indoor workers and 9.3% of managed indoor workers (Abel et al. 2007). Decriminalisation is therefore particularly important in the context of these ongoing risks of violence, particularly in relation to policing practices and access to justice. The remainder of this chapter will explore the ways in which decriminalisation has impacted on the police role, how this has been experienced by sex workers, and what gaps in knowledge continue to exist regarding the impacts of sex workers' experiences of police.

Policing and sex work – the legacy of criminalisation

To fully understand what decriminalisation has meant for sex workers in New Zealand in relation to their interactions with police, it is important to reflect on what the situation was prior to decriminalisation, and why decriminalisation represented such a significant change.

Historical legislation and the role of the police

Historical legislation to regulate the sex industry in New Zealand was based largely on the example of legislation passed in Britain, and meant that street-based sex workers were the most aggressively policed (Eldred-Grigg 1984). Motivated by a desire to address prostitution as a threat to moral order, legislation was passed in New Zealand in the form of the Vagrancy Act 1866 under which a 'common prostitute' who behaved publicly in a 'riotous or indecent manner' could be arrested on the basis that they were an 'idle and disorderly person' and face imprisonment (Eldred-Grigg 1984). The 1884 Police Offences Act later replaced this earlier legislation, which explicitly prohibited 'common prostitutes' propositioning members of the public, thereby reflecting ongoing commitment to policing street-based sex work in particular (PLRC 2008).

A commitment to policing and controlling prostitution in New Zealand historically was not only motivated by concerns regarding morality, however, but also by a perceived threat to public health. This linked to widespread panic surrounding the infectious disease syphilis, and a belief that the disease was a direct consequence of '*promiscuous sexual contact with diseased prostitutes*' (Walkowitz 1980: 48). In the late 1800s Contagious Diseases Acts were passed in New Zealand, Britain and Australia in response to these concerns about the potential impacts of prostitution (Ryan 2005). This legislation afforded police and medical professionals the power to alert a justice of the peace to a woman suspected of being a 'common prostitute'. The Act gave these individuals the authority to take women to a lock hospital, forcibly if necessary, to be examined and she could be detained in the hospital for up to three months (Ryan 2005). This approach obviously meant that street-based sex workers were more aggressively policed due to their visibility. The contagious diseases legislation and the vagrancy legislation represented the first significant legislation passed directly in relation to prostitution in New Zealand (Jordan 2005), and essentially set the scene for a legacy of conceptualising sex workers as dirty, diseased, dangerous and requiring state control. While the focus shifted somewhat in the late 19th century, with a desire to 'rescue' and 'save' sex workers who were 'repentant', those who did not want to be rescued were still considered to require aggressive policing and legal sanctions to control their behaviour (Bartley 2000). The legislation framework thereafter focused on limiting the scope of the sex industry through regulation.

From the latter part of the 20th century to the point of decriminalisation, working as a sex worker in New Zealand was essentially not against the law; however sex workers could be criminalised on the basis of related offences, such as soliciting (offering sexual services to another person in a public place) which was encompassed in the Summary of Offences Act 1981 (Robinson 1987). Within this context street-based sex work was heavily policed due to the perception of street work as a public nuisance, representing a threat to social order and morality (Robinson 1987). Other legislation included the Crimes Act 1961 (Section 147) which prohibited brothel keeping, the Crimes Act 1961 (Section 148 (a)) which outlawed living on the earnings of the prostitution of another person and the Crimes Act 1961 (Section 149) which prohibited the procuring for financial gain a woman or girl to have sex with a man who was not her husband (Robinson 1987). In addition, charges could be brought against those operating covertly as prostitutes within massage parlours under the Massage Parlours Act 1978 (Robinson 1987). Therefore, it was not illegal to work as a sex worker; however, it was impossible to work legally due to this related legislation. If charged under the Summary of Offences Act 1981 (Section 26) a maximum penalty of a $200 fine was imposed, while the other offences could carry up to a five-year jail term (Robinson 1987). Sex workers who were convicted under the Massage Parlours Act 1978 were also subsequently banned from working in massage parlours again and, as a result, were forced to work on the street if they wished or needed to continue working. This legislation cemented a societal understanding that sex work was not considered a legitimate occupation and defined the police role in relation to the sex industry as one of control and punishment, as opposed to care and protection.

Criminalisation, policing and sex worker safety

It is well -documented that sex workers are vulnerable to experiencing violence in their work, with the risk heightened in street-based sex work where sex workers are more visible to the public and often working autonomously (Benoit and Millar 2001; Krüsi et al. 2014; Sanders 2004a; Shannon et al. 2009). One UK study which compared the experiences of on-street and off-street sex workers found that 81% of the 115 on-street sex workers surveyed had experienced violence compared to 45% of 125 sex workers working indoors (Church et al. 2001). Higher levels of violence in street-based sex work may in part relate to the diverse risks and perpetrators street-based sex workers manage while working in the public space – meaning that they not only manage risks of violence from people who approach them as clients, but also from passers-by who abuse and harass them, protestors and vigilantes, and street associates (Armstrong 2014b). However, violence doesn't only relate to the location of sex work but also to the legal framework in place. In contexts in which sex work is criminalised, sex workers also manage the risk of arrest, which again is heightened for street-based sex workers who are most visible. In the context of ongoing risks of violence, a number of studies have documented the strategies developed by sex workers to manage risks of violence (Armstrong 2014a; Dalla et al. 2003; O'Neill and Barberet 2000; Phrasisombath et al. 2012; Pyett and Warr 1999; Sanders 2001, 2004b; Williamson and Folaron 2001). Such strategies may include the process of 'screening' clients, either in person or on the phone to build a picture of the person and attempt to approximate the risk of violence with that individual, and/or collect identifying information as an additional security measure. Safety strategies may also include decisions about where and when to work, and notifying others of working patterns and whereabouts.

It is argued that criminalised frameworks impede the use of safety strategies amongst individual sex workers through policing presenting an additional risk to the already substantial hierarchy of risks managed (Sanders 2004b). This risk is amplified for street-based sex workers who are the most visible group of sex workers and also long-regarded as the most threatening and problematic, and thus in need to control. In criminalised contexts, the policing of street sex work does vary between different areas and cities (Hubbard 2006). However, in some contexts police do unambiguously pursue sex workers on the street in order to arrest and remove them from the public gaze (Benson and Matthews 2000; Hubbard 2004; Rosen and Venkatesh 2008; Sagar 2007; Sanders 2004a; Sullivan 2008; Wotton 2005). Avoiding the police is, therefore, an additional daily hazard for street workers working in this context of criminalisation and the possibility of being arrested is a genuine risk. As a consequence, it has been argued that screening strategies are undermined since sex workers must work quickly and position themselves discreetly in order to avoid the gaze of authorities (Chapkis 2000; Hubbard and Sanders 2003; Kinnell 2006). While street-based sex workers are the most vulnerable to aggressive policing in criminalised contexts, those working indoors also manage this risk daily in the knowledge that being arrested could have significant consequences for future employment, travel and relationships.

Prior to the decriminalisation of sex work in New Zealand, sex workers continually managed the risk of arrest and criminalisation and while this was amplified in the street sector, it was an ever-present risk in all sectors of the sex industry. The police were therefore positioned as a risk to be managed, rather than a source of help and support in the context of risks of violence. The situation pre-decriminalisation therefore mirrors, at least to some extent, the current situation in several countries such as the UK where many activities associated with sex work remain criminalised. One of the key aims of decriminalisation was to create a safer environment for sex workers, and as such this required a fundamental shift in the policing of sex work. The next section of this chapter explores how the policing of sex work has changed in the decriminalised context.

Decriminalisation and policing

Street-based sex work

The most significant change in relationship between police and sex workers post-decriminalisation has been observed in the street sector, where sex work occurs in the open space and as such there are more opportunities for police to come into contact with sex workers. Street-based sex workers have reported that they now feel more respected by police and that instead of representing a threat police now occupy a position from which they can demonstrate a commitment to sex worker safety (Armstrong 2016). This has been particularly evident in Christchurch where relationship building between police and sex workers has occurred in very difficult circumstances, with the murders of four women working on the streets since 2003. The murder investigations in Christchurch stand in stark contrast to those conducted in previous years in other countries with less liberal legal frameworks in place, for instance the widespread critiques of the investigation into the whereabouts of women who went missing in Vancouver's downtown eastside over a 20-year period from the early 1980s (Oppal 2012). In all four Christchurch murders, a perpetrator was arrested and charged, and the police demonstrated publicly their commitment to investigating and achieving justice for the women and those close to them. These investigations were supported by information sharing from clients and sex workers, which would be very difficult if the sale or purchase of sex was criminalised (Armstrong 2016). In one of these cases, the police undertook over 1000 interviews, which resulted in the conviction of one perpetrator (Abel 2014b). However, police believe that more perpetrators were involved and the investigation is continuing, eight years after Mellory Manning's body was found in December 2009. Decriminalisation has therefore enabled a more trusting environment in which all parties can be more open to communicating with authorities, in the interests of addressing violence and preventing further violence against sex workers.

In the street sex work context, decriminalisation has also meant that the police can be called on to help resolve disputes between sex workers and clients – for instance over payment and services provided (Armstrong 2016). In 2014, it was reported in the New Zealand media that a client had been escorted to an ATM by police to withdraw money so that a street-based sex worker could be paid the amount that had been agreed on. The police officer interviewed emphasised that police would assist sex workers in the same way that they would assist any other service industry workers managing a dispute of this type (Wynn 2014). This is a significant change, as it has been noted that when sex work is criminalised disputes over payment or services provided are more likely to spiral into violence since the risk of arrest means that police cannot be called on to mediate in these situations (Kinnell 2006).

Indoor sex work

The police do not routinely enter brothels in New Zealand for no good reason, and do not participate in large raid and 'rescue' operations as occurs in some other countries where sex workers and/or clients are criminalised. Police can enter establishments with a warrant if they consider that an offence is or is likely to be committed in relation to the use of persons under the age of 18, or if there are concerns that the establishment does not hold an operators certificate.[1] Thus, police play no overt role in policing brothels, and those working in them can now call on police if they do experience violence, which was very difficult before the law change. Since indoor sex workers do not routinely come into contact with police in the course of their work, there is little evidence available on how their interactions with police have changed since decriminalisation.

Reporting violence

In contexts in which sex work is criminalised, the risk of criminalisation presents a significant barrier to sex workers reporting violence (Pyett and Warr 1997; Kinnell 2008; Wotton 2005). Thus, in a decriminalised context such as New

---

1 Under the Prostitution Reform Act, every operator of a sex work business must obtain an operator's certificate

Zealand's, a fundamental aim is to make it easier for sex workers to report violence to police. Research conducted in 2007 to evaluate the impacts of the PRA found that although sex workers were still reluctant to report violence to the police, there was a perception that now sex work was decriminalised, these reports would be taken more seriously (Abel et al. 2007; PLRC 2008). The perceptions of street-based sex workers interviewed in 2008/2009 supported this, and several women suggested that they would not hesitate to report violence to police now that sex work was decriminalised. One woman noted that while she did not report being attacked prior to decriminalisation she would do so if it happened now:

> It builds a relationship I think with the police um in the fact that I feel confi-
> dent enough now to go to them if need be, if anything you know went down
> whereas before you wouldn't. You would not because chances are you're
> going to be arrested. . . . So I guess it's closed a bridge there. . . . Sort of made
> each other approachable. . . . If it happened now I would report it. I would
> definitely do that now – Shania
>
> (Armstrong 2016: 10–11)

It is also important to acknowledge the role that that the PRA has played in strengthening relationships with and confidence in police among those work-ing closely with street-based sex workers. Research conducted to evaluate the impacts of the PRA found that while some sex workers may still be reluctant to report violence to police, they did tell another person – most commonly a friend, co-worker, or NZPC worker (Abel et al. 2007). A street-based sex worker inter-viewed in 2009 recalled an experience that she did not initially report to police but later reported with support from outreach workers from a youth organisation:

> A car went past me and they pulled out a rifle. . . . And I had a friend with me
> who witnessed it as well. And the cameras and stuff had seen it. . . . I reported
> it to [youth workers]. . . . And they took me down to the police station and
> made some complaints which I'd never done before. And . . . it just felt good,
> I mean having them idiots going past and doing that. I mean they're prob-
> ably one out of many who do that. And it's not only guns, it's bottles too. . . .
> Everyone's got opinions on the police but yeah I did actually have a little
> respect for them after that. I mean at least those little boys can't go around
> shooting people – Claire
>
> (Armstrong 2015: 295).

Sex workers have also used the PRA to bring to justice police who have offended against them. In 2009, a police officer was convicted and sentenced to imprisonment for abusing his police power to force a sex worker to provide sexual services free of charge (Booker 2009). The criminalisation of sex work provides an environment in which police power can be easily exploited, and as such it can be argued that decriminalisation shifts the balance of power so that sex workers are not as disadvan-taged (Armstrong 2016). The fact that sex workers can now challenge corrupt and abusive police officers clearly demonstrates the level of trust that decriminalisation has engendered, and indicates a wiliness among some police to proactively tackle violence against sex workers regardless of the identity of the perpetrator.

Ongoing challenges

The decriminalisation of sex work has undoubtedly improved the relationship between police and sex workers in New Zealand. However, the history of criminalisation has left a long legacy and it would be inaccurate to suggest that there are no remaining challenges. Criminalisation created a context in which relationships between police and sex workers, particularly in the street sector, were defined by fear and distrust. The law change cannot be expected to heal the scars of criminalisation overnight.

As highlighted in the previous section of this chapter, although there have been some significant improvements in the police approach to interacting with sex workers, there have been isolated reports of individual police officers sexually abusing sex workers. While decriminalisation has provided a context in which police can be proactive about supporting sex worker safety, it cannot prevent individual officers from making decisions to abuse their power in this way. For instance, the actions of Nathan Connolly, who was sentenced to two years' imprisonment in 2009 for forcing a woman to provide sexual services free of charge in order to avoid her being charged with driving offences. And rape allegations made against a Senior Detective in 2014 in addition to repeated attempts to access information about the complainant on a police database (Booker 2009; Kidd 2014). However, hopefully, in time, the commitment to supporting sex workers among some individual officers will lead to wider cultural shifts through sending a message to potential perpetrators that this type of behaviour will not be tolerated.

Another challenge that exists relates to the police approach to working with street-based sex workers. It has been noted that while police demonstrating that they care for the safety of street-based sex workers is welcomed, at times this can be experienced as overbearing and police visibility is considered to represent a potential barrier to attracting clients (Armstrong 2010). Working effectively to support the safety of street-based sex workers in a decriminalised environment therefore requires discretion from police in their approach, ensuring that sex workers know that they are available, while not having a conspicuous presence on the street that interferes with business.

While decriminalisation has helped to break down barriers between police and sex workers, the stigma that is still associated with sex work presents an additional barrier to sex workers reporting violence since sex workers still fear being 'outed' in media coverage of court cases (Abel et al. 2007). The stigma associated with sex work has a long history that has embedded deeply entrenched norms regarding women's sexuality. A change in law cannot reverse this long legacy, and this requires far broader social and cultural change (Armstrong 2015). Thus, while decriminalisation provides a safer environment to report violence, stigma continues to place a limit on the effectiveness of this legislative change.

There are also some limitations to what the police can do to address the most prevalent but more subtle forms of violence that sex workers experience, particularly verbal abuse directed at those who work from the street. Key informants interviewed in a 2009 study demonstrated that while some were committed to doing whatever they could to address verbal abuse directed at street-based sex workers, there was a perception amongst street-based sex workers that this type of abuse was, to some extent, inevitable and that there was little that the police could do to address it (Armstrong 2011, 2015). Indeed, while the police can take action if they witness verbal abuse taking place, the scale of verbal abuse that street-based sex workers experience means that it is very difficult to respond to all of these incidents. However, if police do consistently respond to incidents whenever possible to do so, then this should demonstrate to potential perpetrators that this behaviour is not unacceptable.

There are also specific limitations to police working to support the safety of migrant sex workers. As previously noted, those with temporary work or study visas are not permitted to work in the sex industry. This means that there are still sex workers in New Zealand who are working illegally and these sex workers do not benefit from the rights afforded to other sex workers by the PRA. The precarious legal status of migrant sex workers means that they are arguably more vulnerable to exploitation than other sex workers, and the law presents a significant barrier to them reporting violence (Roguski 2013). This part of the PRA was not supported by NZPC but was included in the law to satisfy some politicians who were concerned about trafficking and/or endorsed a xenophobic fear of an influx of migrant sex workers post-decriminalisation. Since decriminalisation, one study has been conducted specifically focusing on the experiences of migrant sex workers and this research found that a majority of migrant sex workers had entered New Zealand of their own volition, chosen to undertake sex work and were happy overall with their conditions of work (Roguski 2013). Anecdotal reports suggest that police and immigration officials do not aggressively monitor and target sex work businesses in New Zealand in search of illegal workers. Decriminalisation arguably provides a context in which sex workers who are working legally, and clients, can contact authorities if they do suspect that a migrant sex worker is being exploited. Nevertheless, the capacity for police to support migrant sex workers who are exploited or subject to violence remains hamstrung by their illegal status. Only when the law changes and all sex workers in New Zealand are afforded the same rights and access to justice under the PRA, will police be ideally positioned to support the safety of *all* sex workers.

Concluding comments

The decriminalisation of sex work in 2003 set New Zealand apart by becoming the first full country to completely decriminalise sex work. The decriminalisation of sex work in New Zealand was motivated by a desire to create safer work environments for sex workers. This chapter has explored how the decriminalisation of sex work has impacted the policing of sex work, specifically how sex workers interact with police and their ability to report violence.

The decriminalisation of sex work has undoubtedly had a positive impact on the relationship between police and sex workers, most notably in relation to the street-based sex industry. Street-based sex workers interact with police more often due to their visibility. They are also the most vulnerable group of sex workers in terms of being targeted with violence and therefore had the most to gain from decriminalisation. However, sex workers in all sectors of this industry have benefitted from decriminalisation, in that eliminating the threat of arrest has removed a significant barrier to reporting violence and harassment.

While it is clear that the law change has had a positive impact, a number of barriers continue to limit the effectiveness of the police role in supporting sex worker safety. The law change has not (and cannot) removed deeply engrained stigma towards sex workers, or pockets of police culture containing individuals who feel empowered to exploit sex workers. Decriminalisation represents a first step in challenging stigma and provides a context in which the power balance is shifted at least to some extent, and sex workers are better placed to challenge those in positions of authority who seek to exploit them. A future change that could assist in further strengthening the police approach to supporting sex workers, and challenging negative attitudes among individual police personnel, is a shift towards defining violence against sex workers as hate crime. Such an approach has been in place in Merseyside in the UK since 2006 and even in a criminalised context, this has helped to build greater trust in police and work towards redefining the police role in relation to the protection of sex workers, at least to some extent (Campbell 2014). The adoption of this approach in New Zealand's decriminalised context could further strengthen the police approach to responding to sex workers who are victimised, and also influence further positive change within wider society regarding how violence against sex workers is perceived.

It is important to note that there are still existing gaps in knowledge regarding how particular groups of sex workers perceive and experience police in the decriminalised context – particularly transgender sex workers, male sex workers and migrant sex workers. Further research into the perceptions and experiences of indoor sex workers is also important. There may now be different experiences and perceptions, given that over 10 years has passed since the law was changed and a majority of sex workers will now have started working in the sex industry in the context of decriminalisation. It is possible that those who began working in the decriminalised context may have even more confidence in the police since their experience is not clouded by memories of criminalisation and an ever-present risk of arrest. New Zealand represents a unique context in being the first country to fully decriminalise sex work, and as such ongoing research is essential to continue to build evidence regarding the longer-term impacts of this change. However, given the evidence currently available it is reasonable to conclude that decriminalisation has had a positive impact on policing practices, and other countries should strongly consider adopting a similar model of full decriminalisation to prioritise sex workers' rights and safety.

References

Abel, G. (2010) *Decriminalisation: A harm minimisation and human rights approach to regulating sex work.* Unpublished doctoral dissertation. University of Otago, Dunedin.

Abel, G. (2014a) 'Sex workers utilisation of health services in a decriminalised environment', *The New Zealand Medical Journal*, 127 (1390), 30–37.

Abel, G. (2014b) 'A decade of decriminalisation: Sex work "down under" but not under-ground', *Criminology and Criminal Justice*, 14 (5), 580–592.

Abel, G., and Fitzgerald, L. (2010) 'Risk and risk-management in sex work post-Prostitution Reform Act: A public health perspective of the PRA', in Abel, G., Fitzger-ald, L., and Healy, C. (Eds.) *Taking the crime out of sex work: New Zealand sex workers' fight for decriminalisation*. Bristol: Policy Press, pp. 239–259.

Abel, G., Fitzgerald, L., and Brunton, C. (2007) *The impact of the Prostitution Reform Act on the health and safety practices of sex workers*. Christchurch: Department of Public Health and General Practice, University of Otago.

Abel, G., Fitzgerald, L., and Brunton, C. (2009) 'The Impact of decriminalisation on the number of sex workers in New Zealand', *Journal of Social Policy*, 38 (3), 515–531.

Abel, G., Healy, C., Bennachie, C., and Reed, A. (2010) 'The Prostitution Reform Act', in Abel, G., Fitzgerald, L., and Healy, C. (Eds.) *Taking the crime out of sex work: New Zealand sex workers' fight for decriminalisation*. Bristol: Policy Press, pp. 75–84.

Armstrong, L. (2010) 'Out of the shadows (and into a bit of light): Decriminalisation, human rights and street-based sex work in New Zealand', in Hardy, K., Kingston, S., and Sanders, T. (Eds.) *New sociologies of sex work*. Farnham: Ashgate, pp. 39–55.

Armstrong, L. (2011) *Managing risks of violence in decriminalised street-based sex work: A feminist (sex worker rights) perspective*. Unpublished doctoral dissertation. Victoria University of Wellington, Wellington.

Armstrong, L. (2014a) 'Screening clients in a decriminalised street-based sex industry: Insights into the experiences of New Zealand sex workers', *Australian and New Zealand Journal of Criminology*, 47 (2), 207–222.

Armstrong, L. (2014b) 'Diverse risks, diverse perpetrators: perceptions of risk and expe-riences of violence amongst street-based sex workers in New Zealand', *International Journal for Crime, Justice and Social Democracy*, 3, 40–54.

Armstrong, L. (2015) '"Who's the slut, who's the whore?" Street harassment in the workplace among female sex workers in New Zealand', *Feminist Criminology*, 11 (3), 285–303.

Armstrong, L. (2016) 'From law enforcement to protection? Interactions between sex workers and police in a decriminalised street-based sex industry', *British Journal of Criminology*, 57 (3), 570–588.

Bartley, P. (2000) *Prostitution: Prevention and reform in England, 1860–1914*. London: Routledge.

Benoit, C., and Millar, A. (2001) *Dispelling myths and understanding realities: Working conditions, health status and exiting experiences of sex workers*. British Columbia: Uni-versity of Victoria.

Benson, C., and Matthews, R. (2000) 'Police and prostitution: Vice squads in Britain', in Weitzer, R. (Ed.) *Sex for sale: Prostitution, pornography, and the sex industry*. New York: Routledge, pp. 245–264.

Booker, J. (2009) 'Guilty verdict for police officer who extorted free sex from prostitute', *New Zealand Herald*. Available at: www.nzherald.co.nz/nz/news/article.cfm?c_id=1and objectid=10609983 (Accessed 1 November 2016).

Campbell, R. (2014) 'Not getting away with it: Linking sex work and hate crime in Mer-seyside', in Chakraborti, N., and Garland, J. (Eds.), *Responding to hate crime: The case for connecting policy and research*. Bristol: Policy Press, pp. 55–70.

Chapkis, W. (2000) 'Power and control in the commercial sex trade', in Weitzer, R. (Ed.) *Sex for sale: Prostitution, pornography and the sex industry*. New York: Routledge, pp. 181–201.

Church, S., Henderson, M., Barnard, M., and Hart, G. (2001) 'Violence by clients towards female prostitutes in different work settings: Questionnaire survey', *British Medical Journal*, 322, 524–525.

Dalla, R. L., Xia, Y., and Kennedy, H. (2003) '"You just give them what they want and pray they don't kill you": Street-level sex workers' reports of victimization, personal resources, and coping strategies', *Violence Against Women*, 9 (11), 1367–1394.

Duff, M. (2014) 'Sex worker gets $25,000 over harassment', *The Dominion Post*. Available at: www.stuff.co.nz/business/industries/9777879/Sex-worker-gets-25-000-over-harassment (Accessed 30 November 2016).

Eldred-Grigg, S. (1984) *Pleasures of the flesh: Sex and drugs in colonial New Zealand, 1840–1915*. Wellington: Reed.

Hubbard, P. (2004) 'Cleansing the metropolis: Sex work and the politics of zero tolerance', *Urban Studies*, 41 (9), 1687–1702.

Hubbard, P. (2006) 'Out of touch and out of time? The contemporary policing of sex work', in Campbell, R., and O'Neill, M. (Eds.) *Sex work now*. Cullompton, Devon: Willan Publishing, pp. 1–32.

Hubbard, P., and Sanders, T. (2003) 'Making space for sex work: Female street prostitution and the production of urban space', *International Journal of Urban and Regional Research*, 27 (1), 73–87.

Jeffreys, E., Fawkes, J., and Stardust, Z. (2014) 'Mandatory testing for HIV and sexually transmissible infections among sex workers in Australia: A barrier to HIV and STI prevention', *World Journal of AIDS*, 2, 203–211.

Jordan, J. (2005) *The Sex industry in New Zealand: A literature review*. Wellington: Ministry of Justice.

Kidd, R. (2014) 'No charges after top cop accused of rape', *Stuff*. Available at: www.stuff.co.nz/national/9916964/No-charges-after-top-cop-accused-of-rape (Accessed 30 January 2017).

Kinnell, H. (2006) 'Murder made easy: The final solution to prostitution?', in Campbell, R., and O'Neill, M. (Eds.) *Sex work now*. Cullompton, Devon: Willan Publishing, pp. 141–168.

Kinnell, H. (2008) *Violence and sex work in Britain*. Cullompton, Devon: Willan Publishing.

Krüsi, A., Pacey, K., Bird, L., et al. (2014) 'Criminalisation of clients: Reproducing vulnerabilities for violence and poor health among street-based sex workers in Canada – a qualitative study', *BMJ Open*, e005191, 1–10.

O'Neill, M., and Barberet, R. (2000) 'Victimisation and the social organisation of prostitution in England and Spain', in Weitzer, R. (Ed.) *Sex for sale: Prostitution, pornography and the sex industry*. London: Routledge, pp. 123–137.

Oppal, W. (2012) *Forsaken: Report of the missing women commission of enquiry: Executive summary*. British Columbia: Library and Archives Canada.

Phrasisombath, K., Thomsen, S., Sychareun, V., and Faxelid, E. (2013) 'Risks, benefits and survival strategies-views from female sex workers in Savannakhet, Laos', *BMC Public Health*, 12 (1004), 1–12.

Prostitution Law Review Committee. (2008) *Report of the prostitution law review committee on the operation of the Prostitution Reform Act 2003*. Wellington: Ministry of Justice.

Prostitution Reform Act. (2003) Available at: www.legislation.govt.nz/act/public/2003/0028/latest/whole.html#DLM197821 (Accessed 11 July 2017).

Pyett, P., and Warr, D. (1997) 'Vulnerability on the streets: Female sex workers and HIV risk', *AIDS Care*, 9 (5), 539.

Pyett, P., and Warr, D. (1999) 'Women at risk in sex work: Strategies for survival', *Journal of Sociology*, 35 (2), 183–197.

Robinson, J. (1987) 'The oldest profession', in Cox, S. (Ed.) *Public and private worlds: Women in contemporary New Zealand*. Wellington: Allen and Unwin in association with the Port Nicholson Press, pp. 177–191.

Roguski, M. (2013) *Occupational health and safety of migrant sex workers in New Zealand*. Wellington: Kaitaki Research and Evaluation.

Rosen, E., and Venkatesh, S. A. (2008) 'A "perversion" of choice: Sex work offers just enough in Chicago's urban ghetto', *Journal of Contemporary Ethnography*, 37 (4), 417–441.

Ryan, A. (2005) 'From dangerous sexualities to risky sex: Regulating sexuality in the name of public health', in Hawkes, G., and Scott, J. (Eds.) *Perspectives in human sexuality*. South Melbourne: Oxford University Press, pp. 203–216.

Sagar, T. (2007) 'Tackling on-street sex work: Anti-social behaviour orders, sex workers and inclusive inter-agency initiatives', *Criminology and Criminal Justice*, 7 (2), 153–168.

Sanders, T. (2001) 'Female street sex workers, sexual violence, and protection strategies', *Journal of Sexual Aggression*, 7 (1), 5–18.

Sanders, T. (2004a) 'The risks of street prostitution: Punters, police and protesters', *Urban Studies*, 41 (9), 1703–1717.

Sanders, T. (2004b) 'A continuum of risk? The management of health, physical and emotional risks by female sex workers', *Sociology of Health and Illness*, 26 (5), 557–574.

Shadwell, T. (2015) 'Man charged with failing to use condom with prostitute', *The Dominion Post*. Available at: www.stuff.co.nz/national/crime/67464897/man-charged-with-failing-to-use-condom-with-prostitute (Accessed 21 November 2016).

Shannon, K., Kerr, T., Strathdee, S., Shoveller, J., Montaner, J., and Tyndall, M. (2009) 'Prevalence and structural correlates of gender based violence among a prospective cohort of female sex workers', *British Medical Journal*, 339, b2939.

Sullivan, B. (2008) 'Working in the sex industry in Australia: The reorganisation of sex work in Queensland in the wake of law reform', *Labour and Industry*, 18 (3), 73–92.

Walkowitz, J. (1980) *Prostitution and Victorian society: Women, class, and the state*. Cambridge: Cambridge University Press.

Williamson, C., and Folaron, G. (2001) 'Violence, risk, and survival strategies of street prostitution', *Western Journal of Nursing Research*, 23 (5), 463–475.

Wotton, R. (2005) 'The relationship between street-based sex workers and the police in the effectiveness of HIV prevention strategies', *Research for Sex Work*, 8, 11–13.

Wynn, K. (2014) 'Police help short-changed sex worker', *New Zealand Herald*. Available at: www.nzherald.co.nz/nz/news/article.cfm?c_id=1and objectid=11292537 (Accessed 21 July 2015).

5 'Not in our name'

Findings from Wales supporting the decriminalisation of sex work

Tracey Sagar and Debbie Jones

Introduction

Several countries across the globe have English law at the very foundation of their legal systems (Australia, Canada and New Zealand for example), thus it is hardly surprising that in line with the English law, 'prostitution' has been closely associated with a public nuisance discourse in so many countries, with a tradition of managing and containing 'visible' street-based sex work in particular (Hancock 1991; Kantola and Squires 2004; Scoular 2010; Abel et al. 2010; Campbell 2015). However, unlike parts of Australia and New Zealand which have adopted a progressive approach to sex work through either licencing (Australia) or the removal of sex work laws (New Zealand), England and Wales (like Canada) have remained steadfast in their position that visible sex work is offensive, injurious and a self evident public nuisance, thus commanding criminal law sanctions (Wolfenden 1957). In England and Wales a system of partial criminalisation seeks to 'manage' sex work through outlawing a variety of visible activities such as soliciting and loitering in a public place under the Street Offences Act 1959 and kerb crawling and soliciting under the Sexual Offences Act 1985. It is an approach that was re-emphasised in the late 1990s and beyond under the then New Labour government where sex work was not only held up as a public nuisance but also took on the mantle of behaviour that was *anti-social* causing harassment, alarm and distress to members of the wider community (Crime and Disorder Act 1998). Under the New Labour government communities were urged not to tolerate prostitution; the government even supported community activism against sex workers through the state backed 'Street Watch' community/policing initiative which had a primary aim of displacing sex workers outside of the community, and it urged local authorities and the police to work with members of the community to curb undesirable behaviour through the implementation of anti-social behaviour orders (ASBOs) preventing sex workers from engaging in 'prostitution' and excluding them from entering specified geographical areas (Sagar 2005, 2007). All of this took place within a new era of policing underpinned by the concept of *community safety*.

Somewhat ironically, conceptually *community safety* moved the focus of crime prevention from property to *people* – it re-focused attention to the safety needs of those in the community (Squires 1997). Achieving community safety was dependent on local people working with the police and other agencies to undertake coordinated action to resolve local problems. For the police, this partnership approach shared accountability for local issues but in doing so it meant that problems requiring community/police action were also selected at the local level, and primarily this meant that they would be set by the respectable middle classes i.e. those who were much more likely to engage with the police (Brake and Hale 1992: 77, cited in Squires 1997) to the detriment of others. Focusing on what and who the community needed protection *from* resulted in individuals and groups being either *inside* or *outside* of the community and this was and continues to be problematic for sex workers, and particularly so while sex work laws and policies are swathed in public nuisance/community protection discourse which prioritises the needs of the community – over and above for example the safety of sex workers.

It is hardly surprising therefore that sex work policy reforms in England and Wales which are shrouded in protective speak (recognising the vulnerability and exploitation of sex workers, the need for welfarist interventions and support to leave the industry, see Home Office 2004 and 2006) have in fact had severe consequences for sex workers. What could outwardly be regarded as a form of progressive governance given that the needs and protection of sex workers appear to be elevated has been criticised by Scoular and O'Neill (2007) for utilising social 'inclusion techniques' which in truth are much more about 'risk management' and 'responsibilisation'. For example, today under the law of England and Wales sex workers (vulnerable or not) can be ordered by the court to engage with support workers to find ways to exit sex work (see, section 17 Policing and Crime Act 2009). In this instance, good citizenship requires individual change – ceasing to engage in sex work. In short, as Scoular and O'Neill (2007) bluntly explain, inclusion was never really on offer to sex workers. Instead the reforms reflected the moral and political communitarian vision of the then New Labour government, leaving sex workers on the road to nowhere – lacking good citizenship, beyond community and consequentially de-prioritised in Community Safety initiatives. Indeed, putting the final nail in the coffin, the then New Labour government throughout the policy development process declared sex work to be a public nuisance and the *in*tolerance of sex work in the community was encouraged, as well as zero tolerance policing initiatives (see Home Office 2004, 2006).

At the same time, however, a different model of regulating sex work was being implemented across Europe, underpinned by a neo-abolitionist perspective (Scoular and Carline 2014) that defined 'prostitution' as male violence against women and the epitome of male patriarchal domination (male and trans sex workers are not the focus of this agenda, see Whowell 2010). Several European countries in the late 1990s and the first decade of the new millennium outlawed the purchase of sex (for example, Sweden in 1999; Norway in 2009; Iceland in 2009) and what has become known as the 'Swedish' or 'Nordic model' has found a firm place on the political radar within Europe with Northern Ireland and France most recently adopting the model in 2016. To date, England and Wales (two countries which share the same criminal legal system) have refrained from criminalising the purchase of sex per se (see Home Office 2008), but as already noted, there is in place a re-structured legal framework designed to meet the call to provide protection for sex workers from the violence inflicted by male exploiters and tougher measures have been implemented to protect against exploitation through laws that seek to deter men from purchasing sex (see for example, section 14 Policing and Crime Act 2009). As Carline (2009) points out, meeting the vulnerability of sex workers through criminal measures which target clients still sends forth a strong message that buying sex is morally unacceptable.

Of course a problem of some significance is presented where sex workers are on the one hand perceived to be vulnerable and exploited and in need of assistance, and on the other creators of public nuisance and offenders against the community. This is because prioritising community interests can serve to negatively impact on the safety of sex workers – where sex workers are forced out in geographical terms from residential areas (through ASBOs and more recently Criminal Behaviour Orders under the Anti-Social Behaviour Act 2014 for example, and zero tolerance policing including operations targeted at clients), their vulnerability is heightened (Sanders 2009). Furthermore, it is true to say that concerns within the academic community are unremitting regarding the compulsory nature of section 17 engagement and support orders and the ability of criminal justice interventions to 'exit' sex workers from the streets (Scoular and Carline 2014) as well as reducing sex work through client targeting (Sanders et al. 2009). And while further policy guidance on responding to sex work was offered in 2011 from the then Coalition government which did (once again) emphasise the need to provide holistic multi-agency support for sex workers to facilitate exit from sex work, it also followed the long-standing trend of governments in underlining the negative impact sex work can have on communities and made it clear that local resources should be utilised to prevent sex work from taking place (Home Office 2011). In sum, despite the contemporary shifts in law and policy from enforcement to welfarist models of social control, sex work continues to be regarded as a crime against the community and protecting the community from sex workers remains at the heart of sex work policy in England and Wales (Sagar and Jones 2013a). The upshot is that the legal and policy framework regulating sex work in England and Wales is full of contradictions and this in turn presents a labyrinth to be negotiated in policing terms.

This chapter challenges the premise that sex work is a crime against the community necessitating punitive control. It draws on findings from the research project 'Sex Work Research Wales', a 4-year study that took place across Wales between 2010 and 2014.[1] Setting out to fill gaps in knowledge in Wales regarding the location of both on and off street sex work, the research also sought to understand the extent of the negative impact of sex work on Welsh communities as well as policing responses. Analysis suggests that sex work (both on and off street) is neither a policing priority nor a contested community issue in Wales. The importance of the findings are as follows. First, they add to an increasing body of local research highlighting the willingness of residents living in red light areas to share community space/try new and less punitive ways of managing sex work (see for e.g. Bellis et al. 2007; O'Neill et al. 2008; Sagar and Jones 2013a; Sanders and Sehmbi 2015). Second, at a national level in Wales the data signals a more tolerant attitude to sex work and this calls strategies of zero tolerance prescribed by governments into question. The findings here confront many of the 'community protection' concerns which underpin the need for legal controls and which tend to be brought to the surface when the necessity of regulatory laws and policies are deliberated (see Wolfenden 1957; Criminal Law Revision Committee 1984; Home Office 2004, 2006). Thus, the discussion which follows here is very timely given the current review of sex work laws invoked by the House of Commons Home Affairs Committee (2016). At the time of writing the Committee is carefully considering the potential of both the Nordic and New Zealand sex work frameworks in particular. Contributing to this debate, our findings from Wales lead us to argue that abolitionist policies that criminalise the purchase of sex (Nordic model) may not easily be supported by the position that sex work is a public nuisance/damaging to communities. Instead we maintain that the indicators of community toleration presented in this chapter pave the way for the recognition that sex workers have the right to work safely within an inclusionary society and offer support for decriminalisation.

Sex work in Wales: A brief overview

Wales is a devolved nation of the United Kingdom bordered by England to its east. As a devolved nation, it has its own responsibility in matters of health and other social programmes such as education and well-being. However, in matters of criminal law Wales is governed by the law of England and Wales (unlike Scotland which has its own criminal legal system). Being a small nation with an estimated population of just over three million (UK Population 2016), there has been a tendency for sex work-related issues to be subsumed within policy and practice derived from and developed within England. And, it is true to say that until the last 10 years or so very little was known about sex work in Wales. In 1997, the then New Labour government's mantra of local areas are best placed to resolve local problems, together with an importance on evidence-based local policies, brought about the development of local Community Safety Partnerships in Wales and consequentially some years later multi-agency approaches came into being with the aim of tackling a wide variety of local issues including sex work. Collaborations between academics and stakeholders began to take place in the pursuit of evidence-based sex work policy in Wales from 2008 onwards. For example, the authors of this chapter have worked alongside a wide range of local agencies (statutory and third sector) to provide base line data on sex work in Wales. Yet, unsurprisingly given the 'local' focus, this work was patchy and tended to take place in the nation's capital, Cardiff (see for example Sagar et al. 2010; Sagar and Jones 2010). In an attempt to provide some much needed national base line evidence, a 4-year project 'Sex Work Research Wales' (SWRW) led by Gibran UK (a third sector organisation working to support people in the Criminal Justice System) in partnership with Swansea University took place between 2010–14 (funded by the Big Lottery Innovation Fund Wales), the findings of which are the focus of this chapter.

Following an outline of the project's methodology, key findings of the project are presented. Importantly, the findings reported from Wales are primarily concerned with the policing of sex work and public perceptions of sex work. Arguing that sex work in Wales does not present as a perpetual community nuisance which needs to be eliminated, we suggest the time is right to leave behind our obsession with nuisance and enforcement, and embark on a process of legal and policy reform which recognises sex workers as members of the community – deserving emotional and physical security.

Methods

The study

Adopting a multi methods approach the 'Sex Work Research Wales' (SWRW) study was divided into 2 phases. Phase 1 had a number of aims: to geographically map the areas in Wales where sex work took place both on and off street; identify whether sex workers were the target of police operations in Wales; locate areas of Wales where sex work was a community concern; identify multi-agency sex work focused partnerships across Wales; and to consider service provision for sex workers from the perspectives of service users. Phase 2 provided in-depth research which aimed to: understand how local areas with significant sex work populations responded to and managed sex work within a multi-agency capacity; work with local organisations to engage with sex workers; provide in-depth understandings of sex workers' experiences alongside of the opinions and impact of sex work on local communities in a case study area. This chapter draws on the project data specifically concerned with policing sex work and community perceptions of sex work. In this way we are able to provide: an overview of sex work in Wales; police responses to visible sex work activity; indicators of community discontent at sex work across Wales; and community views and opinions of sex work.

Engendering social change: action research

The study was underpinned by an Action Research (AR) ethos – influenced by the ground-breaking work of O'Neill and Campbell's (2004) community study of the impact of street sex work in Walsall. Stepping away from traditional methods of social science research, O'Neill and Campbell opened up their study to community participants who they trained to carry out the research in partnership with them with the purpose of generating new understandings and social change. Similarly, SWRW sought to address the power imbalance from research that is carried out 'on' participants to one that is inclusive and potentially empowering – conducting research 'with' those who are the subject of the study. SWRW trained 10 peer/community researchers (sex workers and members of the wider community) to carry out interviews and administer questionnaires with sex workers, residents and members of the business community (the latter of which forms the focus of this chapter). Peer researchers also assisted with data analysis.

Data collection methods

As already noted, this chapter does not report on the findings from all of the elements to the study (for the full report see Sagar et al. 2014) but focuses on the following aspects of data collection:

Phase 1

Data was collected from:

a) Community Safety Partnerships through the completion of a questionnaire;
b) Two sister websites and newspapers across Wales utilising a three 'one day count' approach (Stanko 2001);
c) Freedom of Information Requests to all four Welsh Police Forces (South Wales, Dyfed Powys; Gwent and North Wales);
d) A survey administered to all four Police force areas in Wales to identify areas where sex work takes place and to assess levels of community discontent.

Phase 2

Provided a more detailed examination of responses to sex work within the South Wales area (identified by Phase 1 as the area within which sex work was most prevalent). During this phase of the study, semi-structured interviews were conducted with stakeholders in Cardiff, Newport and Swansea.

The city of Swansea was identified as the area which would most benefit from SWRW partnership work (responses to sex work were only just developing in this area and little was known about community perceptions and opinions of sex work). In this final stage of the project, questionnaires were carried out with businesses and members of the community in relation to the impact of sex work in Swansea.

Response rates

Phase 1

A total of 17 out of 22 Community Safety Partnerships responded to our survey. Three partnerships requested that we apply for information via the Freedom of Information (FOI) Act 2000 which we duly did. Data from Community Safety Partnerships were also triangulated through counting sex worker advertisements online and in newspapers. Three one-day counts took place between December 2010 and April 2011.

All four police forces took part in the research. In particular FOI requests were focused on information relating to numbers of people cautioned/arrested/released without charge/charged with soliciting or loitering under the Street Offences Act 1959 between July 2009 and August 2010.

A further aspect of the mapping phase of the project included the identification of sex work within 891 Welsh wards (neighbourhoods defined for electoral purposes) with the aim of assessing the impact of sex work on local communities from a community policing perspective. With the assistance of Gwent Police, North Wales Police and Dyfed Powys Police local police officers/Police Community Support Officers (PCSO's) who had responsibility for a geographical ward were contacted and completed a questionnaire. While agreeing to administer the questionnaire, South Wales Police opted for an internal approach drawing on the experience of Detective Inspectors in the Public Protection Departments throughout South Wales Police. The survey was designed to elicit: demographic information; dichotomous (yes/no) responses in relation to the identification of prostitution in the ward and open-ended response options that sought to understand the impact and prevalence of prostitution on local communities. The return rate for North Wales Police was approximately 89% with sex work identified in nine wards; Dyfed Powys approximately 81% with sex work identified in four wards; Gwent Police approximately 77% with sex work identified in 12 wards. In relation to South Wales Police sex work was identified in two wards.

Phase 2

Phase 1 identified that sex work was most prevalent in the South Wales region and thus South Wales became the focus of phase 2 of the research. Sixteen stakeholder organisations took part in the research: Cardiff (4); Newport (6); Swansea (6). This chapter draws on interviews with key stakeholders across South Wales in the context of multi-agency partnership work and local responses to sex work.

Phase 2 also included a case study. Swansea was selected due to it having both street-based and off street sex work with an atypical market in that there appeared to be considerable mobility between off and on street markets which was strongly associated with drug use. Furthermore, little was known about the impact of sex work on Swansea residents or community perceptions and opinions regarding the existence of sex work in the community. A self-completion questionnaire was chosen to survey the opinions and attitudes of residents and businesses (likely to be affected by sex work) within the case study area. Residents were provided with the opportunity to complete the questionnaire by return of post as well as face-to-face completion with our community researchers. The questionnaire's answer options were designed to elicit: demographic information; dichotomous (yes/no) responses in relation to knowledge of prostitution; Likert scale questions and options for qualitative in depth responses aimed at extracting data in relation to the more complex understandings of street-based 'prostitution' and solutions to it. In terms of content the questionnaire assessed: the prevalence of street sex work; attitudes about sex work and sex workers including views about the safety of sex workers; the impact of sex work on the quality of life of the respondents; and understandings of the respondents in relation to local responses to street sex work.

Sampling

The overall sampling framework for the study was a hybrid of self-selecting, opportunistic, snowballing and targeted. Such sampling frameworks are not unusual in studies relating to the study of sex work (Shaver 2005). In relation to the Swansea case study, the population from which the sample for the study was drawn was identified from local stakeholder knowledge including police and sex work outreach services and interviews with sex workers. In total 58 residents and businesses took part in the research either through completion of a postal questionnaire or through face-to-face methods.

Analysis framework

A quantitative software package was used to present descriptive statistics; however, more meaningful data was extracted from qualitative responses and analysed using a thematic framework.

Ethical approval

Ethical approval for the study was granted by the College of Health and Human Sciences, Swansea University.

Findings

Mapping sex work

Street-based work

As already noted, part of the geographical mapping process included survey responses from Community Safety Partnerships in Wales and front line service providers. A total of 155 *street-based* workers were estimated across Wales by Community Safety Parternships; however this figure was met by an increased estimate of up to 263 by service providers. Areas identifying more than 10 street-based workers included Carmarthenshire (estimated range 10–30); Cardiff (estimated at 100); Newport (estimated at 50); Swansea (estimated at 40).

Off street sex work establishments

The majority of Community Safety Partnerships as well as service providers had little awareness of *off street* activity in their areas. Front line service providers however were able to estimate the number of off street establishments at approximately 67 with responses indicating that Cardiff, Newport and Swansea had the most concentrated number of off street sex work establishments – Cardiff (estimated at 10); Newport (estimated range 10 to 20); Swansea (estimated range 10 to 11).

Internet enabled sex work/newspaper advertisements

Having carried out research in Wales for several years, the study anticipated that both Community Safety Partnerships and stakeholder services would have negligible awareness of less visible forms of sex work such as internet enabled sex work – by this we mean those establishments and agencies which advertise their services online as well as those who offer sexual services and who work independently and advertise online. We were also aware that sex workers utilise other mechanisms of advertising such as newspapers. Employing our three 'one-day count' approach we collated data from two sister websites as well as newspaper advertisements across Wales. Data revealed:

a)   57 establishments
b)   1195 sex workers advertising online
c)   209 sex workers advertising in newspapers (data cross checked with online advertisements for duplication).

Through this method we were able to present regional analysis which confirmed sex work was concentrated in South Wales, 40% in Cardiff; 14% in Swansea and 14% in Newport with the rest of Wales standing at 32%. Furthermore, and very importantly, we were also able to confirm that sex work took place *in all 22 local authority areas in Wales*. However, we are very careful to point out that we certainly do not hold out our findings as a true and accurate representation of sex work in Wales – the figure is likely to be much higher. To clarify, SWRW carried out three one-day counts on only two sister websites in Wales and it is important to recognise that escort agencies and sex workers thought to be working independently are also known to operate through social media networks such as Facebook and Twitter and individuals advertise sexual services on their own websites.

Policing responses to sex work

The FOI requests to the four police forces in Wales asked for information on prostitution offences as well as sex work activity warranting police action. Dyfed Powys Police did not hold any information on prostitution-related offences or police operations. Both Gwent Police and North Wales Police had not issued any cautions or made any arrests or released any individual without charge for soliciting or loitering offences. Neither force had carried out any police operations targeted at sex workers or their clients. South Wales Police had issued cautions for the offences of 'soliciting' and 'loitering' to 16 females but no arrests had been made, thus there had been no charges or convictions. Overall the requests revealed that sex work was not a target of police operations in Wales, with only 16 cautions being issued across the whole of Wales. Thus, it could not be said that sex work was a policing priority, or an activity warranting a zero-tolerance approach and the use of punitive sanctions.

Wards in which sex work is a community issue

With the assistance of the four Police Forces in Wales, data was collated from local police representatives and Detective Inspectors of South Wales Police to identify in which of the 891 wards in Wales sex work was taking place, and furthermore whether or not this had been presented as an issue for the wider community.

Sex work was identified as taking place or having recently took place in *only 27 out of 891 Welsh wards*. Sex work was not identified as a community issue at all in the Dyfed Powys and North Wales Police areas. Furthermore, evidence suggested that within those 27 wards, sex work was only an issue for the community in *six wards* – four in Newport and two in Cardiff. Police responses also made it clear that sex work was a concern for a very small minority of residents within those six wards. For example, it was confirmed by South Wales Police that between January and May 2011 only three residents had raised concerns about sex work in the Cardiff wards of Grangetown and Splott at Community and Partners Together Meetings (PACT). Similarly, Gwent Police reported that: three residents had raised concerns about sex work in Pillgwenlly; four–five residents reporting they had *seen* street workers in Victoria; two residents had complained about a brothel in Always; three residents had complained about a brothel in Beechwood. These latter complaints regarding brothels had arisen due to sex work establishments popping up in quiet residential areas. Importantly, as highlighted in the following section, in the six wards where sex work was raised as a cause of community concern, the police forces concerned were actively engaged in multi-agency partnership work.

Multi-agency responses to sex work in the South Wales region

As already noted, phase 2 of the project focused on the South Wales region where data suggested sex work was most concentrated and in particular on three Welsh cities which are connected by the M4 motorway – Newport, Cardiff and Swansea. Only Cardiff and Newport had developed a multi-agency response to sex work, with informal multi-agency work at the time taking place in Swansea. We asked stakeholder agencies/services in these areas to share with us their understandings of sex work focused partnership work as well as their views and opinions regarding the benefits and limitations regarding the delivery of multi-agency work.

Cardiff was found to have strong multi-agency partnerships which had come together to form the Cardiff Sex Worker Forum in 2008 with the aim of delivering a coordinated response to sex work. Focusing primarily on *street sex work*, a key aim of the Forum (which was reiterated by all stakeholder participants) was to uphold and enforce the law, respond to community need and the vulnerabilities of street-based workers – ensuring justice for ALL the community. Thus, community safety was interpreted broadly by Forum members to include a public health duty to protect sex workers and to keep sex workers safe. South Wales Police and Forum partners had also made a commitment to keep sex workers out of the criminal justice system and had developed a 'Diversionary Pathway' – where a sex worker may receive a police caution with a provision to engage with support services, and where an application for a section 17 engagement and support order was seen as a *last resort*. In this way, the partners believed that they could respond to the complex needs of sex workers and improve their safety and well-being – whether a sex worker remained in sex work or chose to exit.

A multi-agency 'prostitution group' had been established in Newport which was chaired by Gwent Police but it did not meet regularly and tended to come together where an issue required attention – therefore it was reactionary rather than strategic. However, there was a clear will amongst all agencies/services to support sex workers as *members of the community*. Gwent Police did not actively seek to deploy punitive sanctions against sex workers; however anti-social behaviour was not tolerated and several ASBOs had been invoked against both street sex workers and their clients. A significant issue was that off-street brothels popped up in residential streets and thus the police had elected to adopt a pragmatic approach – if establishments operated quietly and discreetly then the police would visit and monitor but take no formal action (a traffic light approach). Gwent Police representatives also described the development of a 'code of conduct' – an informal contract between the police and off street establishments which had reduced anti-social behaviour, kept sex workers safe and encouraged good sexual health practices, as well as providing consistent standards across the city.

As for Swansea, an increase in intelligence relating to the numbers of sex workers picked up in custody had led to a multi-agency focus on sex work. At the time of the research South Wales Police and front line services were actively working together. Particularly there was a general consensus that drugs and sex work was inextricably linked in Swansea with a great deal of mobility between on and off street sex work which correlated with periods of 'stability' or 'instability' and drug use. Regarding visible street-based sex work, the police response was to invoke section 27 of the Violent Crime Reduction Act 2006 to move individuals on where they were causing anti-social behaviour that involved the use of drugs and or alcohol – although police representatives acknowledged that this was an outdated approach and far from ideal. As for off street establishments in the area (shop front style), South Wales Police sporadically visited premises to ensure that sex workers were safe.

The findings across the South Wales region were very clear in highlighting that precious resources were targeted at *either* the off-street market (Newport and Swansea) or the on street market (Cardiff) but not both and this presented a serious limitation to the development of an all-encompassing sex work strategy in the three cities. All participants acknowledged the need to develop a regional response, to share intelligence and good practice and in the words of one participant 'to prevent a catastrophe like Ipswich'. However, all three areas did adopt a harm reduction approach and in negotiating the needs of sex workers as members of the community their safety was a priority. It could therefore be suggested that these findings fly in the face of our former contentions that sex workers are outside of community and that their needs are de-prioritised against the needs of the wider community. However, as the data presented thus far indicates, sex work is not a policing priority because it is not a significant community issue in Wales. Indeed, as the following results from our case study illustrates, members of the wider community did not deem sex work to be a community nuisance.

Community perceptions of sex work and the impact of sex work on community

As already noted, 20 residents and 38 businesses provided their views and opinions of on and off street sex work in the Swansea study area.

Resident responses

Street sex work was identified as a crime and disorder issue by only two respondents. The majority of respondents either 'didn't know' sex work took place in the area ($n = 8$) or believed that the numbers of sex workers in the locality were less than 10 ($n = 10$). The overwhelming majority of respondents indicated that they either 'hardly ever' or 'never' saw street sex workers ($n = 16$). While one respondent identified street sex work as an issue which affected the quality of their 'everyday life', others who saw street-based sex workers were clearly concerned about their safety, for example:

> I think that sex workers need to be protected. . . . I think that the safety of sex workers should be the main priority and that we should try to understand the reasons behind why people sell sex so that we can protect their welfare.

I have no personal experience of prostitution but I also think that in a free world people should be free to do whatever they wish to make a living – as long as they are safe!

R83

In terms of nuisance one participant explained:

Just the odd kerb crawler. Not a great nuisance but not very nice either. We have more nuisances from the drop-in centre across the road, but this has calmed down now though.

R02

As for off street sex work, the majority of respondents were aware of sex work in the locality but none of the respondents expressed strong opinions (either positive or negative) about off street work. Indeed, residents appeared to adopt a pragmatic approach:

Swansea has a number of well known establishments and they all are 'behind closed doors'. I have no objection to them operating, it is far better than moving prostitution onto the streets.

R84

Business responses

Crime and disorder in the area was identified by businesses as being primarily anti-social behaviour associated with drug and alcohol use. Out of 38 businesses, 25 were 'not aware' of street-based prostitution with 12 indicating they were 'aware', and one indicating that they 'didn't know'. Furthermore, street-based sex work was not identified as an issue having a negative impact on business:

The street sex workers I am aware of are females but they have never been a problem for this business.

B58

I am aware that it does go on, but it does not affect me.

B67

Friends of mine have said that they've seen street based prostitution taking place around here, but I haven't. It has not made an impact on the business here at all.

B12

The majority of business respondents indicated that they perceived that there were five or less off-street establishments in the locality ($n = 29$); seven respondents didn't know and only one respondent believed that there was over five. None of the respondents reported that indoor establishments had a negative impact on their business.

Nuisance versus safety

Responses (residents and business) did not indicate that sex work was a community concern. Only four respondents out of 58 (two residents and two businesses) agreed with the statement 'I think prostitutes are a nuisance' with the overwhelming majority ($n = 51$) of respondents indicating that they 'disagreed' with the statement.

The perceptions of residents and businesses regarding sex work were found to be very similar to those reported in survey on community perceptions of sex work in Cardiff by Sagar et al. (2010) in that there was a clear divide in opinion as to whether or not people 'should be allowed to buy and sell sex', but with a significant percentage indicating that they worried about the safety of sex workers in the area. Interestingly in Swansea, analysis showed that although 92.3% of the sample either 'hardly ever' or 'hardly ever to never', see street-based sex work, many of these participants also believed that people should *not* be allowed to buy and sell sex, suggesting therefore an objection towards sex work even though they hardly ever or never witnessed it. Yet, in stark contrast, the idea that sex workers are a nuisance received the least conformity and this does not fit with the presumption that sex work is inextricably linked to community nuisance. Furthermore, businesses and residents had firm ideas about different ways of approaching sex work – other than criminalisation:

I think this type of business should be monitored and taxed like any other. Stop keeping this type of work in the shadows, it will never go away.

R83

I think people should be able to buy and sell sex in a controlled environment.

B53

I think that prostitution should be made safer by regulating the health aspects of the work, ensuring that the sex workers are consenting adults, taxing the industry as a whole and then using the income from this taxation to help sex workers leave the industry if they wish to. Sex work should be decriminalised in general.

B35

A main theme arising throughout the responses was a worry and concern about the health and safety sex workers:

Prostitution should be legalised so workers are safe. It is inevitable so it should be legalised.

B68

I think prostitution will always take place but there should be a safe place provided for both the sellers and buyers protection . . . sex workers should have a safe place to work in outside of the city centre, like a managed zone. Sex work is always going to happen so they should have somewhere safe to work.

B63

I think prostitution should be regulated like it is in Amsterdam to make sure that the sex workers are safe and that they have a safe place to work.

B47

Discussion and conclusions

The findings presented in this chapter clearly suggest that although sex work takes place in every local authority area of Wales, it is not a priority for law enforcers. Sex work is only a contested community issue in a handful of wards and for a very small minority of residents within those wards (see also Sagar and Jones 2013b). Findings from the Swansea residents and business survey also suggested that while the principle of being allowed to sell and buy sex may be opposed by members of the community, the actual negative impact of sex work is negligible. Instead, for the police who work in a multi-agency capacity and for the community who live in areas where sex work takes place, sex work is primarily a welfare and safety issue – suggesting widespread support for harm reduction rather than criminalisation.

Importantly, the findings in this chapter provide more than a snapshot of a period of time in Wales – they offer a foundation for both legal and policy reform. In policy terms the findings evidence a clear will within communities to prioritise the safety and well-being of sex workers. And, while it is true to say that multi-agency approaches and community safety initiatives are often *very* localised and therefore fragmented, the building blocks for an inclusive sex work *Strategy for Wales* are in place. In stating this we are careful to note that the 2016 National Policing Chiefs' Council's (NPCC) guidance on policing sex work is to be welcomed with its harm reduction ethos, its call for sex workers to be treated with dignity and respect (para. 5.23), its call for the community to be involved in decision making (para. 5.18), its warnings against police operations that might lead to the displacement of sex work (para. 5.22) and its message that criminal sanctions should be a last resort (para. 5.26), and in Wales it is perhaps true to say that the approach of the NPCC is already embedded to a significant extent. However, as Alex Feis-Bryce has already emphasised in this Part I of this book, this is merely guidance and does not represent a straightjacket for police forces by any means. Thus, while the guidance has the potential to steer collaborative work in a positive way, we nevertheless argue that a *National Strategy for Wales* is now appropriate, not least because it could formalise regional and local responses and provide some much needed steering to improve information sharing and communication across Police Force areas, something that appears to have been overlooked in the NPCCs guidance. The guidance does call for '*a bespoke intelligence picture for each local area*' as well as '*investigative and intelligence-building partnerships and information exchange protocols with key partners*' (para.5.28), but our evidence suggests that there is little information sharing between Police Forces and within Police Forces pertaining to different sex work localities. We consider a National coordinated approach could facilitate information sharing, and that is particularly important in Wales given the mobility of sex workers who are known to work for example along the South Wales M4 corridor.

In terms of potential legal reform, we also welcome the interim report on prostitution from the House of Commons Home Affairs Committee (2016) which proposes the decriminalisation of the sale of sex, changes to brothel keeping laws to enable sex workers to work together in order to enhance their safety, and the removal of previous convictions from sex worker's records through amendments to the Rehabilitation Act (p. 21 paras. 58 and 59). The Committee's final report is keenly awaited; it will consider the *purpose of the law* on 'prostitution' and in doing so draw on robust evidence (for which the Committee has called). Importantly, in pursuit of legal reform, the Home Affairs Committee has recognised that different legal systems are founded on different moral values and that this was particularly true with regard to the 'sex buyer law' (Swedish or Nordic model) (p. 37 para.11), but that the law of England and Wales makes no such moral judgement. Indeed, referring to the approach of the Wolfenden Committee back in 1957, we would argue that any legal reform based primarily on moral values would be a very slippery slope. As the 1957 Committee pointed out, 'there must remain a sphere of private morality and immorality which is, in brief and crude terms, not the law's business' (para. 60). The 1957 Committee also made it clear that to try to enforce any *pattern of behaviour* was not a function of the law. And although this subsequently led to a fierce debate regarding public versus private morality, with Lord Devlin (1959) for example arguing that even private acts are subject to legal sanction if they are considered to be immoral by the popular majority, and Professor Hart (1961) conversely warning of the dangers of moral populism, the principle of 'harm' won out, that is criminal laws must be based on the principle of harm to others (see Feinberg 1990). Indeed, if we had departed from this legal philosophy in 1957 we would have been unlikely to witness the decriminalisation of homosexuality in 1969, or the legal recognition of same sex marriage in 2013 for example. The Home Affairs Committee did appear to be more positive with regard to the New Zealand decriminalisation model – which had 'resulted in a number of benefits and which sent out 'a clear policy message' (2016: 39). However, the Committee stressed that the model required further evaluation to assess the extent to which elements of it might be transferred to England and Wales, and in this regard the potential risk of increased public nuisance will command attention.

The findings documented in this chapter clearly illustrate that from the community perspective *morality* and *nuisance* are very different things. There may well be a divide within communities regarding the morality of sex work, but there is in Wales a common consensus that sex work is not a public nuisance and when sex workers are visible, the overriding concern is likely to be sex worker's safety. Thus, laws criminalising the sale and purchase of sex on the presumption of public nuisance (an argument that has been raised by consecutive governments) cannot be said to be necessary or supported in Wales. Instead, our research supports an approach which departs from criminalisation towards a community justice focused approach which is more closely aligned with decriminalisation and the approach adopted in New Zealand. We accept that decriminalisation cannot reduce stigma overnight, nor can it put a stop to sex workers being subjected to violence, nor can it eliminate the risk of anti-social behaviour. It can however improve relationships between the police and sex workers and lead to increased reporting of violence (see Abel et al. 2007; Abel 2014). This is a much better fit with the overarching aims of community safety and community justice in Wales, which like New Zealand, is a small nation with a relatively small number of sex workers.

References

Abel, G. M. (2014) 'A decade of decriminalization: Sex work "down under" but not underground', *Criminology and Criminal Justice*, 14 (5), 580–592.

Abel, G., Fitzgerald, L., and Brunton, C. (2007) 'The impact of the Prostitution Reform Act on the health and safety practices of sex workers', *Report to the Prostitution Law Revision Committee*, Department of Public Health and General Practice, University of Otago, Christchurch. Available at: www.otago.ac.nz/christchurch/otago018607.pdf (Accessed 11 July 2017).

Abel, G., Fitzgerald, L., Healy, C., and Taylor, A. (Eds.) (2010) *Taking the crime out of sex work: New Zealand sex workers fight for decriminalization.* Bristol: Policy Press.

Bellis, M. A., Watson, F. L. D., Hughes, S., Cook, P. A., Downing, J., Clark, P., and Thomson, R. (2007) 'Comparative views of the public, sex workers, businesses and residents on establishing managed zones for prostitution: Analysis of a consultation in Liverpool', *Health and Place*, 13, 603–616.

Campbell, A. (2015) 'Sex work's governance: Stuff and nuisance', *Feminist Legal Studies*, 23 (1), 27–45.

Carline, A. (2009) 'Ethics and vulnerability in street prostitution: An argument in favour of managed zones', *Crimes and Misdemeanours: Deviance and the Law in Historical Perspective*, 3 (1), 20–53.

Crime and Disorder Act. (1998). Available at: www.legislation.gov.uk/ukpga/1998/37/contents

Criminal Law Revision Committee. (1984) 'Prostitution in the street', *16th Report*. Great Britain: Home Office.

Devlin, P. (1959) *The enforcement of moral*. Oxford: Oxford University Press.

Feinberg, J. (1990) *The moral limits of the criminal law: volume 4: Harmless wrongdoing*. New York: Oxford University Press.

Hancock, L. (1991) 'Legal regulation of prostitution: What or who is being controlled?', *Sex Industry and Public Policy: Proceedings of a Conference* held on 6th–8th May 1991. Australian Institute of Criminology, Canberra A.C.T. Available at: http://dro.deakin.edu.au/view/DU:30030969 (Accessed 11 July 2017).

Hart, P. (1961) *The Concept of Law*. Oxford: Clarendon Press.

Home Office. (2004) *Paying the price: A consultation on prostitution*. London: Home Office.

Home Office. (2006) *A coordinated prostitution strategy and a summary of responses to paying the price*. London: Home Office.

Home Office. (2008) *Tackling the demand for prostitution: A review*. London: Home Office.

Home Office. (2011) *Review of effective practice in responding to prostitution*. London: Home Office.

House of Commons Home Affairs Committee. (2016) *Prostitution third report of session 16–17*. London: House of Commons. Available at: www.publications.parliament.uk/pa/cm201617/cmselect/cmhaff/26/26.pdf (Accessed 11 July 2017).

Kantola, J., and Squires, J. (2004) 'Discourses surrounding prostitution policies in the UK', *European Journal of Women's Studies*, 11 (1), 77–101.

National Police Chiefs' Council. (2016) *National policing sex work guidance*. Available at: www.app.college.police.uk/app-content/major-investigation-and-public-protection/prostitution/ (Accessed 11 July 2017).

O'Neill, M., and Campbell, R. (2004) *Working together to create change: Walsall prostitution consultation research: A participatory action research project.* Walsall: Walsall South Health Action Zone. Available at: www.staffs.ac.uk/schools/art_and_design/safe tysoapbox/images/full_report.pdf (Accessed 11 July 2017).

O'Neill, M., Campbell, R., Hubbard, P., Picher, J., and Scoular, J. (2008) 'Living with the other: Street sex work, contingent communities and degrees of tolerance', *Crime Media and Culture: An International Journal,* 4 (1), 73–93.

Policing and Crime Act. (2009) *Rehabilitation Act.*

Sagar, T. (2005) 'Street watch: Concept and practice – civilian participation in street prostitution control', *British Journal of Criminology,* 45 (1), 98–112.

Sagar, T. (2007) 'Tackling on-street sex work: Anti-social behaviour orders, sex workers and inclusive inter-agency initiatives', *Criminology and Criminal Justice,* 7 (1), 153–168.

Sagar, T., and Jones, D. (2010) *Reaching out to female street sex workers in Cardiff: Findings from 'engagement events'.* For and on behalf of the Cardiff Sex Work Forum, Swansea University. Available at: https://cronfa.swan.ac.uk/Record/cronfa17433 (Accessed 11 July 2017).

Sagar, T., and Jones, D. (2013a) 'The local governance of street sex work in the United Kingdom: Views from the shop floor', *International Criminal Justice Review,* 23 (3), 132–148.

Sagar, T., and Jones, D. (2013b) 'Priorities for the minority? Street-based sex work and partnerships and communities together (PACT)', *Criminology and Criminal Justice,* 13 (4), 431–445.

Sagar, T., Jones, D., and Harris, E. (2010) *Community perceptions of street sex work in Cardiff.* Cardiff: Swansea University. Available at: https://cronfa.swan.ac.uk/Record/cronfa17433 (Accessed 11 July 2017).

Sagar, T., Jones, E., Jones, D., and Clarke, L. (2014) *Sex work research Wales 2010–2014: Summary of findings.* Available at: www.gibran-uk.co.uk/past-projects/sex-work-wales (Accessed 11 July 2017).

Sanders, T. (2009) 'Controlling the anti-sexual city: Sexual citizenship and the disciplining of female sex workers: Special issue "urban safety, anti social behaviour and the night-time economy"', *Criminology and Criminal Justice,* 9 (4), 507–525.

Sanders, T., O'Neill, M., and Pitcher, J. (2009) *Prostitution: Sex work, policy and politics.* London: Sage.

Sanders, T., and Sehmbi, V. (2015) *Evaluation of the Leeds Street sex working managed area.* University of Leeds. Available at: www.nswp.org/sites/nswp.org/files/Executive%20Summary%20Leeds,%20U%20of%20Leeds%20-%20Sept%202015.pdf (Accessed 11 July 2017).

Scoular, J. (2010) 'What's law got to do with it? How and why law matters in the regulation of sex work', *Journal of Law and Society,* 37 (1), 12–39.

Scoular, J., and Carline, A. (2014) 'A critical account of a "creeping neo-abolitionism": regulating prostitution in England and Wales', *Criminology and Criminal Justice,* 14 (5), 608–626.

Scoular, J., and O'Neill, M. (2007) 'Regulating prostitution: Social inclusion, responsibilization and the politics of prostitution reform', *British Journal of Criminology,* 47, 764–778.

Shaver, F. M. (2005) 'Sex work research methodological and ethical challenges', *Journal of Interpersonal Violence,* 20 (3), 296–319.

Squires, P. (1997) *Criminology and the 'community safety' paradigm: Safety, power and the limits of the local'.* the British Criminology Conferences: Selected Proceedings. Volume 2. Papers from the British Criminology Conference, Queens University, Belfast, 15–19 July 1997. Available at: www.britsoccrim.org/volume2/012.pdf (Accessed 11 July 2017).

Stanko, E. A. (2001) 'The day to count: reflections on a methodology to raise awareness about the impact of domestic violence in the UK', *Criminology and Criminal Justice*, 1 (2), 215–226.

UK Population. (2016) Available at: http://ukpopulation2016.com/wales (Accessed 11 July 2017).

Violent Crime Reduction Act (2006) Available at: https://www.legislation.gov.uk/ukpga/2006/38/contents (Accessed 26 October 2017).

Whowell, M. (2010) 'Male sex work: Exploring regulation in England and Wales', *Journal of Law and Society*, 37 (1), 125–144.

Wolfenden. (1957) *Report of the Committee on Homosexual Offences and Prostitution.* Cmnd. 247. London: HMSO.

Part II

Policing Operations, Enforcement and Austerity

6 Policing the absence of the victim

An ethnography of raids in sex trafficking operations

Julia Leser

Introduction

It is another sunny morning in July in a small German city somewhere in the middle of the country. Two vice squad police officers, having entered the apartment of Sumi and Lulu, are now sitting at their living room table, copying personal details of Sumi's passport into a data sheet. A third officer is standing in front of Lulu's room, knocking impatiently. 'Sorry, I'll be out in five minutes', Lulu says. She is still working with a client. In contrast, Sumi, a Thai woman in her late fifties, seems to have had a rather quiet morning right until the police stopped by. Now she is joking with the officers and telling them about her favourite papaya recipes. The officers seem to be hesitant to look at Sumi in her sexy nightgown. As they finish copying Sumi's passport and stand up, Sumi slaps the officers' bottoms. Both of them blush a little, giggling their good-byes on their way out.

Obviously, being entertained by Sumi has not been the vice squad's main objective for visiting the sex workers' apartment today. Rather, Sumi and Lulu's place was just one of their destinations on the raid the vice squad is conducting on a day in July 2015. The vice squad performs these raids regularly upon various sites in which prostitution takes place, searching – of course – for victims of human trafficking.

We all have heard of trafficking. We do seem to *know* what a victim of trafficking is and what she looks like: the characteristics of the innocent, mostly young and migrant women are adding up to constitute the ideal victim (Christie 1986). Further, we seem to *know* that trafficking is a crime conducted upon young girls who are forced into prostitution – so do the police, and that is why this particular vice squad is looking for victims of trafficking in brothels and sex workers' apartments on this summer morning.

In this chapter, the victim is understood as a relational 'object of knowledge' (Bacchi 2012) that emerges from practices and that can be analysed in regard to certain theoretical premises. First, knowledge is always already situated and localised (Hacking 1999). Its differing framings and contexts affect the way we come to understand certain situations and act upon this emerging knowledge. In the case of human trafficking, it has become clear that anti-trafficking campaigns and initiatives tend to frame phenomena of irregular migration and sex work within the context of organised crime, violence and exploitation of women, resulting in the subjectification of primarily Eastern European women as 'victims of trafficking' (Berman 2003). Many authors have described and analysed the 'ideal victim' discourse that produces these 'victims' as young, innocent and naively acting women (Blanchette et al. 2013, Doezema 2000; Jakšić 2008; Pates and Schmidt 2007). In media representations, these discourses are condensed into specific narrative patterns that are repeated and reproduced continuously. Snajdr (2013) has termed these patterns 'master narratives' of human trafficking that draw upon specific and analysable techniques of moralisation and emotionalisation. Second, knowledge production is ubiquitous and central to state practices: gathering knowledge about its subjects and representing it in policies, laws, maps and documents is a *sine qua non* for the state's exercise of power and control over its subjects, as it has been frequently underscored by Foucault. In this case, the state has to *know* the victim of trafficking in order to govern it accordingly. Third, as we know from science and technology studies, knowledge is never exclusively objective, rational nor universal – but quite the contrary: the pathway of producing knowledge is determined by (competing) practices, interactions, interferences, errors, irrationalities, discontinuities, inconsistencies and failures. In this process, subjects and objects are 'by-products' or 'provisional results' (Latour 2007: 94) and objectivities are always plural.[1] Fourth, and to introduce and apply a term proposed by Mariana Valverde, 'bodies of knowledge' are always dynamic compositions of different elements (e.g. expert and everyday knowledge) and therefore 'hybrid' (Moore and Valverde 2000), rendering the knowledge production process – once again – plural and heterogeneous (Valverde et al. 2005). In sum, the victim can be understood as a relational object of knowledge, which means that the so-called victim of human trafficking (in this case) is an emerging composition of various and partly competing institutional logics, bodies of knowledge and their relations. What a victim is (and what is not) is thus negotiated and enacted in knowledge practices.

In state institutions (such as the police), these practices actualise in the form of categorisation and classification of women in sex work.[2] Through standardised operating procedures, but always depending on the police officers' framing, purpose and motivations, the domain of the victim is constituted and defined. Further, the practices of policing reflect upon the self-conception of the intervening state of law: especially within the area of human trafficking, those regulating practices and techniques intertwine with questions of migration control, moral conceptualisations of sex and sex work, the task of securing social order, as well as sanctioning violations to fundamental rights. As recent ethnographic studies of the state have shown, the state is essentially reproduced in state officials' practices (Sharma

---

1   With regard to the state's knowledge production practices, Miller & Rose illustriously articulated: 'Governing is not the 'realization' of a programmer's dream. The 'real' always insists in the form of resistance to programming; and the programmer's world is one of constant experiment, invention, failure, critique and adjustment' (Miller & Rose 2008, 39).

2   The fact that states need to know their subjects in order to function and therefore have to classify their populations has been described by James Scott with the concept of 'legibility': 'Legibility is a condition of manipulation. Any substantial state intervention in society [...] requires the invention of units that are visible. [...] Whatever the units being manipulated, they must be organized in a manner that permits them to be identified, observed, recorded, counted, aggregated, and monitored' (Scott 1998, 183).

and Gupta 2009; Hansen and Stepputat 2001; Schlichte and Migdal 2005). Thus, an ethnographic study of police raids can allow for a more complex account on how policing practices contribute to enacting state-ness and co-producing certain subjectivities – always within the scope of order and disorder.

For my analysis, I have used ethnographic methods (participant observations) in order to retrace policing practices in the field of human trafficking: how do the police come to *know* what a victim of trafficking is? During raids, how do they perceive specific situations and what do they make of it? What instances raise their suspicion? How do they legitimise their practices? I conducted participant observations within a vice squad in a German city for six months in 2015 and observed their raids in sex trafficking operations within that period of time, complementing my field protocols with 25 qualitative semi-structured interviews with various policing agents, administrative officials and social workers who work in specialised counselling centres for 'victims of human trafficking'.[3] But I began my research with a striking paradox: the German city I chose for my inquiries seemed to have had, quite in contrast to it being a relatively small city, a massive problem with human trafficking – the city accommodated three specialised counselling centres for human trafficking victims, a specialised police unit (whose head of department was invited to participate in talk shows on TV on the matter of trafficking), as well as an institutionalised round table with various state officials that had been implemented in order to fight the crime of trafficking. In short, the situation was highly problematised, but on taking a closer look into the official crime statistics, I noticed that the numbers did not match the alleged high scale proportions of the issue. In fact, the last case of trafficking that led to the conviction of the accused in front of a court of justice dated back to 2013 – two years before the time I started my research. For six months in 2015, I accompanied the vice squad officers on their raids upon sites of prostitution, searching for victims of trafficking. But as I did, no victim was ever found, and I started to become aware that I was witnessing the peculiar and highly paradoxical practice of *policing the absence of the victim*.

The legal and organisational framework for policing trafficking in Germany

In order to frame the main results of my ethnographic inquiries, I shall start with a few remarks about the German legal and organisational arenas that embed the state's handling of the issue of trafficking. The German legislation concerning human trafficking has been readjusted in 2005 in accordance to the European *Protocol to Prevent, Suppress and Punish Trafficking in Persons, especially Women and Children* (UNODCCP 2000). Until this legislative reform became ratified, the German law sanctioned human trafficking solely in the form of coercion of human beings into prostitution. In 2005, for the first time, the trafficking of human

---

3 The data I draw on in this chapter have been collected as part of the DFG/ANR-funded research project 'Institutionalising Human Trafficking' that has been conducted in France and Germany from 2014 until 2017 under the direction of Mathilde Darley and Rebecca Pates. The main ambition of this project is to question how the category of the 'victim of human trafficking' is being applied and translated into local institutional practices.

beings for labour exploitation was punishable by law as well, as the definition of trafficking had been broadened and moulded into two distinct legal paragraphs: *§232 Criminal Code* for human trafficking for the purpose of sexual exploitation, and *§233 Criminal Code* for human trafficking for the purpose of labour exploitation. In this chapter, I concentrate on the practices of identifying victims of sexual exploitation, which have been far more often identified as such than victims of labour exploitation. While legal measures against labour exploitation have been taken, the number of cases for labour exploitation recorded with the national crime statistics is far lower than the number of cases regarding sexual exploitation. In 2013, the Federal Criminal Office (*Bundeskriminalamt*, BKA) finalised 425 cases of human trafficking for the purpose of sexual exploitation, while it finalised only 53 cases of human trafficking for the purpose of labour exploitation. This does not necessarily reflect the actual situation concerning forced labour, exploitation and trafficking. In fact, trade unions generally estimate that the number of persons who have experienced trafficking into labour exploitation outside the sex industry by far outnumber those who have experienced trafficking within prostitution.[4] Still, institutional agents like the police strongly focus on victims of trafficking into prostitution within their framing and their practices.

In Germany, there are no national guidelines for the identification of victims of human trafficking (GRETA 2015). To formally identify a victim, law enforcement agencies themselves are responsible. In some of the German states, law enforcement agencies and counselling centres for victims of human trafficking have arranged formalised cooperation agreements that help clarify the routines and procedures of identifying victims. In order to do that, local and state police officers, representatives of health and social service agencies, and support service providers or counselling centres have installed round table meetings at communal and state levels, where issues such as law implementation, victim identification and responsibilities are discussed on a regular basis.[5]

In Germany, different police forces are engaged in the enforcement of anti-trafficking laws. The Federal Criminal Police Office (*Bundeskriminalamt*, BKA), and the Criminal Police Offices of the 16 states (*Landeskriminalämter*, LKA), investigate trafficking cases within their departments for organised crime. The BKA engages in the investigation and prosecution of transnational organised crime networks, often cooperating with EUROPOL and INTERPOL as well as with other countries' police agencies. It also offers training for local police officers on human trafficking and victim identification. The LKA serves as a superordinate agency for the criminal investigation departments that leads investigations within cities and communities. If a local police force is engaged with a trafficking case that goes beyond their range of operations, i.e. that is connected to victims or perpetrators in other communities, states or even countries, the LKA (and, in international cases or those spanning various German states, BKA) gets involved.

Generally though, the processing of human trafficking cases starts either with counselling centres to whom sex workers report as trafficked victims or within

---

4 In our research project 'Institutionalising Human Trafficking' we have analysed several reasons for this in Pates et al. (2016).

5 Regular does mean frequent. In most instances, round table meetings occur once or twice a year.

local criminal investigation departments. In interviewing police officers, they emphasise that the local authorities work within clearly marked jurisdictions, geographically as well as organisationally.[6] Human trafficking here is not located within the sub-department of organised crime (as it is in BKA and LKA), but in most cities within the sub-department of the vice squad. In the city that I have been researching, for example, the vice squad is responsible for all kinds of sexual offences, child pornography, surveillance of registered sex offenders and all kinds of offences related to prostitution. Human trafficking, for the vice squad here, belongs to the latter. As police departments are always limited in their resources, there is only one officer in this vice squad who manages the task of investigating all kinds of offences related to prostitution. The organisation of local police offices seems strictly hierarchical, with all its routines in order and all responsibilities neatly distributed. But those structures will change and adapt due to criminogenic trends and discourses, shifts in criminal policy and legislation, as well as innovation in investigation technologies, as the interviewees indicated.

Routines, standards, and 'doing the state'

So, what do vice squads do in order to fight human trafficking? The very first thing that will come to mind (if one has watched too many crime thrillers and/or read a certain amount of detective stories) is the practice of raiding brothels. In media representations, '[r]aids personify the master narrative of trafficking by casting state agents in the role of saviours rescuing victims from criminals' (Hill 2016: 44). Hill argues that the media usually covers a raid as a 'spectacular performance of state power that purports to show evidence of trafficking and the need for proactive policing' (Hill 2016: 45). Raids, in this perspective, might be associated with a large number of police officers in full gear storming into a badly lit brothel, saving young girls from the hands of those ruthless men who exploit them and thus making the world a much better place. To foreclose, the reality is by far less spectacular. If we want to look into police practices as a means of 'doing the state', we have to acknowledge that police work is done in the first place through the filling out of forms and that "catching bad guys' takes up a small fraction of police forces' time' (Valverde 2010: 76). Police officers are among other things 'street-level bureaucrats' (Lipsky 1980) and police forces are one of the bureaucratic organisations that make up the state in its organisational form (Bierschenk 2016: 155). The state, as we know from Migdal and Schlichte,

> is a field of power marked by the use and threat of violence and shaped by
> 1) the image of a coherent, controlling organization in a territory, which is a
> representation of the people bounded by that territory, and 2) the actual practices involving those staffing its multiple parts and those they engage in their
> roles as state officials.
>
> (Migdal and Schlichte 2005: 15)

---

6 City states (Hamburg, Berlin, Bremen) are the exception. Here, an LKA unit is responsible for any case of human trafficking.

The state is thus not a homogeneous entity but a conglomerate of various state agents, their practices and knowledges, which do not have to match actual ideas of the state. The same is true for the police: we can distinguish between certain ideas about the police (such as the popular representations of police raids stated above) and – more or less – daily police practices. For Bierschenk, police practices are always 'guided by common sense, localised, verbally derived and relayed background knowledge as well as by their accumulated professional experience' (Bierschenk 2016: 166). And:

> Police officers are not only law enforcement officials, but also protectors of the social order, educators of society, relationship operators and knowledge workers. Likewise, the description of the police as a (state) bureaucratic organization only applies partially. Rather, the daily functioning of the police and daily police work are characterized by a tension between formal norms and informal practices, a tension which applies to all state organizations.
>
> (Bierschenk 2016: 170–171)

What distinguishes the police from other state organisations is the monopoly of the use of the force of law, or, differently put, their 'legal lawlessness' (Brodeur 2010: 9). Brodeur defines the police as follows:

> Policing agents are part of several connected organizations authorized to use in more or less controlled ways diverse means, generally prohibited by statute or regulation to the rest of the population, in order to enforce various types of rules and customs that promote a defined order in society, considered in its whole or in some of its parts.
>
> (Brodeur 2010: 130)

Policing thus includes all kinds of police practices that do not ultimately rely on the use of force, but are illegal to everybody except the police, such as detentions, arrests, seizures, confiscations, surveillance, interrogations and so on. In this sequence, a police raid is defined as an unannounced entering of certain premises that includes the search for illegal activities or criminal suspects as well as the checking of the identities of all encountered persons. By law, it is forbidden to enter an apartment and do an ID check. But according to police law, this ID check is legitimate if a person sojourns in a particular place in which the police assume ongoing criminal activity. The interviewees stated:

> We perform raids and we enter apartments because we assume that in these apartments crimes are being committed. That is the basic principle.
>
> (Interview vice squad 10, May 11, 2015)

> The police law allows us to enter apartments. Even if the residents do not want us to. Against the wishes of the residents we can at any time enter and control certain places if there is the assumption of a concrete threat. This includes places in which the activity of prostitution is pursued.
>
> (Interview vice squad 11, May 11, 2015)

The raid is thus a practice that is – in its capacity to enter residential property and check IDs of citizens – forbidden to everybody but police officials. According to police law a raid is legitimate if the police assume the existence of criminal activities in the to-be-controlled places. The police law further suggests that places in which prostitution is (assumed to be) practised are generally suspicious.[7]

All vice squads have particular standard operating procedures when it comes to enforcing anti-trafficking laws. The vice squad police officers have been working within the field of prostitution-related crime for a long time and have gathered a certain pool of experiences. In the course of their careers, they have attended special BKA (Federal Criminal Office) training courses, they have experienced a number of trafficking trials from which they learned what factors are relevant in a case to achieve the conviction of the accused, they know how to process files and collect evidence, and they know whom to consult when certain issues emerge. But they also – depending on their personal interests and motivations – have read scientific literature concerning the topic of trafficking, they have paid attention to the news, they might have watched documentaries or movies on television, so that they have amassed a vast pool of everyday experience and knowledge about those 'victims of human trafficking'. According to Valverde, administrative knowledge is always an 'in-between, hybrid epistemological category' (Valverde 2009: 20). The officers have, over the span of their career, developed particular victim epistemologies as well as certain routines and standard operating procedures that help them in finding these 'victims'. When I asked one of the officers in Kassel how he identifies a victim, he just answered while pointing a finger to his forehead: 'It is all in my head'.

As all legislative prose does, the German anti-trafficking laws allow for a great deal of interpretation. In my interviews and observations I have learned that law enforcement agents identify the key aspects of the criminal law on trafficking selectively and translate the language of the Criminal Code according to their own needs, responsibilities and preferred modes of practice. This process of translation takes place within their nexus of professionalised and everyday knowledge. One of the officers explained this translational process as follows:

> Whereby do I recognise the state of helplessness, for example: was the door [to the woman's workplace] shut or open? Was he [the assumed trafficker] outside shopping or drinking a couple of beers with his buddies, well, then the woman could have used this opportunity to run down on the street and seek help. Or do I have to look at other signs of helplessness, maybe the woman's inability to talk properly, her state of intelligence [. . .] But like it is written in the Criminal Code: if another person's, i.e. the prostitute's, state of helplessness is exploited, i.e. she was forced to come to a foreign country, that means she is typically Bulgarian or Romanian. She is helpless because she doesn't speak German, she doesn't know our culture, and is only allowed to stay within the walls she was put in. So if this person has been coerced into taking up or continuing work in prostitution, that means that those women are recruited in Bulgaria under the pretence that they can work in Germany

---

7 This is stated in the *Hessian State Police Law* §18 Abs. 2 Satz 1b HSOG (German: *Hessisches Gesetz über die öffentliche Sicherheit und Ordnung*).

as a waitress. And when they arrive, they are told that they have to work in prostitution. And they don't want to do that. Maybe they have been working as prostitutes before they came here, but now they don't want to anymore, and then we are talking about coercion. And that means they are not allowed to keep their money but have to give it to the trafficker [. . .] or maybe she shows signs of injury [. . .] But the legal definition is difficult; often, the lines of human trafficking are blurred. It is our job to carve out those lines using interrogation techniques. And we always have to have a possible trial in mind: what will be the outcome? Which things does the judge want to hear? At what point does a conviction of the accused become possible?

(Interview vice squad 10, May 11, 2015)

This quote shows that this knowledge about the alleged victim here is a hybrid corpus of the officer's own experiences, his expert knowledge and partly corresponding to the 'ideal victim narrative' – or 'master narrative', as Snajdr (2013) has termed it – of the helpless, young and Eastern European woman. He also translates the legal definition in a way that fits the police's practices of interrogation, proper filing and securing of evidence that has to be presented in court later. In the very moment he has to classify the victim, he already questions the probability if the victim's particular features will be sufficient to prove the case in court and will lead to a conviction. He has witnessed many trials that were unsuccessful and therefore has developed a routine of classifying practices in accordance to his anticipation of the criteria applied during a trial. The practice of the raid is embedded in these logics: I will show that the raid actually includes a set of practices and bodies of knowledge, performed according to particular and localised logics and objectives, that in turn have complex consequences and implications and help to understand police practices of control within the frame of making (in)securities and (dis)order and as techniques of governing.

Problematisations and paradoxes

As previous research has shown, the main catalysts for law enforcement investigations in human trafficking are indications by the victims themselves or by third parties (Herz 2005: 10). Still, many vice squads perform raids as a proactive means of investigation. In the city I have been conducting my research, the officers focus on home-based prostitution and visit known apartments on a regular basis, which usually means every month. In those operations, usually three to six officers visit up to fifty apartments on one day. The raid as police practice is what Farrell and Pfeffer (2014) have called a 'traditional vice squad strategy' that is commonly being utilised by vice squads that proactively look for victims of human trafficking. Within the police departments Farrell and Pfeffer have researched in the United States, they noticed that the officers usually fail to identify possible victims during their raids, because the raid as an investigative strategy is traditionally designed for exposing offences such as illegal residence or non-existing work permits in the area of prostitution.

The raids I participated in showed similar results. The procedure of the raid consisted of entering the apartment of the sex workers, asking for their passports, copying the details of their passport into a form sheet, calling the police headquarters to check if the women are registered sex offenders and, concluding, asking the women if everything was okay, to which they would reply 'yes'. Let us look at one example from the field protocols[8]:

> In an apartment building, first floor. The first officer rings the bell to an apartment that belongs, according to a sign on the door, to 'Jana'. The other two officers and I hide next to the door. Jana opens the door.

Jana: 'Occupied!'

Officer: 'Just a moment, we are the police. Can I have a look at your passport?'

Jana: 'I'm with a client right now, but okay, just a second.'
> Everybody enters the apartment.

Jana: 'Come into the kitchen, quick!'
> The first officer starts to copy the details from the passport Jana had just given to him.

Officer: 'From Belarus. Where are you born?'

Jana: 'Kobrin. K-O-B-R-I-N. And I live in Berlin.'

Officer: 'Nationality is Belarus.'

Jana: 'Yes.'

Officer: 'And you live in Berlin, in which street?'

Jana: 'Hindenburgdamm.'

Officer: 'Hinder . . . .?'

Jana: 'Hindenburg. I believe that was a chancellor back in the days. (laughs)'

Officer: 'How long are you planning to stay here for work?'

Jana: 'Not long. This is just a job on the side, but it is legal.'

Officer: 'What is your main job then?'

Jana: 'I'm a beautician. Just think, what kind of jobs do non-Germans do here? Hairdresser, beautician, and this here. This is my second job so to say.'

Officer: 'Can I take a picture of you?'

Jana: 'Why?'

Officer: 'For our files only.'

Jana: 'Do I have to?'

Officer: 'No, it's optional.'

Jana: 'Then no. You already have the picture in my passport, don't you?'

Officer: 'Your telephone number?'
> Jana dictates her number.

Officer: 'Anything else, is everything alright? Do you have problems with certain men in this building who want to take your money?'

Jana: 'Of course, Romanians, Bulgarians . . . (laughs)'

Officer: 'That is what I thought.'

Jana: 'No, everything is just fine.'

Officer: 'Okay then, thank you. We will not bother you any longer. Bye-bye!'
> Everybody leaves the apartment.
>
>   (Field protocol raid, February 24, 2015)

---

8 The names of all participants have been changed in order to respect their anonymity.

So, what happened during these raids was either one of the following possibilities:

a) The woman examined would have her personal identification documents in order, which meant that the police would copy these details into their form sheet, include a photograph of her and a remark of her current whereabouts. After the raid was finished, the officers would enter the gathered data into a police database exclusively used for the purpose of registering people working in prostitution (and searchable by name by police officers nation-wide).

b) The woman did not have a valid passport or other acceptable means of identification, which the officers would deem as problematic, because they would have to detain her, bring her to the station and find a way to identify her. In this situation, the woman's emotional demeanour was decisive to the officers' further procedure: if the woman acted apologetic and remorseful, the officers would leave her with a warning. If, on the other hand, the woman without proper means of identification would act rather bluntly and showed no signs of contrition, the officers would take her to the station and treat her like an offender to immigration laws. They explained that they interpreted the woman's behaviour as disrespectful and therefore had 'to teach her a lesson'. Here, the situational assessment includes an affective dynamic (the officers' 'gut feelings') that influences their classification practices (Leser et al. 2017: 25).

c) The woman did not have her passport, but somebody else did. When interviewing the officers, they would indicate that a woman not in possession of her own passport would be a sign that she could possibly be a victim of trafficking. In the situations I observed during the raids, the woman asked for her passport would sometimes call for a friend to bring it, and the police officers would have to wait for a few minutes until another woman would enter the apartment and showed the passport to the officers, whose suspicion was in turn not raised, because the third-party in possession of the raided sex worker's passport was a women as well, and not a male 'trafficker'. The gender dynamic weighs heavily into the officers' classification practices: reproducing the master narrative of trafficking, in which 'heinous male predators molest [. . .] female captives' (Jones 2010: 1144), the officers seem to assume the proper victim to be female and girlish and the proper trafficker to be male and ruthless. Here, the master narrative operates as a simplifying device regarding the situational assessment of the (possible) victim's features, particularly its gender and age. It also suggests that male victims and female traffickers are 'invisible' (Jones 2010, 2014) – not only in the 'master narrative', but also in the state practices.

d) The woman examined had a passport, but the crosscheck with the headquarters' databases revealed that the woman was a registered offender and wanted for arrest. In that case, the police would arrest her and take her to the station in order to initiate the proper detaining procedures.

We can see from these options above that the objective of 'identifying possible victims' has to be understood quite literally: in the centre of the raid as a police practice (or rather: a set of practices) stands the identification of migrant women engaged in sex work in form of checking their documents, i.e. their names, age, and nationality. In this way, they become registered as prostitute migrant women in police databases later on and as such, they are approached as subjects who might be in danger (every prostitute migrant women *could be* a victim of trafficking) and someone who is dangerous, threatening (possible offender and/or disrupter of the social order) *at the same time*. This process of identification involves the registration and classification of a distinct target group and contains means of formalising persons into data sheets, accumulating and processing these data into databases. Thus, this process first and foremost produces knowledge about a target population in order to make this group more manageable via gathering this group into a database. Second, different conclusions about the identified parameters are drawn according to the logics of policing practices to perform a situational assessment: could this be a possible victim of trafficking? Is she helpless? Or is she dangerous or disruptive regarding the social order? These parameters do not only include technical details about a person's age, nationality and gender, but also certain affective behavioural features of the controlled person.

While the raid as such constitutes a standardised operating procedure in vice squads, the officers who engage in performing the raid have – to a certain extent – discretionary powers as street-level bureaucrats (Lipsky 1980) in direct contact with the controlled population, i.e. they can prioritise certain locations and times for the raid. In the raids I observed, police officers focus strongly on Bulgarian and Romanian women in sex work as problematic and therefore as target populations for raids. Thus, they control apartment buildings that these women inhabit more often than e.g. brothels where Germans work. Bulgarians and Romanians are, as they stated in interviews, more prone to be victims. When the officers talk about their target groups for finding victims in terms of nationality, they almost exclusively refer to women from Bulgaria and Romania, explaining that these women are more helpless than Germans and thus more easily exploitable.[9] In the interviews, the police officers clearly identify Romanians and Bulgarians as the primary target group of potential victims, but paradoxically, in the raids these women do not come to the attention to the officers as victims, but as offenders. In two instances they found Romanian women without passports or other proper means of identification, but did not perceive the missing passport as a sign of being trafficked, but instead took both of the women to the station, treating them as possible offenders to immigration laws. In another instance the crosscheck with police headquarters revealed that the Romanian woman they just checked was an offender wanted for trafficking in France, leaving the officers perplexed because of her gender. A female trafficker, they commented, was highly atypical.[10] In none of the raids I observed, was a

9   In the official statistics regarding formally identified victims of trafficking, Germans are equally represented as Bulgarians and Romanians are: In 2015, out of 416 identified victims, 98 were Romanian, 97 were German, and 71 were Bulgarian (BKA 2015). But building up such a statistic also means to produce certain narratives of who does what to whom, where they are from, and how to intercept the criminals. Thus, clear narratives are produced concerning women and men from certain countries with particular migration statuses (Pates et al. 2016, Blanchette et al. 2013).

10   Although 'the United Nations found that an overwhelmingly disproportionate number of human traffickers were in fact not males, but females, and that female traffickers may outnumber male traffickers worldwide' (Jones 2014, 147).

'victim of human trafficking' identified. The officer told me afterwards in an interview that they in fact never have been successful in finding a victim during a raid:

> The ways of coming to the attention to the police as a victim are different. Mostly the women just self-report. But within the eight years I have performed raids, I never met a victim who would reveal herself to us.
>
> (Interview vice squad 11, May 11, 2015)

Yet, they persist in their regular raids. And these raids are insofar 'traditional', as Farrell and Pfeffer (2014) are calling it, as they constitute standardised operating procedures that have existed in the vice investigations' repertoire for a long time and that form the officers' actions and expectations of what will happen during their operations. It could be assumed that the search for evidence of human trafficking is not the main objective of their raids, and that they rather check on violations of immigration laws. These practices, rather than developed in order to identify victims of trafficking within the area of commercialised sex, seem to be quite an unchanged continuation of traditional practices developed in times when the whole commercial prostitution sector as such was criminalised and controlled mainly via repressive policing.

We thus have to look further into the logics and legitimisations of these practices: why are raids still performed when no victim was ever found? Why is there such a strong focus on Bulgarians and Romanians? If success does not legitimate the raids, what does?

Producing order and deviant subjects

Let us look at another example from the raids I have been observing: three officers and myself went to raid a local apartment building where sex workers rent an apartment to work in (in this instance it was an apartment building where mostly Bulgarian women used to work). The police officers went into every apartment, rang the bell and checked the passports of every single sex worker they met. As we went from one apartment to another, we finally arrived at the last one where the officers found themselves confronted with a different situation than in the other apartments they checked so far. They rang the bell and a Bulgarian woman opened the door, letting us in. We went into the kitchen and found five Bulgarian men sitting around the kitchen table, smoking and eating food. I felt that the officers were suddenly very tense. They started questioning the men, what they were doing here and so on. Then the officers started discussing among themselves and after a while they announced that they wanted to check all the men separately in the room next door. One of the policemen and I waited in the kitchen, while the other two went into the room next door, calling in the Bulgarian men one after the other. They body-searched them and checked their passports. It took them quite a while to get done with that. While I waited in the kitchen, I asked the police officer who was waiting with me why they were doing this. He pointed out to me that he noticed a piece of tinfoil on the kitchen counter when he came in. He explained that they suspected this piece of tinfoil was used to wrap some kind of drug, and he suspected that drug to be weed. If those men in the kitchen were in the possession of drugs like that, they have to check them, he explained. So they did, and after about half an hour they were done, and they started searching the kitchen and the rest of the apartment for more leads and evidence. They found nothing. The piece of tinfoil turned out to be just a piece of tinfoil that had been used for cooking. They did not find any drugs. It turned out that the woman living and working in this apartment had invited her friends over for dinner and that was it (Field protocol raid, April 14, 2015).

In this example, several things are striking. First, the officers make ad hoc legitimisations for their practice of raiding (mostly private) apartments. The tinfoil as a lead to drug use was their legitimisation for a full check of the apartment including every person who was there at the time. Second, while this instance has nothing to do with victims of trafficking, it illustrates how the policing practices revolving around trafficking produce particular (dis)orders, specific subjects and norms. And third, more specifically, it (re)produces the target population, that is Bulgarians and Romanians, as an inherently suspicious group. So they raid within a narrow and focused area where they assume to find these populations in order to perform control upon them and, if possible, 'catch the bad guys' they associate with this population. That Bulgarians and Romanians stand as a metonym for disorder and crime becomes more apparent in an interview done with a vice squad officer in another city:

> We started raiding in the 1990s. It was cruel. It was so cruel. We found mattresses, in apartments with fifty square metres we found up to twelve mattresses on the floor. Fourteen-year old girls in prostitution. And in some parts you couldn't stand for more than three seconds on one spot because it was too sticky. It was the meanest of the mean. [. . .] We faced this problem very early, all those disgusting buildings. A lot of people cashed in on it, those who had residential property in those areas to let. We had some foreigners who those houses belonged to, they really cashed in on it. And I had colleagues who had been to Plovdiv, Bulgaria, and they told me how bad it was there. They were really disturbed by it. We just had to go against it. We had to force an extended presence on the curb.
>
> (Interview vice squad 20, July 28, 2015)

Even when control is not as explicit as in the example above, the presence of the officers and their visibility is central to the raids and strategically utilised for maintaining and (re)producing order.

Particularly in the field of prostitution and human trafficking, police officers I interviewed had difficulties to not involve their own personal beliefs and opinions – things they came to *know* through their own personal interests, which interlace with their practices and institutional discourse, which in turn results in this 'institutional fiction' that highly resembles Snajdr's 'master narrative' (2013), recalling images of femininity, youth, innocence, vulnerability and poverty. For example:

> The traffickers start to prepare their merchandise in the country of origin. They selectively target women they want to deliver into Western European countries. Sometimes they chose women from Bulgarian orphanages who

don't have any relatives left, so nobody will look for them if they go missing. Of course they take an advantage of the women's economic distress. The women are generally very poor, most of them have children and struggle in order to support their own families. They don't have a proper education. Some of them are illiterate and cannot write or read. All of that makes them prone to become a victim. Another important thing is the women's self-image and their role as women in Bulgaria which is defined in totally different ways as it is in Germany. They don't really perceive themselves as victims because they don't know better. The women obey the men, they follow them anywhere and fulfil their duties towards their husbands.

(Interview vice squad 11, May 11, 2015)

In the police officer's explanation, the Bulgarian woman is especially vulnerable because of the conservative gender roles and beliefs in her country of origin. Those specific problematisations used by the officers are producing normative orders in terms of who is being subjectified as a victim and why (in theory). But most interestingly, the notion of knowledge used for identifying victims (in theory) is not specialised expert knowledge, but common knowledge enmeshed with standard narratives that serves as a clear horizon of expectations (either their own expectations or the expectations they are confronted with when interacting with other institutions), which causes irritation to the officers as they face the more complex realities of their clientele.[11] In their daily practices, these expectations are not met: the controlled population they encounter does not fit the officers imagined criteria of someone being vulnerable and in need of help (a 'true' victim). Rather, they are deemed inherently suspicious – and thus rendering the 'victim' a truly absent figure.

Counterbalancing the absence of the victim

The implementation of anti-trafficking policies and legislations depends on the successful production of a victim in daily policing practices. As we have seen so far, the police seem to fail to 'produce' victims during their regular raids for a variety of reasons, while concurrently these raids seem to serve a different purpose than initially assumed. Still, the failure of the police in producing the assumed high numbers in official crime statistics accordingly is counterbalanced by certain strategies: (i) the vice squads developed alternative modes of data acquisition. The data they gather on their raids in known brothels and sites of home-based prostitution – names, nationalities, birth dates, phone numbers, photographs, whereabouts – were fed into police databases for internal uses, i.e. accessible by other vice police officers across the state; (ii) police officers articulate numbers other than the official statistics which

---

11   Ethnographic research on trafficking in human beings indicates, for example, that smuggling and labour migrations often is blurred with trafficking, that there are many cases of exploited labour into jobs other than sex work, and that it is often unclear where to draw the line between economic exploitation and trafficking. It suggests that victims are coerced by a range of factors including poverty, kinship obligations, fear of violence, debt, or the desire for the trappings of modernity (Jacobsen & Skilbrei 2010, Engle Merry 2015, Skilbrei & Tveit 2008, Zhang 2009). On taking a closer look, it is unclear who the victims are, how big the problem actually is, and what kinds of exploitation are involved.

are almost always estimates or add-ups from the prostitution databases; and (iii), the abstraction from certain numbers, like estimates of city wide working sex workers or the count of Bulgarian prostitutes in a one-day raid, as possible victims of trafficking. In this way, 'victim of trafficking' becomes a certain semantic category which almost always refers to 'migrant prostitute', and thus an indication that is the foundation for most of the numbers and knowledge being produced on trafficking victims. For example, one of the city's counselling centres states that they counsel up to 40 women a year who are mainly Bulgarian and Romanian sex workers, and though they are not officially identified as victims, they are *possible* victims of trafficking. Similarly, the police estimate that there might be up to 400 possible victims of trafficking in the city, which is their estimate of overall sex workers present. What happens here is a transformation of very complex, messy, singular stories into more stereotype overall narratives through the techniques of counting: of classifying and turning them into numbers that can be summarised, allowing for allotting very different things in the same categories and creating 'trafficking victims' in the plural. It can be assumed that the police contain and arrange broader political interests, and through their production of knowledge (in form of databases and statistics), they legitimise their performance of control and securing order – thereby enacting stateness and co-producing certain subjectivities.

Conclusion

As we have seen, the raid is not a singular practice, but a conglomerate of a variety of governmental techniques aimed at the policing and control of migrant women engaged in sex work. It includes techniques of identification, registration and classification of 'problematic' subjects, and draws on particular logics of performing control, maintaining order, of data acquisition and knowledge production in order to make those subjects of control more manageable. In these practices, the 'victim of trafficking' is enacted as a 'relational object of knowledge' along different dimensions: temporal relations concerning the expectation and anticipation of future events (like proving the victim's features in front of a court of justice), situational relations of assessing a person's status along affective and gender dynamics, and performative relations regarding the role-conception of the police officers, of their duties and responsibilities. Meanwhile, the 'master narrative' of trafficking is selectively invoked in the knowledge practices of the officers as a simplifying device, which leads to particular paradoxes in their daily performance. Those women who *should be* typical victims, the Bulgarians and Romanians, do come to the attention of the state not as victims, but more likely as offenders to immigration laws, as disruptors of the social order, as suspicious and deviant. The imaginary figure that police officers come to *know* as a 'true victim', deserving of being rescued, remains absent. But while these policing practices revolve around those rather contrasting forms of subjectivities – the absent victim and the problematic sex worker (possible victim, possible offender and/or disruptor of the social order) – the police and the state as such are being reproduced in a certain way: in being burdened with the task of upholding the social order, they identify (not the victim, but) what is deemed normal, deviant, order-less or morally questionable, in short: what sort of problem requires a response by the state. In practice, this becomes a matter of emphasis, of negotiation, contestation and sometimes even discrete decision. It is a process that incorporates a variety of hybrid bodies of knowledge, institutional logics, interactions and interrelations. And although these practices are unmistakably local, situated and embodied in individual state officials, they assemble a complex composition of how the state is done.

References

Bacchi, C. (2012) 'Why study problematizations? Making politics visible', *Open Journal of Political Science*, 2, 1–8.
Berman, J. (2003) '(Un)popular strangers and crises (un)bounded: Discourses of sex-trafficking, the European political community and the panicked state of the modern state', *European Journal of International Relations*, 9, 37–86.
Bierschenk, T. (2016) 'Police and state', in Bradford, B., Jauregui, B., Loader, I., and Steinberg, J. (Eds.) *The SAGE handbook of global policing*. London: Sage, pp. 155–178.
Blanchette, T. G., Silva, A. P., and Bento, A. R. (2013) 'The myth of Maria and the imagining of sexual trafficking in Brazil', *Dialectical Anthropology*, 37, 195–227.
Brodeur, J. P. (2010) *The policing web*. Oxford: Oxford University Press.
Bundeskriminalamt [BKA]. (2015). *Bundeslagebild Menschenhandel*. Wiesbaden: BKA.
Christie, N. (1986) 'The ideal victim', in Fattah, E. (Ed.) *From crime policy to victim policy*. Basingstoke: Palgrave Macmillan UK, pp. 17–30.
Doezema, J. (2000) 'Loose women or lost women? The re-emergence of the myth of white slavery in contemporary discourses of "trafficking" in women', *Gender Issues*, 18, 23–50.
Farrell, A., and Pfeffer, R. (2014) 'Policing human trafficking: Cultural blinders and organizational barriers', *The Annals of the American Academy of Political and Social Science*, 653 (1), 46–64.
Group of Experts on Action against Trafficking in Human Beings [GRETA] (2015) *Report concerning the implementation of the Council of Europe Convention on Action against Trafficking in Human Beings by Germany*. Available at: https://rm.coe.int/1680631c3b (Accessed 1 October 2017).
Hacking, I. (1999) *The social construction of what?* Cambridge, MA: Harvard University Press.
Hansen, T. B., and Stepputat, F. (2001) *States of imagination: Ethnographic explorations of the postcolonial state*. Michigan: Duke University Press.
Herz, A. L. (2005) *Menschenhandel: Eine empirische Untersuchung zur Strafverfolgungspraxis*. Freiburg i. Brsg, Germany: Max Planck Institut.
Hill, A. (2016) 'How to stage a raid: Police, media and the master narrative of trafficking', *Anti-Trafficking Review*, 7, 39–55.
Jakšić, M. (2008) 'Figures de la victime de la traite des êtres humains: de la victime idéale à la victime coupable', *Cahiers internationaux de sociologie*, 124, 127–146.
Jones, S. V. (2010) 'The invisible man: The conscious neglect of men and boys in the war on human trafficking', *Utah Law Review*, 4, 1143–1188.
Jones, S. V. (2014) 'The invisible women: Have conceptions about femininity led to the global dominance of the female human trafficker?', *Albany Government Law Review*, 7 (1), 143–165.
Latour, B. (2007) 'A textbook case revisited: Knowledge as mode of existence', in Hackett, E. J., Lynch, M., Wajcman, J., and Amsterdamska, O. (Eds.) *The handbook of science and technology studies*. Cambridge, MA: MIT Press, pp. 83–112.

Leser, J., Pates, R., and Dölemeyer, A. (2017) 'The emotional leviathan: How street-level bureaucrats govern human trafficking victims', *Digithum*, 19, 19–36.

Lipsky, M. (1980) *Street-level bureaucracy: Dilemmas of the individual in public services.* New York: Russell Sage Foundation.

Migdal, J. S., and Schlichte, K. (2005) 'Rethinking the state', in Schlichte, K. (Ed.) *The dynamics of states: The formation and crises of state domination.* Aldershot: Ashgate, pp. 1–40.

Moore, D., and Valverde, M. (2000) 'Maidens at risk: Date rape drugs and the formation of hybrid risk knowledges', *Economy and Society*, 29 (4), 514–531.

Pates, R., and Schmidt, D. (2007) 'Wahrheiten über Opfer: Menschenhandelsdiskurse im Vergleich: HU Berlin: Zentrum für transdisziplinäre Geschlechterstudien: Bulletin Texte', *Der involvierte Blick Zwangsprostitution und ihre Repräsentation*, 35, 90–105.

Sharma, A., and Gupta, A. (Eds.) (2009) *The anthropology of the state: A reader.* Malden; Oxford; Victoria: Blackwell Publishing.

Snajdr, E. (2013) 'Beneath the master narrative: Human trafficking, myths of sexual slavery and ethnographic realities', *Dialectical Anthropology*, 37, 229–256.

United Nations Office for Drug Control and Crime Prevention [UNODCCP] (2000) *Protocol to prevent, suppress and punish trafficking in persons, especially women and children.* Available at: http://www.unodc.org/documents/treaties/UNTOC/Publications/TOC%20Convention/TOCebook-e.pdf (Accessed 1 October 2017).

Valverde, M. (2009) *Law's dream of a common knowledge.* Princeton: Princeton University Press.

Valverde, M. (2010) *The force of law.* Ontario: Groundwood Books Ltd.

Valverde, M., Levi, R., and Moore, D. (2005) 'Legal knowledges of risks', in Law Commission of Canada (Ed.) *Law and risk.* Vancouver, Toronto: UBC Press, pp. 86–120.

7 Trafficking, pimping, sex work and the police

Street prostitutes' perceptions in Las Vegas

Andrew L. Spivak

Introduction

Research on the legality and policing of prostitution has grown considerably since Mcleod's (1982) study encouraged scholars to discuss the extent to which sex work could constitute a legitimate, regulated occupation, as opposed to being an institution that is necessarily victimising. However, recent academic discourse about the criminalisation of sex work is increasingly focused on the popular concept of sex trafficking, and is shaped by social activists, media and policy makers, and even opposing feminist perspectives (Lui 2011).

Popularised as a social problem in the 1990s, concern about trafficking gained momentum both domestically and internationally, and has been associated with policy changes over the past two decades that often reflect some scholars' assumptions that sex workers are mostly (or entirely) comprised of trafficking victims. This conflation of sex work and trafficking has created confusion in the reporting of national statistics in the United States (Adelson 2008), as well as acceptance of a victimisation paradigm among many journalists, social service providers and criminal justice officials. Consequently, policing policy and practice has tended to focus on the 'rescue' of sex workers from their traffickers (Lerum et al. 2012; Marcus et al. 2012; Weitzer 2014).

In a political climate that encourages law enforcement agencies to work toward an end to trafficking (and thus sex work itself) by removing pimps/panderers from society, policing practices tend to begin with sex workers themselves. Frequent interaction between police and prostitutes is certainly not a new phenomenon, and researchers have noted common issues for sex workers related to this interaction – e.g. harassment and sexual assault, reluctance to report customer violence, coercion to be informants (Armstrong 2016; Benoit et al. 2016; Dewey and Germain 2014). However, little research has focused on the extent to which sex workers' interactions with police in recent years reflect paternalistic attitudes, attempts to inform on alleged pimps, or efforts to rescue them from prostitution.

The aim of the present study is twofold: first, to assess the validity of victimisation perspectives by examining the self-reported prevalence of pimping, violence and coercion among a sample of 171 street prostitutes in Las Vegas, Nevada interviewed between 2012 and 2014. Second, to examine these respondents' experiences with police in the context of current literature on police-prostitute interaction and anti-trafficking initiatives. As much anti-trafficking activism in the United States has paid particular attention to juveniles (Curtis et al. 2008; Nevada Assembly 2013; Swaner et al. 2016), the data from this research is well-suited to this goal – 27 of the 171 respondents were juveniles, the rest were between 18 and 24 years' old.

Young sex workers or sex trafficking victims

Narratives about street prostitutes, particularly those who are juveniles and young adults, often reflect conflicting factors that shape entry into prostitution, including both coercion and agency, but in popular conceptions of human trafficking they are constructed entirely as innocent victims stripped of basic human rights, often kidnapped and controlled by a powerful figure (Saunders 2005). This forced prostitution of youth has been an international concern since the1970s, but localised fears of 'sex slavery' in America gained prevalence most recently after the First World Congress Against the Sexual Exploitation of Children in 1996. Soon after, a new classification for youth selling sex – the commercially sexually exploited child, or sex trafficking victim – emerged with new legal codes pertaining to sexual consent laws for minors (Davidson 2005; Schaffner 2005).

The subsequent movement to save youth from sexual exploitation led to the Trafficking Victims Protection Act (TVPA) in 2000, which defined severe trafficking in persons as 'sex trafficking in which a commercial sex act is induced by force, fraud, or coercion, or in which the person induced to perform such act has not attained 18 years of age' (US Department of State 2000). By precluding minors' legal consent in all cases of paid sex and harshly criminalising 'traffickers,' US policy effectively endorsed a victimisation perspective for all juveniles engaged in prostitution.

The following year, a research report from the University of Pennsylvania School of Social Work estimated in 2001 that between 100,000 and 300,000 juveniles may be at risk for sexual exploitation (Estes and Weiner 2001). 'At risk' children included not only runaways, but those who were 'outsiders' or who lived on the Mexican or Canadian borders. Nonetheless, the figure was repeated in venues including the New York Times, USA Today and CNN as the actual number of victims. The ensuing anti-trafficking and CSEC movements included celebrity advert campaigns (which touted the 300,000 figure), television documentaries on 'sex slaves in America', more than $180 million in federal funds to almost 100 groups, including many whose stated agendas were geared toward the abolition of all sex work (e.g. The Polaris Project, Shared Hope and Innocence Lost), and 42 federally-funded law enforcement task forces (Cizmar et al. 2011).

Many of the funded NGOs with political influence were strongly abolitionist toward all types of prostitution (Saunders 2005). Lerum et al. (2012) documented the political struggles by sex workers' rights organisations to resist the damage of anti-trafficking legislation, which equated human trafficking with sex work. As empirical research on sex work increased, scholars questioned the validity of the anti-trafficking movement and the paucity of empirical data from actual sex workers (Cojocaru 2015; Marcus et al. 2012; Weitzer 2014).

Meanwhile, sex worker's rights organisations have striven to legitimise sexual commerce as a vocation (Chateauver 2014), and studies stemming back to the late 1970s have documented the nuanced impact of sex work on the lives of some labourers (Agustín 2007; Brents and Hausbeck 2007; Chapkis 1997; Dalder 2004; Decker 1979; Foltz 1979; Woodward et al. 2004; West 1993). More recently, Agustin (2007) notes that sex work can open the door for many to leave intolerable situations like abusive family members, prejudice and dead-end jobs.

Weitzer (2005) notes that safety, income and overall experience in prostitution or sex work is certainly shaped by both local and global location, as well as socioeconomic conditions. The experience of a Nevada brothel worker may be very different from a 'street walker', a 'high-end call girl' or an undocumented immigrant working in the underground economy. Thus, perspectives that view prostitution through the lens of either oppression or empowerment cannot adequately reflect the diversity of experiences across this population. Rather, 'the type of prostitution is the best predictor of worker experiences', and these subtleties are best revealed when scholars reject the victim/worker dichotomy for a polymorphous perspective (Weitzer 2005: 219).

Issues in police-prostitute interactions

A number of studies have documented sex workers' descriptions of abusive behaviour by police officers, including harassment, sexual coercion and extortion, false arrests and threats of violence. These negative experiences have led many street prostitutes to feel pressure to develop avoidance strategies and view the police as a general threat (Benoit et al. 2016; Dewey and Germain 2014; Nixon et al. 2002; Thrukal and Ditmore 2003; Wagner et al. 2016). Hodgson (2001: 536) suggests that the paramilitary organisational culture of policing agencies leads officers to ' "learned values' of violence and coercion as primary tools for dealing with day-to-day interactions, and sex workers unsurprisingly report lower general confidence in the police than does the general population (Benoit et al. 2016).

Conversely, police often view prostitutes in a negative light. Vice officers are often seen by their colleagues as having reduced status, and female officers have reported feelings of disgust in playing the role of prostitutes in sting operations (Williamson et al. 2007). In a survey of 158 police officers across 10 policing agencies in Pennsylvania, 39% agreed that 'prostitution is immoral and for that reason alone should continue to be illegal'. Additionally, 62% agreed that 'legalizing prostitution will result in an increase in social problems in those areas where it is occurring' (Mentzer 2010: 50).

Nonetheless, sex workers do report developing occasional cooperative relationships with some of the officers they encounter; one 19-year-old who had been engaged in street prostitution in Birmingham, UK, told researchers 'If you are sweet with them then they will be sweet back' (Sanders 2004: 1713). Some workers also describe various degrees of paternalistic attitudes among officers that can reduce the likelihood of arrest, as well as – among older prostitutes – some overall improvement in police treatment over the past few decades (Benoit et al. 2016).

Dewey and Germain (2014) conducted qualitative interviews with street-based sex workers in Denver, Colorado, from which three themes emerged in prostitutes' views about their interactions with police: (i) arrest is essentially indiscriminate, meaning that sex workers, or any woman on the street in areas the police consider to be known for such activity, risk arrest for a number of offences, (ii) they have some ability to develop 'arrest-avoidance skills' in their interactions with police, particularly with regard to recognising sting-operation cues and (iii) police can and often will exceed their authority and engage in harassment and abuse (Dewey and Germain 2014).

Another qualitative survey of sex workers and former sex workers describes a spectrum of general archetypes of police-prostitute interactions that emerged from qualitative interviews with former sex workers, including 'nice cops' who are generally non-abusive and appear to care about protecting workers' general safety, non-responsive officers who, while not abusive, want little to do with prostitutes and seem to be annoyed when they have to deal with them, and perpetrators who engage in abuse and sexual extortion. Finally, nearly half the respondents described having police officers as paying customers. This wide range of descriptions with which sex workers characterise their encounters and relationships with police officers reflects the complexity of criminalisation, as well as culture of policing. Policing agencies engage in a variety of strategies and tactics in dealing with most social phenomena, including prostitution; the use of discretion and non-formal rationality in responding to various situations means that sex workers cannot expect similar handling from every police officer they may encounter (Williamson et al. 2007).

The present study

This research was part of a national study sponsored by the US Department of Justice (USDOJ) through a grant from the Office of Juvenile Justice Delinquency Prevention (OJJDP) to the nonprofit organisation Center for Court Innovation (CCI).[1] The initial studies in New York City and Atlantic City were conducted by scholars at the City University of New York (Curtis et al. 2008; Marcus et al. 2014), after which CCI reached out to researchers at universities and consulting agencies in Miami, the San Francisco Bay Area, Dallas, Chicago, and Las Vegas. The Las Vegas site's research team was based at the University of Nevada, Las Vegas (UNLV). The project began in February 2012 and ended in May 2014, with most interviews occurring in the last five months of that period (Wagner et al. 2016).

Setting

Las Vegas, Nevada has a reputation of being a hedonist destination. Tourists can not only gamble and dine, they can visit one of Las Vegas's highly regulated adult

1 This research was funded by grant #2009-MC-CX-0001 ("The Commercial Sexual Exploitation of Children (CSEC): A National Study of CSEC Prevalence, Prosecution, and Services") from the US Department of Justice (DOJ), Office of Justice Programs, via a sub-award through Fund for the City of New York (FCNY), Center for Court Innovation. The project was conducted under protocol 1306–4498M of the University of Nevada, Las Vegas Office of Research Integrity – Human Subjects.

businesses, including swingers clubs, high-end strip clubs and burlesque shows. This adult industry in Las Vegas is an inextricable part of the city's image, with billboards advertising strip clubs, adult stores, clubs and shows.

The US Census Bureau, in cooperation with the American Community Survey, estimates the city of Las Vegas population in 2015 at 605,097, while the entire metropolitan statistical area, including North Las Vegas, the suburb of Henderson and neighbourhoods in 'unincorporated areas' of the valley (much of which is closer to downtown Las Vegas than some areas within technical city limits) has an estimated 2,035,572 residents (US Census 2015). The city attracts nearly three million tourists each month, creating an average one-sixth increase in the population on the weekends (Las Vegas Convention and Visitors Authority 2012). Most of this increase occurs in primary tourist areas, the hotel-casinos of which are highly regulated with security staff and video surveillance. Though casinos are scattered throughout the Las Vegas valley area, Vegas's nightlife is primarily clustered in two locations: 'the Strip', an icon of modern Las Vegas, and downtown, a historic area that built the city's original reputation, eventually fell into dilapidation, and is now in the midst of gentrification. Though prostitution is illegal in Clark County, which contains the city of Las Vegas, escort advertisements are highly visible on mobile billboards, escort magazines and cards with explicit photos and phone numbers, often handed out by undocumented workers at hotel entrances and busy street corners. Additionally, well-known legal brothels operate in neighbouring counties, some only an hour outside city limits. Nevada is currently the only state in the United States that allows any form of legal prostitution, thus enhancing Las Vegas's reputation as a centre for sexual tourism in the United States (Brents et al. 2010).

While known for its 'Sin City' grandeur, the average household income of $52,601, with 16.2% estimated below the poverty line, is comparable to national estimates. The state ranks 48th in average graduation rates for public high school students with only 68.1% of students in Clark County graduating (Tyler and Owens 2012). Las Vegas is also one of the most transient metropolitan areas in the United States. Until 2000, the decennial censuses asked households whether they had been living in the same state five years earlier. In 1970, only 60% of MSA residents had been living in Nevada five years earlier. This proportion increased to 63% in 1980, 66% in 1990, and 68% in 2000. However, the respective proportions for the nation were 84, 85, 88, and 89% (US Census 2013).

Between August 2005 and May 2007, 226 minors were adjudicated for prostitution or prostitution-related offences in Clark County (Kennedy and Pucci 2008), and one sample (N = 161) of juvenile girls in county detention revealed that 47% had prior involvement in prostitution (Kennedy et al. 2009). Those in the sample who had been sexually exploited were significantly more likely to have experienced a number of challenging disparities, including physical and sexual abuse, hospitalisation for mental health issues, abuse of alcohol and other drugs and being runaways.

Methods

Initial study respondents were recruited by flyers containing a phone number – a toll-free 24-hour '800' number – for potential respondents to arrange an appointment to be interviewed. The flyers asked, 'Have you ever exchanged sex for food, money, housing, or other goods?' The toll-free number was routed to a cell phone and monitored by project staff at all hours. Project staff conducted interviews at respondent-chosen public places, such as coffee-shops and fast-food restaurants. In accordance with institutional review board protocol, at least two researchers were present at all times during these interview meetings.

Research team members (graduate student assistants) initially posted advertisements on Craigslist, Redbook, and Backpage using the same wording as the fliers, although few respondents called in response to these ads. Outreach efforts in neighbourhoods known for prostitution (sometimes called 'tracks' as noted by local police who spoke to our researchers) in which team members walked in pairs of two handing out flyers and speaking to persons on the street, produced some interviews, but progress was slow for several months. In one neighbourhood, some locals suggested that prostitutes would be reluctant to talk because they were controlled by pimps, and several men did appear to be watching over women who were walking along the track. By fall 2013, the pace of recruitment increased and remained steady through the end of the project in May 2014.

As in the original New York study (see Curtis et al. 2008; Marcus et al. 2016), the research design employed a Respondent Driven Sampling (RDS) system to continue recruitment beyond the 'seed' interviews, in which respondents received coupons to distribute to their peers. This sampling method is specifically designed to assess representative characteristics of hidden, underclass populations (Heckathorn 2002). Research assistants, all of whom completed research ethics training (required by the university's institutional review board) and an additional 8–20 hours of ethnographic interview training, conducted the interview protocol, including both closed and open-ended questions. Each respondent received 40 dollars' cash, as well as three coupons with unique numerical codes to pass along to other youth they knew who might be engaged in sex work, and were paid an additional 10 dollars' cash when these coupons were redeemed.

The confidentiality protocol ensured informed consent and anonymity. Upon meeting potential respondents, researchers asked permission to conduct the interview and electronically record it. Most respondents agreed to be recorded, and those who did not were still interviewed. Respondents were read an informed consent statement, and those who agreed to continue (almost all) were then asked to choose a study-participant pseudonym to be written on the informed consent documentation.

The interview questionnaire, designed by CCI, contained 176 questions. Topics included respondent information, making and spending money, market involvement, customers, pimps and market facilitators, network, health and needs, experiences with the police and expectations. Interview times ranged from 45 minutes to several hours, but most were under an hour.

Findings

Interviews revealed a diverse set of participants, who reported varying experiences with pimping, violence and interactions with police. Table 7.1 summarises

Table 7.1 Percentage distribution for selected characteristics

	Overall (N = 171)	Female (N = 107)	Male[1] (N = 64)
Age			
13 to 17	16.4	20.6	9.4
18 to 20	40.9	43.0	37.5
21 to 22	23.4	20.6	28.1
23 to 24	19.3	15.9	25.0
Race/ethnicity			
White	22.2	18.7	28.1
Black	57.3	57.0	57.8
Hispanic	10.5	10.3	10.9
Other/Multi	9.9	14.0	3.2
Last Grade Enrolled In			
< 6	0.7	1.1	0
6 to 8	3.4	4.4	1.8
9 to 11	43.8	43.3	44.6
12 (or GED)	52.1	51.1	53.6
Age at First-Paid Sex			
< 13	3.6	3.8	3.1
13 to 17	67.5	70.5	62.5
> 18	29.0	25.7	34.4
Has a Pimp	12.9	16.8	6.3
Has a Market Facilitator who is Not a Pimp	24.0	23.4	25.0
Ever had a "run-in" with police	82.5	78.5	89.0
Ever Arrested for Any Reason	54.4	50.5	60.9
Ever Arrested for Prostitution	7.6	8.4	6.3
Arrested in the Past Year for Prostitution	4.1	4.8	3.1

1 Three female and two male respondents identified as transgender.

demographic characteristics of the sample, as well as some experiential indicators (e.g. having a pimp, having ever had a "run-in" with police, having ever been arrested).

Interviewees ranged from 13 to 24 (only one respondent was 13). Twenty-eight participants were under 18 at the time of the interview, and 99 were between 18 and 21. Only five respondents (2.9%) were transgender. Just above half of the study participants were African American, the rest primarily white, with some Hispanic and mixed race/ethnicity. Interestingly, just under one-third of over-18 participants did not have their first paid-sex experience until after the age of 18, reflecting a wide distribution of pathways through which the participates had entered sex work.

Particularly surprising was the significant proportion (nearly two-fifths) of study participants who were boys and young men, although this result was similar to findings from other study sites (Swaner et al. 2016). Many of them claimed to engage in sex work with primarily older female clients in exchange for temporary lodging and occasional financial assistance, often in extended arrangements – the researchers began to refer to these youth as 'sugar babies'. They tended to also make money via drug and gang activity, as well, and were not generally influenced by pimping, while boys who saw male clients were more likely to have narratives reflective of victimisation.

Pimping and coercion

The question of what proportion of sex workers have pimps/traffickers and are coerced into prostitution by these third parties has been especially contentious among scholars and activists, and is often central to discussions of criminalisation. While young sex workers are often resistant to acknowledging pimps to authorities, the study's interview protocol contained several questions to ascertain the nuances of participants' living situations and relationships in order to answer this question, such as asking respondents whether someone helps them find customers, provides transportation and/or protection or helps them manage the money they make and/or pay their bills. Even if participants did not think of such persons as pimps – often, respondents considered such people to be roommates, boyfriends etc. – the study referred to the people in these roles, who could reasonably be defined as pimps/traffickers from a victimisation perspective, as 'market facilitators'. About one-third of participants overall, and nearly two-fifths of female participants, had a market facilitator of some kind (see Table 7.1), but less than half of them considered these persons to be their pimps.

Nearly half of respondents acknowledged having help at some point meeting with clients, and this help ranged from pimps to friends and family members. Similar to findings by Marcus et al. (2012), some of the participants described having used 'spot pimps' – people who do not primarily operate as pimps/traffickers, but are involved in 'street life' and sometimes refer clients to sex workers upon request for a referral fee.

About one-quarter of respondents who had pimps/market facilitators indicated that their pimps/facilitators found clients on the internet, and often this was the primary method of doing so. Besides the internet, pimps/facilitators 'worked the streets' or utilised networks of regulars who contacted them when they wanted to arrange to meet the sex worker.

Relationships with pimps/facilitators were varied, from one respondent who said she loved her pimp and desperately wished he felt the same, to another who bitterly hated her pimp. Some market facilitators were considered boyfriends, 'baby daddies', as well as relatives, friends and often friends of friends. Though most pimps/facilitators were men, a few were women, often considered good friends and/or sister figures. In many cases, these female facilitators did not take any money for their management, while male facilitators almost always demanded a cut.

One 17-year-old respondent described having been 'turned out' by a pimp when she was 14. He seemed to be a boyfriend in the beginning and bought her gifts, but eventually she felt that she owed him sex, and then he expected her to have sex with others. When she moved in with him, 11 other juvenile girls lived in the same dwelling. She considered fleeing, but noted that one friend who tried to leave was burned in the face with an iron. She described staying quiet and keeping to herself, avoiding violence. After two years she was able to contact a family member to help her sneak away.

A 22-year-old respondent described her pimp as her 'best friend' and 'protector'. 'He won't ever hit me. He pays the rent, he pays the bills . . . he takes care of everything'. She noted that 'most hoes know to keep their mouth shut and stay in a hoe's place. I don't feel like that and I can talk when I want'. She gave all her money to him, but perceived a sense of freedom with him, believing that he cared for her.

While male respondents rarely described having pimps, one 19-year-old male respondent was willing to discuss a sense of dependency on his pimp. First getting into prostitution after a stint in juvenile detention, he tried working the street on his own but was grateful when he met this man (described as a friend of a friend). He felt a sense of relief 'because he does all the sorting, he does everything for me . . . he handles the money, and the schedule. I just do the job'. The interviewer noted that the respondent was a methamphetamine addict, and his pimp kept in him in supply of meth, as well as lodging and food. Unlike many female youth with pimps, he stated that he did not have strong feelings toward his pimp, but just saw him as a 'go-to' person who made things simpler and easier – he didn't need to worry about arrangements with clients, price negotiation and transportation – and he felt that the job was much safer. Potential clients met independently would sometimes try to jump (assault and rob) or rape him, though he said 'they haven't gotten me yet' regarding his multiple experiences being the victim of attempted sexual assault.

Another female respondent, 23-years-old, met her pimp several years earlier at a time when she was addicted to heroin.

> I was walking home . . . kind of close to where I was but there was no bus on the street so I was forced to walk and he pulled up and said, 'do you need a ride?' and I accepted it . . . it was really nasty outside . . . asked if I'd ever tried being an escort. . . . He had helped other girls do it and you know, you can make one grand in a night . . . during the day, I would go over to his place and he would set me up on the computer and I would do just like, one day and take the money and go home.

She eventually moved in with him and rented a motel room for meeting clients. He 'coached' her, teaching her to find clients online and providing transportation and she gave him half her earnings. She said he was never cruel or disrespectful, and they never had a sexual relationship, although he was equally dependent on her because he was an unemployed 'professional gambler.' 'I liked him, I kind of depended on him. . . . If I didn't wanna spend money on something, he'd buy it for me, or food. Took me to California, paid for us to stay there'.

While some respondents worked with steady pimps, others worked with different pimps as they moved in and out of prostitution. One 18-year-old respondent only conducted three paid sex transactions in her life – each arranged with a different pimp. The first time, when she was 17, the arrangement was set up by her friend's boyfriend (whom she knew was pimp): 'I was with one of my friends and she was telling me that she did it and stuff. She was with this guy, and she said he was taking care of her, giving her money and food and she didn't have to worry about any of that stuff. And at that time, I was out on the streets and I needed money'. She chose not to stay with him, and so he took all her earnings (about 50 dollars) but did not attempt to claim ownership over her. The second time she sold sex, her mother (also a prostitute) set it up to help support her (the mother's) drug habit: 'Mom introduced me to him, my mom does it all the time. I got 50 or 40 dollars'. She had to give 30 dollars of it to her mother. The third and final time she sold sex, she met the client through a female classmate who arranged the meeting. They met at a Motel 6, and he paid her 30 dollars (20 of which she had to pay to the classmate).

Another 18-year-old described working with her boyfriend, who helped her find clients, make ads online and negotiate pricing. They share the money, and he does not work with anyone else. This type of boyfriend/pimp role was common among respondents with facilitators, and few indicated conditions that appeared coercive.

One very young respondent, a 15-year-old, was tricked into her first paid sex experience by a female friend/pimp. She had moved in with the friend after being sexually abused by a relative. The friend had been engaged in prostitution herself for a while, meeting clients online, and set up the engagement with the respondent unaware of what was expected until she met him: 'I was angry at first, when she set me up. But then I got paid and it was alright'. She continued to engage in paid sex intermittently, allowing her friend to make appointments when she needed money, but did not feel pressured to do so. The two friends shared household expenses, but the respondent never paid a direct proportion of her earnings in exchange for the arrangements.

About two-fifths of participants had seen or been involved in a conflict, physical fight or potentially violent altercation, while working. As one participant put it, these conflicts could be over anything: 'Someone stepping on someone's shoes, gang banging, you see all types of shit, being on the street'. Of the types of altercations participants described, about a third were with customers, primarily over money. An additional fifth were with pimps, and the rest involved domestic violence, between other prostitutes, gang-related incidents, clients' partners and employees of businesses who kicked them off the premises for soliciting. A few descriptions appeared to support the perception of pimp-related coercion. For example, one respondent told a story about beating up another prostitute, causing that prostitute's pimp to approach her about the altercation, a tense situation because she 'can't look in his eyes, because this mean you's his bitch'. When asked how she learned this rule, she told the interviewer that she has several family members involved in street prostitution. Her sister was a 'ho', her mom used to be, her father was a pimp and the rest of her family is 'full of gangbangers'.

Only 34 participants described specific strategies to avoid conflict or protect themselves in conflicts. About two-thirds of these said that they 'walked away' or 'keep to [themselves]' or 'avoid drama'.

Overall, young sex workers in Las Vegas describe a varied distribution of experiences involving pimping/trafficking and coercive/violent conditions. A few respondents appear to fit the common image of the trafficking/pimped youth – violence and coercion are present and often a significant part of their narratives – but many more have engaged in sex work with some degree of autonomy.

Interactions with police

Interactions with police officers were common among participants, with less than one-fifth of respondent having never had any 'run-ins' with police (see Table 7.1). This proportion was a little higher among the 27 juveniles (under 18) participants, seven of whom had never had a run-in. Among this group, truancy, breaking curfew, underage drinking, drug use and shoplifting/stealing were the most common reasons for police interactions. Status offences were actually the most common reason listed for having had a police interaction. Juveniles were also a bit less likely to have been arrested than those 18 and older, only eight of whom had ever been arrested, compared to a little more than half of participants overall. Only one juvenile respondent indicated that she had been 'hassled' for prostitution, stating that she had been stopped and talked to by the police at least four times but never arrested.

Among those 18 and older, the frequency of police run-ins varied greatly. Some participants noted police interactions in their lives as very frequent occurrences, responding with 'too many to count', '3–4 times per week' and 'over one hundred'. Overall, 34 respondents (almost exactly one-fifth) of the sample reported having more than 10 interactions with the police, about a third of whom estimated the interactions above 30 times. Among these participants, the most common reasons for police contact were offences including shoplifting, battery, domestic violence, larceny, possession of drugs, jaywalking and trespassing. Male respondents reported the most contact with police, especially for non-prostitution related activity, while female respondents were much more likely than males to have run-ins for solicitation. Thirty participants reported having had run-ins with police specifically due to sex work and 13 of these had been arrested for prostitution, seven of these within the past year. Those who were stopped by police tended to give fake names to officers, while those actually arrested were more likely to give the police accurate identification. Participants described police as hassling them when they walked 'the tracks' (areas common among street prostitutes), and often arrested workers while conducting undercover sting operations.

Most of the respondents had strategies to keep away from the police, often noting that they hid or ran away when they saw a cop. Twenty-eight participants indicated that avoiding police was a factor in deciding where to work. One respondent discussed the lengths she took to stay away from cops on the street and those working undercover:

> Yes . . . um . . . like if we see a police officer, or whatever, we'll like go in a store or whatever's closest. And when we meet the tricks. . . . The police officer, they won't let you touch them, like you can't touch a police officer. Right there, so . . . we'll be like, we'll touch them, and we'll tell them we know it's not a police officer.

Another respondent described her impression of the criminal justice system: 'For soliciting you don't really see a judge. You don't do nothing. They hold you for 48 hours and then let you go'. She had been arrested several times, the most recent by an undercover officer. To avoid being picked up by an undercover officer again, she asks new clients to touch her breast before negotiating prices under the assumption that police cannot engage in such behaviour.

Only a few participants discussed substantially negative interactions with the police. One respondent was picked up by an undercover officer who asked her to do something 'disgusting' in order to not arrest her. She refused to discuss what the officer specifically asked her to do, but did say that she told the other officers at the station and they laughed at her. Another respondent said an officer asked her to show him her breasts to avoid arrest. A different respondent described the way charges against her were dropped due to police misconduct: 'I got out of a case because the undercover did too much. Meaning, I gave head to an officer when he was on duty – and he was supposed to be . . . it was too much. He did too much, and he wasn't supposed to do that. So they didn't charge me'. The respondent didn't indicate whether the officer was held accountable in any way.

The accounts of police interaction described by respondents in the study reflected a generally negative impression – avoidance and fear of arrest were common themes when discussing police – although most did not report having experienced the kinds of egregious abuse found in past studies.

Discussion

The aims of the present study were to (i) assess the validity of victimisation perspectives by examining the self-reported prevalence of pimping, violence and coercion among a sample of 171 street prostitutes in Las Vegas, Nevada, and (ii) to examine these respondents' experiences with police in the context of current literature on police-prostitute interaction anti-trafficking initiatives.

In addressing the first aim, the interviews reveal that young street-based prostitutes in Las Vegas, similar to their counterparts in New York, Atlantic City, Miami, Chicago, Dallas and San Francisco (Swaner et al. 2016), have experienced coercion and violence from pimps and customers at a level of prevalence that gives only partial validity to the victimisation/trafficking perspectives fueling anti-trafficking (and abolitionist) activism. Even when carefully inquiring about relationships and living arrangements, less than half report having pimps/facilitators or 'facilitators' who might be considered as such. While many of the workers interviewed described violent day-to-day circumstances, few appeared to be under the power of a controlling facilitator, without agency in their activities. Respondents described many of the facilitators as friends, family and acquaintances whom they had approached for help themselves, and/or with whom they had simply lived and shared expenses. Often, these facilitators had introduced them to sex work (sometimes because they'd been doing it themselves), but others entered the participants' lives after they'd already become involved in prostitution. Nonetheless, recent anti-trafficking statues allow authorities to bring trafficking charges against all such persons for nearly any level of assistance, with especially severe penalties if the youth is under 18 (Nevada Assembly 2013; Nevada Attorney General 2016).

Regarding the second aim, the study produced two notable findings from participants' descriptions of police interaction. First, while day-to-day contact with police was as prevalent as in past studies, and more than half the sample had experienced arrest, the sample of youth in Las Vegas did not indicate as much police abuse as might have been expected. While 15% of Williamson et al.'s (2007) survey of incarcerated women reported having been coerced into sex with police officers, only one of the Las Vegas participants indicated this kind of victimisation. General harassment was relatively common, however, as well as descriptions of avoidance strategies in relation to vice operations, similar to respondents in Dewey and Germain's (2014) study. Second, none of the participants indicated having been pressured by authorities to reveal traffickers/pimps in exchange for easier treatment upon arrest. The study did conclude before the recent state-level anti-trafficking statute, so this element of police-prostitute interaction may be changing, and only a very small percentage of the sample (7.6%) indicated that they'd been arrested for prostitution. More than four of every five participants who had ever been arrested had never been arrested specifically for selling sex, and arrests for prostitution are the cases in which anti-trafficking initiatives and attitudes would be most likely to play a role in police treatment.

Conclusion

Overall, the extent to which social attitudes, activism and policy surrounding sex trafficking affects police-prostitute interaction is largely unexplored. This analysis of findings from a study of young sex workers in Las Vegas, Nevada, has indicated that the victimisation perspective's narrative about sex workers is limited and incomplete, and that experiences with police, while not as bad as in some studies, are still more negative than positive.

The research discussed above also highlights the continued stereotypes and alarmist social constructions of those involved in third-party organisation of sex work activities. In this sample, few individuals appear to be under the control of a facilitator, and where facilitators are involved these relationships are tied up with kinship, family, friendship and other complex relationships. Policing agencies that hope to deal more effectively with this vulnerable population, especially regarding safety and public order, would benefit from a more evidence-based understanding of sex workers' circumstances than is often currently held.

References

Adelson, W. J. (2008) 'Child prostitute or victim of trafficking?', *University of St. Thomas Law Journal*, 6 (1), 96–128.

Agustin, L. M. (2007) 'Introduction to the cultural study of commercial sex', *Sexualities*, 10 (4), 403–407.

Armstrong, L. (2016) 'From law enforcement to protection? Interactions between sex workers and police in decriminalized street-based sex industry?', *British Journal of Criminology*, 18 (1), 1–19.

Benoit, C., Smith, M., Jansson, M., Magnus, S., Ouellet, N., Atchison, C., and Casey, L. (2016) 'Lack of confidence in police creates a "blue ceiling" for sex workers' safety', *Canadian Public Policy*, 42 (4), 456–468.

Brents, B. G., and Hausbeck, K. (2007) 'Marketing sex: US legal brothels and late capitalist consumption', *Sexualities*, 10 (4), 425–439.

Brents, B. G., Jackson, C., and Hausbeck, K. (2010) *The state of sex: Toursim, sex and sin in the new American heartland*. New York. Routledge.

Chapkis, W. (1997) *Live sex acts: Women performing erotic labor*. New York. Routledge.

Chateauver, M. (2014) *Sex workers unite: A history of the movement from stonewall to slutwalk*. Boston, MA: Beacon Press.

Cizmar, M., Conklin, E., and Hinman, K. (2011) *The village voice*. Available at: www.villagevoice.com/2011-06-29/news/real-men-get-their-facts-straight-sex-trafficking-ashton-kutcher-demi-moore/ (Accessed 11 July 2017).

Cojocaru, C. (2015) 'Sex trafficking, captivity, and narrative: Constructing victimhood with the goal of salvation', *Dialectical Anthropology*, 39 (1), 183–194.

Curtis, R., Terry, K., Dank, M., Dombrowski, K., and Khan, B. (2008) *The CSEC population in New York City: Size, characteristics, and needs*. Report submitted to the National Institute of Justice, United States Department of Justice. New York: Center for Court Innovation.

Davidson, Julia O'Connell. (2005) *Children in the global sex trade*. Cambridge: Polity Press.

Decker, J. F. (1979) *Prostitution: Regulation and control*. Littleton, CO: Rothman.

Dewey, S., and St Germain, T. (2014) '"It depends on the cop:" Street-based sex workers' perspectives on police patrol officers', *Sexuality Research and Social Policy*, 11 (3), 256–270.

Estes, R. J., and Weiner, N. W. (2001) *The Commercial sexual exploitation of children in the U.S., Canada, and Mexico*. University of Pennsylvania School of Social Work. Available at: www.sp2.upenn.edu/restes/CSEC_Files/Exec_Sum_020220.pdf (Accessed 11 July 2017).

Foltz, T. (1979) 'Escort services', *California Sociologist*, 2, 105–133.

Heckathorn, D. D. (2002) 'Respondent-driven sampling ii: Deriving valid population estimates from chain-referral samples of hidden populations', *Social Problems*, 49 (1), 11–34.

Hodgson, J. F. (2001) 'Police violence in Canada and the USA: Analysis and management', *Policing: An International Journal of Police Strategies & Management*, 24 (4), 520–551.

Kennedy, A.M., Klein, C., Bristowe, J. T.K., Cooper, B.S., and Yuille, J.C. (2009) 'Routes of recruitment: Pimps' techniques and other circumstances that lead to street prostitution', *Journal of Aggression, Maltreatment & Trauma*, 15 (2): online.

Kennedy, A.M., and Pucci, N.J. (2009) The identification of domestic minor sex trafficking victims and access to services in Las Vegas, Nevada. Vancouver, WA: Shared Hope International.

Las Vegas Convention and Visitors Authority. (2012) *Year-to-date executive summary*. Available at: www.lvcva.com/includes/content/images/media/docs/ES-YTD20128.pdf (Accessed 11 July 2017).

Lerum, K., McCurtis, K., Saunders, P., and Wahab, S. (2012) 'Using Human rights to hold the US accountable for its anti-sex trafficking agenda: The universal periodic review & new directions for US policy', *Anti-Trafficking Review*, 1, 80–103.

Liu, Min. (2011) *Migration, prostitution, and human trafficking: The voice of Chinese women*. New Jersey: Transaction.

Marcus, A., Horning, A., Curtis, R., Samson, J., and Thompson, E. (2014) 'Conflict and agency among sex workers and pimps: A closer look at domestic minor sex trafficking', *The ANNALS of the American Academy of Political and Social Science*, 653 (1), 225–246.

Marcus, A., Riggs, R., Horning, A., Rivera, S., Curtis, R., and Thompson, E. (2012) 'Is child to adult as victim is to criminal? Social policy and street-based sex work in the USA', *Sexuality Research and Social Policy*, 9 (2), 153–166.

Marcus, A., Riggs, R., Rivera, S., and Curtis, R. (2016) *Experiences of youth in the sex trade in Atlantic City*. New York: Center for Court Innovation.

McLeod, E. (1982) *Women working: Prostitution now*. London: Croom Helm.

Mentzer, H. (2010) *Law Enforcement Officers' Attitudes toward female prostitutes and prostitution*. Ph.D. dissertation. The Pennsylvania State University.

Nevada Assembly. (2013) *Assembly Bill 67 (AB67)*. Available at: www.leg.state.nv.us/Session/77th2013/Bills/AB/AB67_EN.pdf (Accessed 11 July 2017).

Nevada Attorney General. (2016) *Human trafficking in Nevada*. Available at: http://ag.nv.gov/Human_Trafficking/HT_Home/ (Accessed 11 July 2017).

Nixon, Kendra, Leslie Tutty, Pamela Downe, Kelly Gorkoff, and Jane Ursel. (2002) 'The everyday occurrence: Violence in the lives of girls exploited through prostitution'. *Violence against Women*, 8 (9): 1016–1043.

Sanders, T. (2004) 'The risks of street prostitution: Punters, police and protesters', *Urban Studies*, 41 (9), 1703–1717.

Saunders, P. (2005) 'Identity to acronym: How child prostitution became "CSEC" ', in Bernstein, E., and Schaffner, L. (Eds.) *Regulating sex: The politics of intimacy and identity*. New York: Routledge, pp. 167–188.

Schaffner, L. (2005) 'Capacity, consent, and the construction of adulthood', in Bernstein, E., and Schaffner, L. (Eds.) *Regulating sex: The politics of intimacy and identity*. New York: Routledge, pp. 189–205.

Swaner, R., Labriola, M., Rempel, M., Walker, A., and Spadafore, J. (2016) *Youth involvement in the sex trade*. New York: Center for Court Innovation. Available at: www.courtinnovation.org/sites/default/files/documents/Youth%20Involvement%20in%20the%20Sex%20Trade_2.pdf (Accessed 11 July 2017).

Thukral, Juhu, and Melissa Ditmore. (2003) *Revolving door: An analysis of street-based prostitution in New York City*. New York: Urban Justice Center.

Tyler, T. G., and Owens, S. (2012) 'High school graduation and dropout rates', in Shalin, D. N. (Ed.) *The social health of Nevada: Leading indicators and quality of life in the silver state*. Las Vegas, NV: UNLV Center for Democratic Culture. Available at: http://cdclv.unlv.edu/healthnv_2012/index (Accessed 11 July 2017).

U.S. Census. (2013) *American factfinder*. Available at: https://factfinder.census.gov/faces/nav/jsf/pages/index.xhtml (Accessed 11 July 2017).

U.S. Census. (2015) *American factfinder*. Available at: https://factfinder.census.gov/faces/tableservices/jsf/pages/productview.xhtml?pid=ACS_15_5YR_B01003&prodType=table (Accessed 11 July 2017).

U.S. Department of State. (2000) *Trafficking Victims Protection Act of 2000*. Available at: www.state.gov/j/tip/rls/tiprpt/2007/86205.htm (Accessed 11 July 2017).

Wagner, B. M., Whitmer, J. M., and Spivak, A. (2016) *Experiences of youth in the sex trade in Las Vegas*. New York: Center for Court Innovation.

Weitzer, R. (2005) 'New directions in research on prostitution', *Crime, Law & Social Change*, 43 (4–5), 211–235.

Weitzer, R. (2014) 'New directions in research on human trafficking', *The ANNALS of the American Academy of Political and Social Science*, 653 (1), 6–24.

West, D. (1993) *Male prostitution*. Binghamton, NY: Haworth.

Williamson, C., Baker, L., Jenkins, M., and Cluse-Tolar, T. (2007) 'Police-prostitute interactions: Sometimes discretion, sometimes misconduct', *Journal of Progressive Human Services*, 18 (2), 15–37.

Woodward, C., Fischer, J., Najman, J., and Dunne, M. (2004) *Selling sex in Queensland*. Brisbane, Australia: Prostitution Licensing Authority.

8 Condoms as evidence, condoms as a crowbar

Synnøve Jahnsen

Introduction

The condom is not a research object that talks, so I could never ask it to reflect on the work it is doing, how it functions and relates to other actors, how it is positioned in the field or how it responds to political and ethical dilemmas, as I have with my human sources for information. Still, inspired by scholars who use 'matter' as their focal point and searchlight in their research, the aim of this chapter is to make the condom one of several 'speakers' of and on prostitution policies. I will do this by interrogating it as a locus for dilemmas, paradoxes, institutional conflict, interaction and exchange, as well as a potential site for negotiation and reconciliation. I will argue that the condom, mute by its defined nature and rarely explicitly discussed in the public debates on prostitution policy, is at the very front line of the ongoing battle between social and criminal justice in prostitution policy area.

Inspired by a larger theoretical debate that is often termed the 'new or neo-materialism' (see e.g. Ahmed 2008; Lemke 2015), I utilise insights from an ongoing debate (rather than a homogeneous style of thought or a single theoretical position) that seeks to overcome naïve representations of epistemological, ontological and political status of research. This means that I am interested in the 'interrelatedness and entanglements of men and things, the natural and the artificial, the physical and the moral' (Lemke 2015: 5), at the same time as I question how scholars are part of or become part of the phenomena they study. The chapter draws on my own experiences and insights from doing a multi-sited field study and engaging with a wide range of stakeholders involved in prostitution and anti-trafficking policy in Norway. I seek to offer a more materialist and reflexive account of prostitution politics by providing one example of what a new materialist account of prostitution politics might look like.

The chapter is organised in two parts, where the two following sections provide descriptions of my fieldwork and relations in and to the field. Here I not only illuminate the myriads of intersections a field researcher has to manage but also how one can become entangled or get lost in its logics. I illustrate this by explaining how I stopped paying attention to the circulation of condoms as a part of a governmental distribution of services and responsibilities. In the second part of this chapter I narrate the punitive turn that is taking place in Norway as a response to international anti-trafficking policies. This part is divided into eight individual sequences, which I refer to as *scenes* from the field. The underlying story is about a woman I name Rita, and how prostitution policies affect her life as she becomes a target for competing institutional logics and professional mentalities, seeking not only to offer assistance and help, but also to control and manage the prostitution market and in order to prevent human trafficking. By using examples from fieldwork conducted at multiple sites, the aim is to show how local and national actors report diverging views in terms of what "success" means in the field of prostitution and anti-trafficking policies. By zooming in on Rita and her story, the aim is to describe how and why changes in policy lead to dilemmas and conflicts. By looking at an object that is explicitly constructed to offer protection and safety, my aims to explore the discrepancy between the rhetoric of officially stated anti-trafficking policies as protecting women and the local and institutional realities that are reported by those whose profession is to implement them.

Relationships to and in the field – both sides now

The recent history of the activities I have observed is the implementation of the United Nations Convention against the trafficking of persons, especially women and children that was introduced in 2000, and the following ratification by the Norwegian government in 2003 that introduced a set of legal changes as well as governmental initiatives to coordinate and anchor the new policies. At the time, as I started doing my first field observations of the police, the Norwegian government had already launched four governmental action plans against human trafficking and more recently introduced a ban against the purchase of sex. By this, Norway followed the Swedish example with unilateral criminalisation (for more information about the 'Nordic model' and Norwegian prostitution policies, see Skilbrei and Holmström 2013; Jahnsen 2014; Jahnsen and Skilbrei 2017 a, b).

To investigate the relationship between international, national policies and local practices as part of my PhD project, I conducted field studies in two police districts, with two municipal service providers for prostitution and one religious organisation doing street-based outreach work. My empirical enquiry formally began in January 2010 and ended in August 2010, with follow-up study in 2011. As part of my fieldwork I spent approximately 400 hours in the field and formally interviewed 21 representatives from the police and 17 representatives from the social service providers. While the establishment of special anti-trafficking units are a relatively new form of organising police efforts against prostitution, specialised welfare services for sex workers and victims of trafficking can be dated back to the early 1980s. Already then, representatives of municipal welfare services and volunteers in the Church City Mission responded to concerns over minors being exploited in street prostitution and sought to offer rehabilitation to women in prostitution in the form of housing and education (Jahnsen 2014).

In addition to digging into these recent institutional histories I also observed several court case proceedings open for the public, ranging from the rare prosecution of sex purchase, to the relatively more common prosecution of pimping and trafficking. In addition, I interviewed political stakeholders at both local and national level and attended various forums that facilitated training and sharing of knowledge among representatives of a larger network of agencies, both in the field of specialised services for sex workers and in the field of human trafficking. Formal interviews came in addition to the numerous field conversations, email correspondence and engagement in social media platforms that allows researchers to observe and take part in conversations with members of global and local social movements, from sex workers rights activists and their allies to radical feminists seeking to push their agenda forward on all levels of governance. Like a wicked impersonation of the singer-songwriter Joni Mitchell, I sought to understand 'both sides' of how the local practices and politics were enacted and how they played out. It was at once highly polarised and reminiscent of the American feminist sex wars, yet distinctively marked by Nordic criminal justice and welfare regimes.

It is the observations of how local police officers and social workers talk about their work to each other and to me, the researcher, as well as the way they go about doing their work that form the backbone of my study. This allowed me to not only study the 'human face' of a policy aiming to curb the prostitution market, but also the mind-set of the street-level bureaucracy and their exercise of discretionary powers (Lipsky 2010). Doing field observations allowed me to not only study the work of the newly established anti-trafficking task forces in the police, but also to study how they interacted and intersected with other parts of the police organisation, as well as external agencies. Data from observations was supplemented with a series of group and individual interviews conducted at the premises of their working environments as well as while driving in a patrol vehicle. As such the data is rich in its contextual descriptions and contains information about why police officers on the street might not find time to prioritise anti-trafficking policing and enforcement of the sex purchase act, even when this is a set target for a shift.

Because this chapter deals with policing of foreign women, and not only sex workers per say, it is important to mention that I am a Norwegian citizen and was born in one of the cities I conducted my researched in, Bergen. Norway is a small and closely-knit society with a population estimated to be around 5 million. The largest city, the capital city Oslo, is estimated to be the size of 647,676, while Bergen, the second largest city, has an estimated population of 275,112 (SSB 2015). Being a native speaker, it was relatively easy for me to access information about what we can refer to as a multi-agency field, but also to be included by police officers and social workers, as my west coast accent provides me with a very distinct local identity. In Norway people from Bergen are known for being direct, outspoken and at times pushy, a stereotype that has its downsides, but which provided me with extra leeway when asking direct and sometimes uncomfortable questions about a controversial topic. Being a local myself also had the research effect that some things were never spoken explicitly about, yet communicated in body language and facial expressions, assuming that I already knew the answer to my question or the context of which a particular utterance, for example about local distinctions between police districts and local mentalities. While feeling a sense of belonging in Bergen, I would simultaneously find myself lost in the streets of Oslo as this city in some respects was 'foreign' territory for me at the beginning of my fieldwork. I knew parts of the city from previous visits, but learned to know its outskirts and backstreets while being a 'backseat police observer', exploring it through the 'gaze of the police' (Finstad 2000). While observing and interviewing the police, I found myself positioned in various roles, treated as an apprentice or a student of policing at times, while others approached me as a friend or ally, and as such as someone to whom they could trust, confide and complain to. A common topic in my field notes is therefore the lack of funding, recourses, competence and mandate to do 'proper police work'. Even those who showed signs of reluctance towards me or saw researchers as outsiders or 'matter out of place' would still find it useful to share their perspectives on this matter. As discussions about what exactly constitutes 'proper police work' in Norway is related to wider debates on the ongoing police reforms in Norway and implementation of new management philosophies, these are topics that are beyond the scope of this chapter, yet are important to mention as relevant context for future studies.

Here it is more important to stress that I for periods have been embedded as a social service provider in the field, both due to a pre-existing involvement in voluntary work and due to not being able to fund the final stages of my PhD project. Lack of funding forced me to seek a position as a special advisor at Pro Centre, which is both the provider of municipal welfare services in Oslo and the national resource centre for knowledge on prostitution. For a period of six months at the end of 2013 my role was to consult on legal and political matters as well as develop educational programmes, both aimed at the general population and involving the staff (social workers, case handlers, nurses, doctors and administrative staff). During my time at Pro Centre I was involved in receptionist and clerical work as well as interacting with women who visited the drop-in centre. This means that my interactions in the field have varied from having the role as a distant observer on the outside to being the one who prepares and serves food, listens to stories, offers help with accessing and using a computer, or even simpler tasks such as handling a laundry machine. In some cases, all I did was allow someone to cry or pray for a loved one while holding on to my arms.

Although all interactions in the field have not been recorded for research purposes, I mention them here as doing simple chores for someone allows the growth of friendships and alliances, but also for the exchange of knowledge and information. These relations have undoubtedly informed my perspectives of what constitutes interesting research questions, as many of the conversations I have had with sex workers have directly or indirectly informed me about how some groups of women relate to the police as one of many representatives of the Norwegian state, a state which for many is foreign and as such a strange and confusing one. For example, a common misunderstanding I have encountered is that many women think it is illegal to sell sex in Norway, which is a sign that many have limited access to correct information about their rights and legal status in Norway.

That the livelihood and mere existence on Norwegian territory for many is challenged by the threat of expulsion, challenges the traditional modes of social services provision to marginalised populations. In addition, it alters ideas about what it means to be a social service provider at a prostitution outreach centre. The most obvious change is the demand for information on legal rights and access to welfare services for non-citizens. There are several reasons for this, but the development in Norwegian prostitution markets is the most noticeable explanation. Over the last two decades Norwegian society has become increasingly marked by the general demographic change where migrants have constituted as much as 70% of the net annual growth in the population (SSB 2015). During the same period the prostitution markets have gone from being populated mostly by Norwegian citizens to mainly consist of migrants, where Nigerian women have been among the largest and most visible growing groups (see e.g. Pro Sentret 2015). Not all parts of the migrant population have migrated through formal paths to citizenship and some are regarded as 'irregular migrants' or 'visitors'. These groups are considered particularly vulnerable for exploitation, as they have no legal access to the regularised Norwegian labour market. Thus, a frequent discussion among social care providers and case handlers for potential victims of trafficking would be about how to provide correct information in a complicated legal terrain with crossing jurisdictions; and how to handle communication and provision of information that might sometimes shatter the dreams of someone hoping to stay permanently in Norway. As such my informants in the social services would find themselves 'stuck between a rock and a hard place' while learning how to deal with the mismatch between the official policies of the Norwegian immigration regime and the needs of the women they were supposed to help.

The Norwegian condom

While many aspects of providing welfare services are changing, some parts are fairly stable. In particular, providing condoms has been and is still among the core tasks of the outreach teams as well as a visible aspect of the service that is provided at the drop-in centres. In Norway the harm reduction and HIV prevention programmes that were developed in the early 1990s to a large degree still function to secure funding and a political status of the social care and service providers, irrespective of the changes that are taking part in the justice sector and immigration regime. Come rain come shine, condoms are what outreach workers bring when they enter the streets on late nights, visit the massage parlours and knock on the doors of apartments on the indoor market. Those sex workers who come to visit the drop-in centre will equally find condoms in different shapes and for different purposes. The condoms are free of charge, and usually there are no limits in terms of how many condoms you can take. Sometimes, if you are lucky, you will find them in different colours and tastes and a variety of shapes and sizes, from large, snug, thick, thin to standard. One of them is even called the Norwegian condom' (Norwegian *Norgeskondomet*). This condom is carefully packaged in a 'Norwegian design' inspired by the most popular hand-knitted pattern in Norway, the Marius pattern, considered to be a design icon that communicates Norwegians' love for the freedom one can seek outdoors, in the Norwegian nature.

The condoms are supplied by The Norwegian Directorate of Health and are available to organisations and private persons. If you go online and manage to fill out the form (available in Norwegian, not English), you can order them to your home address. The Norwegian Directorate of Health write on their home page that they target risk populations and that they consider these to be adolescents and young adults under the age of 25, people who buy and sell sex, refugees and asylum seekers, men who have sex with men and people living with HIV and their partners, as well as prison inmates. There is no available information on how The Norwegian Directorate of Health evaluates or measures their success or to what extent they succeed in their attempts to provide information about the importance of finding the right condom, to avoid allergic reactions against latex or even what it means that their condoms are 'carefully tested during production' to ensure that the quality is within international quality standards (Helsedirektoratet 2017). Faced with the lack of information, one is left with the impression that the quality of the national policies in this area can be measured in the quality of the condoms themselves and that the governing principle in the national HIV strategy is about avoiding condoms that burst.

For the social workers and nurses who engage with sex workers, the act of distributing condoms is so integrated in their work that it is hardly talked about. It is a thing that is both a part of and constitutes the drop in centre as a social and material space, much like the couch, the candle lights, the flowers, the constant supply of biscuits and the smell of home-made waffles. Being both a part of and an observer of this space, I noticed that condoms would be put in a bowl, free to grab as one passed, under a sign saying 'Safe Sex or No Sex. No Negotiation!' clearly stating the imperative attitude of the Norwegian state seeking to install a form of self-regulation among sex workers in exchange for free condoms.

Once I got used to seeing the sign and while I eventually became part of the almost daily routine of making sure to fill the bowls of condoms, I stopped noticing what I was doing, how the condoms circulated or where they came from. Now, as years have passed since my time as a worker among social workers, nurses and doctors, it is easier for me to revisit my field notes to answer some of my initial questions, questions that I pushed aside as I became increasingly engaged with the field. The aim of this chapter is to linger at the act of supplying condoms, in order to highlight some of the conflicts that exist in the prostitution and anti-trafficking policy field, and also what insights we can draw from the conflicts of which condoms are part.

Scene 1: a bag filled with condoms

By the time I met 'Rita' and learned to know the story that will unfold below, I had been doing fieldwork for about four months. I had started out researching local outreach programmes targeting sex workers before I eventually started spending most of my days together with the newly established anti-trafficking team. As I entered their office early one Monday morning, it was unusually messy, and 'Erik' the team-leader, seemed both frustrated and excited. Excited to tell me what was going on, and frustrated by the workload with which he was now presented.

Some unexpected events had taken place over the weekend, he explained to me, before he continued by adding, as he had many times before, how complicated this type of police work is. His back was crunched as he was sitting on a chair opposite to me while talking about the different items on display in front of us. 'How am I supposed to know which items belong to which person? This is a mess!'

Erik showed me a suitcase, some clothes, a hairbrush and several bathroom items, beauty accessories and some excessively high-heeled shoes, before he pointed at a black bag in the corner and said 'that belongs to the municipal out-reach team' before rhetorically asking 'should it be returned to the social work-ers?' By now he had removed himself from the chair as he opened the bag to show me its content. It contained condoms. More condoms than I was able to count or estimate, but I recognised them. Strictly speaking the condoms did not belong to the social workers. Rather they were part of a rather unrestricted supply from the state aimed at so called 'risk populations'. Right now they were not doing much prevention, rather they constituted part of the exhibit of evidence that appeared before us and might eventually contribute to deciding the women's judicial fate. From a police perspective the condoms constituted part of the forensic evidences that proved that prostitution in fact was taking place in an apartment that had been raided over the weekend.

Scene 2: condom as a crowbar

Knowing the realities of outreach work and the peer-to-peer strategies of the municipal social workers told me that the fact that one of the women who was arrested was in possession of a bag of condoms indicated that one of them consti-tuted a key person for the municipal outreach team for social services. Through her, or rather through providing her with condoms, they were able to reach a number of persons they otherwise would have difficulties to reach. As anticipated, 'Silje' from the social services soon appeared at the police station.

In conversations about what type of work they do, social service providers and outreach workers often refer to condoms as an essential part of a health perspec-tive on prostitution, some referring to it as a 'crowbar', a tool to open up con-versations about other problems, besides the spread of STIs. For them providing someone with a condom was also giving them the key to open up the possibility for dialogue. If they did not accept it immediately, there was still a chance they would return at a later stage when they actually needed help. Besides providing protection against STIs, handing out condoms is presented as a way to send a message integral to the empowerment strategy most service providers sought to enforce, signalling that help and assistance is available without trespassing sex workers right to privacy and to not be in contact with them. For an increasing part of the sex worker population however, this offer constitutes their only access to public health care in Norway and as such provides an opportunity to access ser-vices to which other irregular migrants might not get access.

'What the police often fail to see', a social worker explained to me, 'is how intertwined the many political agendas become at the micro level where face to face encounters constitute the institutional practices and interactions with marginalized communities'. She continued to explain how important it was to speak confidentially without being morally judged. The patient-doctor privilege provided that space. Conversations with sex workers might start out with the question of whether they needed condoms but hopefully would end up with an offer for more medical assistance and individual follow up with a case handler. 'Talking about bodily issues may lead to conversations about abusive boyfriends, violent clients as well as economic debt' one of the nurses at the drop-in centre explained. While a social worker in a district that did not have a drop in centre, but instead offered rides to a clinic at the local hospital explained that 'Sometimes, I get the best conversations when we are on our way to the hospital'.

The social workers and nurses also told me they were alarmed that some of the communities they engaged with were growing increasingly reluctant to accept the offer of public services and explicitly unwilling to accept the offer of condoms. The social workers interpretation of this related these incidents to the intensified police intervention as part of new anti-trafficking policies, as some women were quite vocal about their fears of being raided and have condoms lying around as an indication of prostitution. Those who had experienced the consequences of prostitution policies in the form of police raids had learned that condoms did not only protect them from STIs, but could also be used against them, as evidence of prostitution. Just like it had for Rita (whom I mentioned above).

Condoms were described as a crowbar (Norwegian brekkjern), a metaphor social workers used to point towards the possibility of developing a relationship between social service providers and sex workers, and these possibilities were pathways to longer conversations and deeper individual change. These conversations might be about motivating women to engage with the legal system or seek assistance as victims of trafficking. Seen this way, the condoms enabled social workers and health personnel to access valuable information about what was going on in sex workers' lives, what challenges they faced and what help they might need to overcome them. This begs the question, if social workers can reach populations and build relationships of trust in ways in which the police are unable, why would the police jeopardise these relationships in their search for traffickers and pimps? In what follows I will return to the story about Rita in order to explain where the answer lies.

Scene 3: bad karma

Rita's prosecutor told me that she should consider herself lucky that the public attorney did not press charges against her for human trafficking and that she 'got away with' a pimping charge. In conversations with me Rita told me that she did not feel lucky. Rather she felt economically disadvantaged. I followed her entire court proceedings, after we first started chatting later that same day as Erik had opened the bag of condoms and told me about the raid. I explained to Rita what I was doing there, that I was not a police officer nor a social worker, but a researcher. She did not really understand so I told her I was writing a book and gave her a card with my picture and the name of my university while explaining to her that I wanted to learn more about her story. Her Norwegian was broken so I offered to follow her into the reception area and helped her fill out a form requesting missing items, as I knew she would have trouble translating the form and filling in all its columns. As we dutifully filled out the forms and I listed all the belongings she was missing, including eyeliners and lipstick to clothes, we both learned more about each other. Rita explained to me how she was getting older and was struggling with a health problem, her heart. She told me that because of her health problems she had felt a need to exit prostitution. So, as an alternative to selling sexual services she had started subletting the apartment she lived in to other women. Some of them travelling, some of them sold sex and this happened sometimes from her apartment. She told me they were usually Thai-women, like herself, who travelled to Norway often in transit to other European countries.

'I thought I was really clever', she told me. She uttered her words while giggling through her teeth, as if she was conveying the ironic twist of the story she wanted to tell me or as if to sooth an open wound. She was the one who had called the police, she explained. She wanted them to resolve a feud that had started between her and her guest. They claimed she owed them money. She could not explain to me how she had ended indebted to them, but I got the impression they had been gambling. Either way, she was not ready to pay them and she wanted them to leave her apartment. After all, she lived there.

So, when her guests refused to leave she called the police and told them that her guest was taking drugs. She called with an expectation that the police would help her, but soon learned that she had just made matters worse. The police raided her flat in search of the drugs, and ended up taking all of them into custody over the weekend. Her guests were gone but to what expense? Not only had the guest robbed her, she claimed, as several of her belongings now were missing. She was now also about to be evicted from her apartment. For her it seemed as if she had brought this upon herself, like bad karma.

Scene 4: condom as evidence

What I knew, but could not disclose to Rita, was that she already, before she called the police, was a listed target as part of what the Norwegian police refers to as 'Operation Houseless' (Norwegian *Operasjon husløs*). I knew, because I had been standing outside her apartment building earlier the very same day she had made the call. I had been invited to observe a young male police officer and the way he worked to reduce the indoor market for prostitution by targeting people from the Thai community. Thus, in my mind she had not brought this on herself and her situation had very little to do with bad karma. That the police had not intervened earlier was more a coincidence. In fact, it might have been a result of my unwillingness to accompany a young male police officer as he sought to enter Rita's apartment. As we parked our car outside her apartment, I told the officer that I would have to wait in the car rather than follow him all the way as he entered Rita's building. He seemed surprised but accepted and left me to wait for him in the car. Quickly thereafter he returned, telling me he had problems finding the right apartment and that he suspected that they knew he was the police and therefore did not open. They might have seen him from the window, he said. I had problems adding the two, not finding the doorbell and them discovering that he was not a client but the police. Later I learned that male police officers usually will bring a partner on these types of assignments – which explained his eagerness to bring me along (as I too could function as witness if anything turned sour or if there were allegations of misconduct). Maybe he did find the door but did not want to enter without me? Beyond pointing out that my unwillingness to follow the police officer all the way into her apartment was rooted in ethical and legal regulations pertaining to Norwegian researchers that prohibits me from entering private spaces uninvited, I will not go further into the details of my field-work concerns here. Instead I want to focus on why Rita's apartment became a police target in the first place. By answering this, I can also explain how Operation Houseless is imagined to work as a form of situational and preventive police strategy against trafficking and how it is mandated by the rather broad definitions of pimping in the Norwegian Criminal Code (*hallikparagrafen* in Norwegian). At the core is the idea that it is possible to prevent trafficking by limiting the market for commercial sexual services. Put simply, the goal of the officer I accompanied was not to raid the apartment nor incarcerate anyone. Rather his target was to document that it was used as a premise for prostitution. This is the first step of an administrative rather than a purely punitive path to intervention and crime reduction in Norway.

Usually Operation Houseless will start with online surveillance of escort pages, before individual women are targeted directly, by police officers pretending to be a customer soliciting for sex. After having made an appointment, the police will check out the premises, which are usually apartments or hotels, with the aim of identifying clients on their way to or from an appointment. As such, the sex purchase law will be part of Operation Houseless. After having entered the premises, the police will often search them to secure forensic evidence, such as mobile phones, photo evidence (of the bed, towels, condoms and so on). In some instances, for example if the operative police unit do not have a forensic investigator on their team, or are unable to secure evidence on the spot, as in the case with Rita, the police will seize evidence for further investigative processes. If there are several persons sharing the premises, like in the case of Rita, the police will usually separate them at the premises or bring them into the station for separate questioning. In Rita's case all of them were taken in for questioning. Because some of the women are foreign citizens, the police will usually also perform identity checks in order to control whether they are legal migrants or temporary visitors, either directly at the premises or supported by teams who specialise in passport residence permits at the police station.

The preferred piece of evidence in Operation Houseless is a confession from a client and/or a sex worker. Having secured a confession that prostitution is taking place, the final step of the operation is to contact the landlord or hotel owner to inform them of their liability, that there is prostitution going on in their property, while simultaneously urging them to terminate tenancy. The police will directly or indirectly remind a landlord of the threats of a pimp indictment.

To sum up, this use of the legal framework is not specifically tied to the issue of the penalization of clients in and off itself, but targets actors who assist, promote or benefit from prostitution. Yet penalising clients is often involved as part of these operations, as a ticket and a confession effectively prove that prostitution is in fact taking place. In Rita's case however no clients had been fined, which meant that the police would need to base their case on other forms of evidence. This is where the black bags of condoms enter as an important piece of evidence in a larger chain of legal proceedings aiming to achieve a particular political goal, namely to fight trafficking.

Scene 5: Operation Houseless

Originally 'Operation Houseless' was an initiative from the anti-trafficking group in Oslo called the STOP project. This project was placed under the Division of organised crime, which allows the use of a rather broad repertoire of police methods when identifying, preventing and prosecuting trafficking and pimping. The STOP project started in 2007 and at the beginning the unit mostly recruited operative staff who had been trained in special operations targeting the drug market (this in contrast to the anti-trafficking unit in Bergen who mostly recruited police investigators). The police would present Operation Houseless as part of a particular system of thought, language and action, where any action can be categorised as either strategic, tactical of operational or all of them at once, and where strategies against trafficking preferable were either preventive, innovative and disruptive, preferably all of these at once. This serves to frame policing of prostitution within a militarised logic where the police are at war, as if the traffickers are the enemies that need to be defeated, simultaneously constructing the prostitution market as a battlefield.

In the beginning Operation Houseless gave the police great results in the capital city, I was told, as some environments simply disappeared. This however demanded constant policing, something for which they did not have the manpower, which eventually led them to prioritise certain groups over certain periods. The police will therefore usually target groups based on ethnicity and/or suspicion of links to other crimes and organised criminal networks. Which nationalities are prioritised varies over time and between police districts and is partly dependent on more overarching prioritisations within organised crime units, as well as efforts to reorganise the national police at large. While Eastern European, Asian and African women are likely targets for police intervention, Norwegian citizens are less likely to be targeted by the police in a systematic way, as they are not considered to be likely victims of trafficking.

Because the unit focused on preventing trafficking rather than investigation and prosecution, their preferred methods usually included cases that never ended up in court. This also means that the volume of this form of policing activity is measured in numbers that are only available inside the police. It simultaneously also makes it cost-effective, as it usually does not add to the burdens of the public prosecutor and justice system. Operation Houseless can therefore also be understood in a larger context where modern forms of policing and crime control increasingly are organised to live up to new management philosophies within policing and a strong emphasis on cost effectiveness, where accountability is often translated into accountancy. Operation Houseless can also be seen as part of a more systematised and targeted use of intelligence and information, where new technologies and the ability to gather information via internet-based advertisements and forums become a precondition for targeted crack down operations on the indoor market. Here there is no regard for the distinction between the spaces where women sell sex, and where they live. This means that making people homeless, like in the case of Rita, not only becomes a legitimate act, but also a necessary step to deter exploitative behaviour.

Essentially the idea is to pre-empt trafficking by disrupting the prostitution market by any legal means. As such the operation can be side-lined with the sex purchase law as one of two ways to 'strangle the market' as one informant put it. For a period, the operation was seen as a success both locally and nationally, mirrored by the fact that the operation is mentioned explicitly in the government's action plan against human trafficking as one of four anti-trafficking strategies (Ministry of Justice and Public Security 2010) which are to:

a)   Identify and prosecute cases of human trafficking and pimping
b)   Reduce available apartments on the indoor market ('*Operasjon Husløs* ')
c)   Prosecute human traffickers for alternative crimes
d)   Enforce the sex purchase law with a focus on its preventative effect on human trafficking, reduction of the prostitution market and changes of attitudes in the population.

As we can see from the list, the official policing strategy is, put simply, to use any legal means to deter traffickers from establishing themselves in Norway. Here policing simultaneously slides from preventing and prosecuting human trafficking to reduce the prostitution market and managing attitudes in the population. This logic is also mirrored at national policy level as the rationale behind the sex purchase ban, where a ban against the purchase of sex is meant to deter traffickers from coming to Norway, illustrated by the following quote from the former Minister of Justice Knut Storberget when it was implemented. 'Human beings are not commodities in a market and by criminalizing the purchase of sex we will make it less attractive for human traffickers to look to Norway' (Ministry of Justice and Public Security 2008). Seen from this perspective, 'Operation Houseless' mirrors a more overarching ambition that there shall be no reason for traffickers to 'look to Norway' as it will not house prostitution activities.

Scene 6: fear and loathing

Operation Houseless seems equally fitting as the name for a broader national strategy that informs the effort to create partnership and alliances between a network of actors who in different capacities regulate and control the prostitution market. According to the police, these alliances constitute a joint effort to prevent the purchase of sex and curb the activities of what the police refers to as 'travelling prostitutes' and potential victims of organised crime (Politiet 2010), making it difficult to separate between the desire to identify victims of trafficking and the desire to control sex workers' mobility. The threat of indictment for pimping has prompted some hotels to enter partnership agreements with the police and others, and also to train their staff in how to monitor the local indoor market via internet advertisements. It is reported that some hotels copy women's passports and contact the police to check if the woman is registered in their databases. According to a media report in the newspaper Stavanger Aftenblad (2010), several hotels in the Stavanger area operate with so called 'blacklists' of women for internal use, in order to avoid customers suspected of selling sex or perceived as being 'difficult'. This practice is reported to occur, although the legality of such practices is highly questionable. In several instances the Norwegian police have also communicated to the public that they need to report suspicious activities, as prostitution may be an indication of trafficking. It is thus not only the police who look for suspicious activity and signs of prostitution and trafficking in Norway.

Scene 7: together against human trafficking?

Historically speaking, the process of 'ridding society' of prostitution is not a novel one. For many, prostitution symbolises the opposite of social progress, the sanctity of the family union and a social democracy based on principles of equality and inclusion. In stead, prostitution symbolises the lack of control, social and moral decay. While hotly contested, Norwegian politicians have traditionally balanced their various forms of idealism with a sense of pragmatism and tolerance towards prostitution (Skilbrei 2012). This pragmatic attitude has translated into a strong support for a social and public health perspectives where harm reduction strategies have been the preferred strategy. This is reflected in my data as social workers and the police seek ways to overcome institutional barriers. For many of my informants working directly with victims of trafficking, there is nothing more valuable than having someone's telephone number and knowing they have a friend who was equally committed to communication across institutional boundaries. One of my informants explained that she had never had a job where she had to network so extensively to get things done. The networking efforts I observed, albeit extensively relying on informal contacts, are also mandated and institutionalised in the form of local coordination units seeking to bridge the gap between various services involved in trafficking cases.

The relationship between the police and the social services for women in prostitution has developed locally over time; there are ties that can be traced back to the 1980s. These relations have mainly focused on dialogue between social services and the police in efforts to reduce violence and crimes against sex workers. The introduction of the special anti-trafficking unit and the organised crime team is seen as a breach of this relationship, and as such the bonds of mutual trust were broken at the same time as cooperation became increasingly shaped by centralised efforts to coordinate anti-trafficking policies at a national level which simultaneously linked it closely to the immigration regime, and as such introduced new partners with which to cooperate at all levels, not only at the departmental level.

It is my observation that the increased political pressure to support the prevention of human trafficking via punitive measures has unsettled a form of preexisting balance between the professions involved in this policy area, as conflicts erupted between those who marshal a zero-tolerance approach against visible street prostitution and those who marshal for tolerance and inclusion. Conflicts may manifest themselves openly in the media or at public meetings, or in the lesser known stories of female outreach workers feeling harassed by patrol police officers who approach them while they are doing outreach work on the streets, as if the mere act of being there is a suspicious act that legitimises stop and search. Such acts can be uncomfortable for those who are not used to handling the police, as it can be interpreted as a form of micro aggression from representatives of professions who devalue or marginalise other professional worldviews – rather than work jointly within a common understanding. Thus, the government slogan 'together against human trafficking' seems to not sit well with those who at the end of the day are out walking the streets.

The clash between perspectives is best illustrated by the dispute that erupted when Tomas Ekman, a Swedish Superintendent and leader of an anti-trafficking unit in Gothenburg visited Norway. 'It's much worse in Norway than in Sweden', he alleged to Norwegian journalists before he continued by stating that 'The pimps send their prostitutes to. . . [the] (outreach centre) Pro Sentret in order for them to receive help, so they can become strong and sell sex several times a day' (NRK 2007). Under the headline 'shocked by Norwegian prostitution' visible street prostitution in Oslo was presented as a case in point that the situation was worse than in Sweden because Norwegians provide health care to sex workers. In Ekman's perspective, providing such welfare services 'was not helping the girls, but the pimps and traffickers', and providing social services to sex workers equals the facilitation of prostitution and as such the opposite of crime prevention. Seen this way Norwegian prostitution policies seems both misguided and naïve whereas potentially on the wrong side of the fight against human trafficking.

His allegations were met with distaste by Liv Jessen, an outspoken leader of the national resource centre Pro Centre. She objected to the conflation between prostitution and human trafficking and commented that 'it is only swedes who believe that the worse you are off, the nobler thoughts you will get' while adding that in a more long-term perspective, maybe sex workers will think 'I am worth something else, I want a better life' (NRK 2007). In this perspective providing social outreach services is not about making women strong enough to be continuously exploited, but rather about empowering them to seek a better life. As such, Liv Jessen as representative of the Norwegian approach to prostitution objected to the competitive tone from the Swedish police commissioner seeking to compare national responses by measuring the visibility of street prostitution. Rather than labelling Norwegian policies as naïve or misguided, the question should be about how society can strike a balance between political, legal and ethical concerns, while at the same time having a realistic understanding of both short-term and long-term effects of various policy instruments. Put simply, efforts to shut down harm reduction initiatives and police harassment marginalised populations seemed as misguided as the medieval belief that withdrawal of blood (bloodletting) from a patient would cure or prevent illness and disease. Put differently: making the situation worse will simply make it worse, not provide a pathway for improvement.

Concluding remarks

Obviously there are many more stories that could be told about Rita and her life in Norway. However, those parts of her story are not mine to tell, which is why I pause her story where our paths last crossed, me observing her leaving a courtroom with her head faced down, yet 'lucky' not to have been prosecuted for human trafficking. In this chapter, I have tried to illuminate how we can relate the incidents that erupted in her life with the political aim to disrupt the prostitution market as a way to prevent human trafficking. Although Rita is a unique individual, her story as a target for various anti-prostitution and trafficking policies becomes one of many stories that unfolded during my fieldwork study about what happens when policy makers leave it up to the professional judgement to rule whether a certain person is seen as worthy or unworthy of assistance and support. The fundamental question this chapter raises is whether it is possible to bridge the gap between service providers and a particular community without approaching someone like Rita, someone with particular ties in her community, ties that not only put her in contact with many sex workers, but also ties that seen from a police perspective are suspicious.

It is commonly assumed that social workers and police officers share their interests in a common fight against trafficking and that the shortcomings of policy makers springs from a lack of knowledge about the consequences of their policies. However, as this chapter has illustrated, there are several examples of competing policy goals and conflicting interests in the field. I have also showed how social workers, health personnel and police officers not only navigate between competing discourses about prostitution, but also between organisations and professional standards. Seen from a zero-tolerance perspective, the questions that arises when faced with someone in the possession of a bag of condoms is not only a question about their role in the prostitution market (seeing Rita as a pimp and potential trafficker, rather than as someone who simply shares a flat and educates her peers about sexual health). It is also a question of whether the act of providing condoms to sex workers is an act aiding to the existence of the prostitution market. The police gaze not only casts a dark shadow of suspicion over anyone involved in the prostitution market, but also on those who seek it out in the role as care givers and social service providers. Seen from their perspective, using condoms as evidence not only threatens their ability to provide welfare services, but it also undermines long-term goals seeking to empower and enable members of marginalised communities, not only to protect themselves from risk, be it STIs, violent clients or boyfriends, but also to exit prostitution, should they desire to do so. Thus, the incommensurability of perspectives is less about disagreeing on the desired outcomes and the joint effort against human trafficking but rather a question of whether a repressive and punitive approach where the police are allowed to define both the problem and its solution is the right way forward.

References

Ahmed, S. (2008) 'Imaginary prohibitions: Some preliminary remarks on the founding gestures of the new materialism', *European Journal of Women's Studies*, 15 (1), 23–39.

Barad, K. (2007) *Meeting the universe halfway: Quantum physics and the entanglement of matter and meaning*. Durham and London: Duke University Press.

Finstad, L. (2000) *Politiblikket*. Oslo: Pax.

Helsedirektoratet. (2017) *Bestill gratis kontomer*. Available at: https://helsedirektoratet.no/folkehelse/seksuell-helse/bestill-gratis-kondomer (Accessed 30 September 2017).

Jahnsen, S. (2014) *Innestengt eller utestengt? Norsk prostitusjonspolitikk og kampen mot menneskehandel*. Ph.D. thesis. Department of Sociology, University of Bergen.

Jahnsen, S., and Skilbrei, M.-L. (2017a) 'Norway', in Jahnsen, S., and Wagenaar, H. (Eds.) *Assessing prostitution policies in Europe*. Milton Park, UK: Routledge.

Jahnsen, S., and Skilbrei, M.-L. (2017b) 'Leaving no stone unturned: The borders and orders of transnational prostitution', *British Journal of Criminology*. Available at: https://doi.org/10.1093/bjc/azx028

Lemke, T. (2015) 'New materialisms: Foucault and the "Government of Things"', *Theory, Culture & Society*, 32 (4), 3–25.

Lipsky, M. (2010) *Street-Level bureaucracy: Dilemmas of the individual in public services*. New York: Russell Sage.

Ministry of Justice and the Police. (2008) *Forbud mot kjøp av sex i Norge og i utlandet Pressrelease Pressemelding*. Available at: www.regjeringen.no/no/aktuelt/forbud-mot-kjop-av-sex-i-norge-og-i-utla/id508300/ (Accessed 11 July 2017).

Ministry of Justice and the Police. (2010) *Sammen mot Menneskehandel: Regjeringens Handlingsplan mot Menneskehandel* (2011–2014). Available at: https://www.regjeringen.no/globalassets/upload/JD/Vedlegg/Handlingsplaner/Handlingsplan_mot_menneskehandel_2011-2014.pdf (Accessed 30 September 2017).

NRK. (2007) *Sjokkert over norsk prostitusjon*. Available at: www.nrk.no/norge/sjokkert-over-norsk-prostitusjon-1.3160085 (Accessed 11 July 2017).

Pro Sentret. (2015) *Årsrapport 2014*. Oslo: Municipality of Oslo.

Skilbrei, M.-L. (2012) 'A marriage of convenience between pragmatism and principles: The development of Norwegian prostitution policies', *Sexuality Research and Social Policy*, 9 (3), 244–257.

Skilbrei, M.-L., and Holmström, C. (2013) *Prostitution policy in the Nordic region*. Ashgate: Ambiguous Sympathies.

SSB. (2015) *Folkemengde og befolkningsendringar, 1. januar 2016, berekna tal*. Available at: www.ssb.no/befolkning/statistikker/folkemengde/aar-berekna/2015-12-17 (Accessed 11 July 2017).

Stavanger Aftenblad. (2010) *Hoteller svartelister og utestenger prostituerte*. Available at: www.aftenbladet.no/nyheter/lokalt/stavanger/Hoteller-svartelister-og-utestenger-prostituerte-1961348.html (Accessed 11 July 2017).

9 Gentrification and the criminalization of sex work

Exploring the sanitization of sex work in Kings Cross with the use of ASBOs and CBOs

Lucy Neville and Erin Sanders-McDonagh

Introduction

Introduced in 1998 as part of the Crime and Disorder Act, anti-social behaviour orders [ASBOs] have been used in various locations around the UK to police street-based sex work [SBSW]. This chapter will argue that ASBOs were used regularly in a particular area of north London as part of a targeted policing strategy that focused on the removal of SBSW from key areas in Camden, and were specifically and intentionally utilised in order to remove street-based sex workers (SBSW-ers) from the Kings Cross area. We argue that ASBOs and other punitive measures have been used as a way of sanitising the area, removing 'undesirable' Others that might impinge on the aestheticized areas of consumption that regeneration seeks to create. Drawing on empirical data collected during 2010–12, we argue that SBSW-ers in this area experienced a range of negative impacts because of this policing strategy, putting their health and safety at risk. Against a local backdrop of reduced funding (from 2008 onwards) to support women's services in the third and public sectors, a lack of appropriate drug and mental health services, cuts to housing provision and reduced social work and social care services, this chapter will provide an overview of the ways in which service providers, key stakeholders, and sex workers have been negatively impacted by the use of these punitive measures. We argue that despite suggestions from local government that ASBOs simply seek to assist and support sex workers, these approaches do little to reduce SBSW or help women working in prostitution.

Methodology

This paper draws on ethnographic research conducted over 10 months from 2011–12 with a third sector organisation based in London. The organisation works mainly with young people, but there is a sub-section within the organisation that works specifically with female street-based sex workers. The organisation offers sex-working women a variety of services, engaging them through their twice-weekly drop-in sessions, or their thrice-weekly outreach walks. The drop-in and outreach sessions are normally co-delivered with other local organisations which deal with the same client group, but may have a different focus (e.g. drug-specific projects or homelessness projects etc.). Most of their client base have or have had serious drug addiction issues (heroin and/or crack cocaine), most have been homeless and/or are living in unstable accommodation, many have been in prison, and many have mental health issues. Some of the women access services through both the drop-in and outreach, while others only use one or the other. The aim of the organisation is to support and help women who have high level needs, and are often living chaotic and dangerous lives. They offer a harm-reduction approach to working with sex workers, and work towards stabilising them as much as possible.

To gain a full and varied impression of the complex processes involved in engaging with clients during outreach work, we employed several different methodologies, including mobile interviews, GIS mapping, and formal semi-structured interviews with outreach staff, outreach managers, outreach clients and those working in related services (e.g. local councils and other third sector organisations). Of relevance to this discussion is the use of mobile and semi-structured interviews with staff, workers from related services, and sex working women. The mobile interviews we conducted were semi-structured, using both prepared and ad hoc questions, and involved the use of GIS mapping to plot routes taken and places of specific outreach-related salience. Carpiano (2009) suggests that mobile interviews are most useful when they are used in conjunction with other methods, so in addition to these interviews we also conducted semi-structured, face-to-face interviews with the same staff we went on outreach walks with ($n = 8$), as well as workers from related sectors ($n = 6$) and sex working women at the drop in ($n = 10$). We have anonymised the names and identifying details of all participants.

History of anti-social behaviour orders

Under the Crime and Disorder Act of 1998, Anti-Social Behaviour Orders [ASBOs] were introduced and widely used by police and local authorities across England as a way of managing activities that were not criminalised, but were seen as harmful or detrimental for local communities. Police and local authorities can apply for an ASBO in court for anyone over the age of 10, where a person has acted 'in a manner which caused or was likely to cause harassment, alarm or distress' (Home Office 2004).

ASBOs remain in place for at least two years, although they can be reviewed if 'behaviour improves' (www.gov.uk/asbo). The penalties for not obeying the conditions of the behaviour order (called breaking or breaching an ASBO) vary by age. For young offenders (between 10–16), breaching an ASBO may result in a fine, a community sentence, or possibly a detention and training order that can last up to 24 months. Adult offenders may face fines of up to £5000 or a 5-year prison sentence (or both). Hewitt (2007: 358) reports that around 55% of breaches are punished by imprisonment, and notes that one of the most controversial features of the ASBO system is that it can lead to a person being sent to prison for breaching an ASBO imposed for a non-criminal act: 'a person may be sent down, in other words, not because what s/he did was a criminal offence, but because s/he did it twice'. It is often the case that the punishment imposed for breaching an ASBO is therefore 'far greater than the one the act would have received in its own right' (Hewitt 2007: 357).

In 2014, The Anti-Social Behaviour, Crime and Policing Act greatly expanded law enforcement powers in addressing anti-social behaviour. The Act introduced the Criminal Behaviour Order (CBO) which replaces the Anti-Social Behaviour Order on conviction. While the Act has been heralded by some as "the death of the ASBO", it is important to note that conviction-based ASBOs essentially continue unchanged in the form of CBOs, which carry similar consequences. This legislation leaves ASBOs as a civil order intact – in the form of Injunctions – and allows for a CBO to be applied on 'order of conviction', meaning that once someone has been convicted of a crime, the prosecutor can request an application for a CBO. Historically, ASBOs were considered 'necessary' from a legal perspective if the court takes the view that 'the offence for which the defendant has been convicted is so serious and anti-social that it tends *in itself* to show that an order is necessary' (CPS 2017a, italics added). CBOs rely on essentially the same rhetoric, but, in the words of the CPS, 'the 'necessity' test becomes a 'helpfulness' test' – CBOs are thus aimed at "helping" offenders to desist from engaging in anti-social behaviour (CPS 2017b). As with ASBOs, a court may also look for a pattern of anti-social behaviour and for this purpose, evidence of the facts behind previous convictions and failed interventions (such as a failure to comply with an anti-social behaviour contract) may be probative. Prosecutors may also seek to rely on anti-social behaviour which did not result in prosecutions or convictions. The CBO moves beyond the ASBO insomuch as the court may impose requirements as well as prohibitions (CPS 2017b). Kingston and Thomas (2015: 1) therefore argue that CBOs introduce 'new powers which are believed to be more wide reaching than earlier laws which tried to take on the problem of anti-social behaviour'.

Controversy has dogged ASBOs/CBOs since their inception, partly because the government definition of what constitutes anti-social behaviour is quite broad. A 2006 report from the Home Office lists the following activities as 'anti-social':

> harassment of residents or passers-by; verbal abuse; criminal damage; vandalism; noise nuisance; writing graffiti; engaging in threatening behaviour in large groups; racial abuse; smoking or drinking alcohol while under age; substance misuse; joyriding; begging; prostitution; kerb-crawling; throwing missiles; assault; and vehicle vandalism.
>
> (Home Office 2006: 8)

Such a broad definition means that not only are certain *activities* considered anti-social, so too are the people who carry them out, making anti-social behaviour an ontological condition. For those who have been given ASBOs, being present in certain locations or spending time with 'people who are known as trouble-makers' (www.gov.uk/asbo) can become criminalised activities. In addition, the 2003 guide to ASBOs from the Home Office lists the undermining of economic regeneration as a potential anti-social behaviour (Home Office 2003: 6, 16, 47, 64).

ASBOs and street-based sex work

ASBOs have been widely used across England and Wales as a way of controlling sex work. It could be argued that, *prima facie*, policy developments in the area of sex work and anti-social behaviour appear to be positive. In 2011, for example, the Coalition Government released the *Effective Practice in Responding to Prostitution* (Home Office 2011) guidance, which emphasised holistic, harm-reduction approaches towards SBSW and advocated for punitive measures like ASBOs/CBOs to be used only as a last resort. However, in practice it is not clear that this guidance has been implemented – at least not unilaterally and equally across various local districts. While there is no national data available on ASBOs, research from Young et al. (2006) provides data from 2002–06 on ASBO applications in the Kings Cross area and found that while 17 women had been issued orders for prostitution, only three ASBOs had been given to kerb crawlers, despite kerb crawling being specifically mentioned as a key 'anti-social' activity in Home Office Guidance.

Kingston and Thomas (2015: 3) point out that the new 2014 Act allows for local powers to respond to 'local concerns', which is likely to increase the incoherent approach that individual councils and police force areas have taken to manage prostitution and street-based sex work, and may increase the already punitive approaches that exist across England and Wales. Just as the use of ASBOs became commonplace nationally as a way of responding to SBSW, it is likely that many boroughs will continue to use CBOs to manage sex work in their jurisdictions. Instead of promoting the holistic, harm-prevention approaches favoured in the 2011 Home Office report, this tends to create a situation where criminal justice agencies are awarded contracts to deliver highly conditional 'support' for street-based sex workers, firmly dependent on their withdrawal from SBSW (Sagar 2010). Kingston and Thomas (2015: 12) express concern that this new localised control will simply allow 'forces and officers to take a more punitive approach', and in some instances, respond 'more punitively towards sex workers than their clients'.

It should be noted that there is one notable exception to local government management of SBSW in the UK: instead of penalising either workers or clients, Leeds has pioneered a 'Managed Area' approach. Under this scheme SBSW-ers are allowed to operate in a designated area of streets during certain hours without fear of arrest or police harassment (Sanders and Sehmbi 2015). A review of the scheme by Safer Leeds concluded that it had been a tentative success, despite proving unpopular with a minority of residents and local businesses. Sanders and Sehmbi (2015) found that the scheme had improved relationships between SBSW-ers and the police, increased levels of Ugly Mug reporting, increased SBSW-ers take up of social and health care interventions, and reduced the number of complaints made by residents with regards to 'nuisance'.

Regeneration and sex work in Kings Cross

The Kings Cross area of London has a long history of prostitution and particular associations with street-based sex work. Located in the London Borough of Camden and in the heart of an area of regeneration, Kings Cross has seen ASBOs being widely used, ostensibly to target drug dealing and visible drug-use, but several reports suggest that sex workers in the area have also been disproportionately targeted (Greater London Authority 2005; Young et al. 2006).

There are clear links to be made between the use of ASBOs/CBOs in Kings Cross, and gentrification and development. Since 'Operation Zero Tolerance' in 1997, there has been a concerted effort to remove both homeless people and street-based sex workers from the area, and this has dovetailed with greater investment in the surrounding locale (Deckha 2003; Hubbard 2004; Holgersen and Haarstad 2009). The Kings Cross Partnership (KXP), funded by the Government Single Regeneration Budget (SRB) was initiated during this period to develop and regenerate the area. Operation Welwyn, jointly funded by the Camden Community Safety Team and the KXP, was established with the remit to 'confront drug and vice crime within the King's Cross area . . . to target specific criminal and anti-social activity and disorder in the ward' (Young et al. 2006: 28).

From 2003, the rate of regeneration in Kings Cross considerably accelerated, most notably since the building of the new Eurostar station. According to London and Continental Railways (LCR), the Kings Cross Eurostar development is the biggest ever single construction project in Britain, and more than £9 billion has been invested in the areas adjacent to the new stations (Holgersen and Haarstad 2009). It should be noted that instead of 'normal' subsidies in return for building the railway, LCR received fixed assets, including land areas along the route with the right to develop these for profit. Holgersen and Haarstad (2009: 359) draw on Lefebvrian's (1973) conceptualisations of the social and political construction of space to argue that in the case of regeneration in Kings Cross, it is important to make a distinction between 'urban space as exchange value and urban space as use value', noting there is a 'difference between groups that appropriate space for the purpose of accumulating capital and groups that appropriate space as a place to live and work'. They report that while there were a number of consultation exercises carried out with the local community about development plans for Kings Cross, these meetings were largely didactic events where planners told local residents about proposed changes and listened to concerns, but essentially ignored the voices of the residents and community stakeholders – there was little meaningful dialogue, and little intention from the planners to make changes in line with concerns raised by the residents (Deckha 2003). Holgersen and Haarstad (2009: 365) argue that 'the structure of the public consultation [in Kings Cross] appears to delimit participatory influence'.

Processes of urban regeneration often redevelop previously 'undesirable' areas to make them safe and clean for white, middle-class populations, a process which is abundantly clear in Kings Cross. Marginal groups like SBSW-ers have no place in the sanitised city – the genteel, well-lit, aesthetically pleasing spaces of Kings Cross have been redesigned for the well-heeled, urban, cosmopolitan traveller. This is a public space with ambiance and class – in St Pancras station itself you could buy a £300 evening dress from Whistles, a £150 tailored shirt at Pink, or a £100 candle from Jo Malone. If you wanted to venture outside, you could walk up the cobblestoned pedestrian pathway to Granary Square where you might bump into art and fashion students from the elite Central St Martins College, have an £18 cocktail while sitting on the terrace of a wine bar, before heading for dinner at the Grain Store where you can pay £20 for a polenta salad. It appears that the area around Kings Cross has been created for affluent, international consumers in mind – arguably developers do not want glossy, sanitised spaces 'polluted' with street homeless, drug dealers or sex workers. As Hubbard argues:

> the fact that public space is designed to meet the wants and desires of affluent consumers while systematically excluding those adjudged unsuitable or threatening. . . [means] sex workers are apparently seen as dangerous threats that need to be eliminated from the sight of the affluent . . . reducing the visibility of sex work in the central city is an obvious way that policy-makers can send out a message that it is ripe for reinvestment.
>
> (2004: 1697–1698)

The ASBO (and now the CBO) has proved to be a powerful tool in the service of 'cleaning up' Kings Cross. Writing in 2006, Young et al. argue that 'ASBOs were introduced as a key feature of the crime and anti-social behavior control effort in the ward. At the time of publication, 218 ASBOs were granted in Camden, greater than any other London borough' (2006: 4). They suggest that urban regeneration was a key driver in the removal of sex workers, beggars and rough sleepers from Kings Cross, and the considerable resources that were put forward from KXP and Camden to 'clean up' the area were clearly related to regeneration efforts. However, Young et al. (2006) observe that while sex work in Kings Cross was noticeably reduced, there was compelling evidence that sex workers either moved location, or sold sex at times that were less likely to be patrolled or monitored. The authors also note what they term tactical displacement:

> tactical displacement occurs when the same offence is committed but in a different way . . . a number of people mentioned that policing initiatives and urban regeneration had driven criminal activity "underground". Sex and drugs, once sold on the street, had not disappeared but continued in hostels, crack houses and in private premises.
>
> (Young et al. 2006: 69)

In line with arguments from Sanders (2009) and Kingston and Thomas (2015), Young et al. (2006) argue that sex workers in Kings Cross who were identified as 'persistent offenders' by police and community safety teams were given the opportunity to engage with services that would ostensibly make them 'good citizens' and remove them from the street. Those that refused to engage with the services offered were then issued with an ASBO as a punitive response to their refusal to meet the required prescriptive standards of coercion set out by the authorities. Young et al. (2006: 81) suggest that prison sentences of 9–12 months were not uncommon for sex workers who entered an exclusion zone breaking the 'good behaviour clause' by soliciting.

Despite clear concerns expressed by their own commissioned research (c.f. Young et al. 2006), a 2005 report from the Greater London Authority and our research with sex workers in the Kings Cross Area from 2010–11 suggest that punitive policing measures, including the use of ASBOs, were still being used for the management of SBSW.

Experiences of sex workers in Kings Cross

In this section, we provide data from our research to argue that despite clear concerns expressed about the use of ASBOs for female sex workers, Camden continued to employ punitive measures for women working in and around Kings Cross. Our interviews and observations suggest that there was a distinct awareness among outreach workers, related service providers, council workers and street-based sex working women that Camden had taken, and continues to take, an extremely hard-line approach towards policing 'antisocial' behaviour and the use of ASBOs. Outreach workers and related service providers generally viewed this with negativity, noting that it did little to help their vulnerable clients and often increased their levels of risk and potential to experience harm. As one service provider noted,

> I think obviously every borough would like not to have any problems – no street drinking, no drug use, no sex working as well. Islington is quite flexible, quite – I think – more understanding than the other boroughs. It's pretty good; I like this attitude more than with ASBOs and everything, you have to work *with* clients and not just say "you can't be doing it".
>
> (Gloria, Service Provider).

One of the support workers described how the team previously had issues working with Camden street services because 'they were very much ASBO-orientated, enforcement-orientated' and the focus on 'bringing [sex working women] back to the police . . . we found it quite difficult to work with'. She noted that

> the [Camden Street Services] workers are really nice, but they had a lot of grief from their managers: 'Where's my stats? Where's my this?' – I think they were under pressure a lot to give people ASBOs and when we were working with them we were finding it quite difficult to talk to some clients, [as the worry was that Camden Street Services] would talk to the police'
>
> (Amy, outreach worker)

Another worker in the sector discussed how she and her colleagues minimise their association with the Street Services Team – 'the ASBO lot' as she described them – and 'don't normally tell [clients that it] is the same organisation as us, because women get very funny about that sort of stuff' (Kelly, service provider). It led to situations where street-working women were reluctant to engage with the outreach teams because 'the women still think that police is police – [they're like:] "we are sex working, they are not going to listen to us"' (Julia, outreach worker). As Kelly puts it:

> Well, [saying you're associated with Camden Street Services is] not the best way to start off with someone [sex-working], because as far as they're concerned it's [one] organisation, [and] if you work for the same people that's what they know – they're like 'I've got an ASBO from that area and now you

want me to tell you about my drug use!' It's a different section, so what we try
and do is to work with them to try and stop these things from happening. . . .
We try and feed in what positive stuff the women are doing, rather than them
saying, 'I saw them on the streets sex working on the [. . .], dah-da-dah, and
we're going to ASBO them', we can say, 'actually, this week, I saw her three
times and we sat down and talked about this, this, this and this happened that
might be different contributing factors'.

(Kelly, service provider)

There was also a high level concern exhibited by service workers in the sector
about the effects of displacement.

I think because, let's say Camden are more 'enforcement' side of things, giving out ASBOs and things like that, so obviously [women previously working in] those areas tend to move a little bit, let's say they cross into Islington
or other areas because they're not comfortable in Camden. . . . I guess with
Camden and Islington they know they get loads of hassle in Camden so they
tend to come this side . . . But now sex workers, they are, like, hiding it a bit
more because of the police, and it's not safe as well. . . . On [. . .] Road, even
a few months ago there were a few girls working there, they were sat down
and I was like, 'Oh, you don't work here anymore?' And they were like, 'No
we don't because we can't be visible like that now' – because the police are
patrolling the area quite a lot.

(Gloria, Service Provider)

The Council took a more pragmatic approach, with one worker noting that it is
difficult to balance the following of 'safeguarding procedures, you know, in terms
of feeding appropriate information to the police, [while] . . . at the same time
guaranteeing and reassuring the local street community that [you] can work with
them effectively' (Chuma, Council Worker), but concluded that 'ultimately our
aim of this unit is to reduce ASB – I mean, that is the ultimately aim, is to reduce
ASB, so. . . [we] effectively. . . [have to be] able to deliver that as well as provide
effective harm reduction'. Concerns here were very much focused on the effect
that street-based sex working might have on the local community.

The sex working women we spoke with who were (or had been) engaged
in street-based sex work also expressed concerns about the Borough's use of
ASBOs. Brenda discussed how 'the police were trying to ASBO me from Kings
Cross, not from Kings Cross, just the red-light district part' and voiced her fears
over what would happen to her in court (as she had breached her order) and how
she would deal with the fallout, particularly if there were financial repercussions.
Many women we spoke with were well aware of the irony of a situation where
they were fined by the courts for breaching an ASBO related to sex working, yet
had no way to pay the fines except by returning to sex work.

I went to court last year and I was told if I appeared out on the street again,
I would go to prison, so that's really scared me. . . . It [street-based sex work]

has got worse, 'cause now they're slinging ASBOs on girls, and that's gotten worse as it's going along . . . they know we've gotta come out, they know if we go to court they know we've gotta come back out on the street and earn that money to pay it [the £80 fine]. And the court just slams it on you and they think you can pay that money immediately, unless you plead with the judge and say you can't pay that straight away, you have to plead to get that cut in half so you can pay it each week.

(Helen, sex worker)

There was also concern that the process of using ASBOs to displace street-based sex workers was making sex workers less safe. Donna described how 'when it got to the end of me working [in Kings Cross], yeah [I did feel unsafe]. It was getting violent, and as I said everybody was getting nicked every night [for soliciting] and things like that, so it got pretty bad' (Donna, sex worker). Helen discussed how the use of ASBOs deterred sex workers from working together for safety, and even from talking to each other to share local information about dangerous punters and general safety.

I been keeping myself to myself 'cause you're better off that way, 'cause if you mix with the other girls, you're liable to get that little bit of friction [from the police]. And if they're taking drugs or anything like that it reflects on you. I know one girl out there but I don't talk to her anymore, because every time I've spoke to her, every time she stopped and spoke to me I kept getting shit from the police. . . . So it was better to back off when I did, I didn't want to be nasty to her, but I just said to her, "Don't come near me, you're gonna get me in trouble".

(Helen, sex worker)

It is interesting to note that we spoke to street-based sex workers before the Leeds managed area pilot, but the Leeds model was already something that some of the sex workers suggested as a viable alternative to the use of ASBOs and the absolute prohibition of street-based sex work.

If they [the police] weren't such a nuisance at times, left us alone, let us get on with what we got to do, it wouldn't be so bad. But they're a bloody nuisance half the time, because as soon as a punter sees them, he won't come near, they won't come near us. . . . They won't legalize it [sex work] and that's why we're getting so much hassle. If they legalized it we wouldn't get that hassle. We wouldn't get that hassle. Give us a block to work on, we would be out of their sight, they put us on a block and we weren't supposed to go out in the street, if we worked on that block, we'd have no problems. We'd have no problems. . . . We would feel safer. If it was [on] camera and videoed we'd feel safer there than what we would be out on the street, a lot safer because then they would know what's happened, if somebody got attacked, they'd know exactly where it's happened, on that spot, and I'm all for that because it should be either legalized or [they should] give us somewhere where we can go and we know we're safe, but out on the street we're not safe because you get these nutters who are out there and you don't know if they're going to turn on you. You know? I'm not being nasty to them, but you do, you get them and sometimes girls get injured or get killed.

(Helen, sex worker)

Discussion

While some of the research done on ASBOs and punitive measures in Camden showed that sex work did decrease in the area over time (London Borough of Camden 2015; Young et al. 2006), it is clear that many sex workers, including SBSW-ers who have high level needs and long histories working in and around Kings Cross, continued to work, but altered their working patterns or moved to unfamiliar places to avoid detection.

To a certain extent, this was seen by the Council as a success, and as Young et al. (2006: 41) note: 'While enforcers recognized that the ASBO was punitive and entailed restrictions on the liberties of the population they were targeting, this was considered an acceptable cost for the gains received by the community as a whole'. It could, perhaps, be argued that the removal of street-based sex workers from certain areas might be seen to 'benefit' a community, but this of course assumes that sex workers themselves are not part of the community. A 1994 MORI survey carried out with Camden residents highlights concerns about crime – specifically noting concerns about burglary and violent crime – but does not mention sex work specifically. Despite this, one of the six strategic objectives implemented by Camden to 'tackle crime and improve community safety' includes a referral scheme for sex workers and clearly indicates that sex work should be understood here as 'anti-social behaviour' (Mutale and Edwards 2003). We would argue that despite Camden's narrative that constructs sex work as an issue of community concern (without any specific data that highlights prostitution as a key issue), there is evidence that not all communities consider sex work to be 'anti-social'. Indeed, even in areas where SBSW is seen as an issue for the community, many community-based approaches have adopted non-punitive measures that seek to control sex work, instead seeking to work with sex workers and their clients to better support them, while at the same time reducing the local 'anti-social' impact of prostitution. In some cases creating dedicated specific areas as a space for SBSW-ers, for example, is an approach that has enjoyed some degree of success (Brown and Moore 2014; Kingston and Thomas 2015; Sanders and Sehmbi 2015). Indeed, recent research has argued that in some communities, sex workers are not seen as 'anti-social', nor as a threat to local law and order, but are embraced and supported (Cooper 2016; Kingston 2013; Pitcher et al. 2006).

Few, if any, sex workers benefitted from the introduction of ASBOs in Camden, and cases where women are coerced into stopping SBSW via the threat of punishment if they continue to sell sex has the potential to create more harm. Many academics have argued that ASBOs do little to stop women working, particularly when they are working to support a drug habit (Hester and Westmarland 2004; Sanders 2005). Instead, and as our evidence suggests, the existence of an ASBO simply forces sex workers to move out of areas where they are used to working and familiar with local geography and people, leaving them to face the additional dangers that come from working in unknown or unfamiliar places (Hubbard 2004; Hubbard and Sanders 2003; Kingston and Thomas 2015; Sanders-McDonagh and Neville 2012). Not only does working in unfamiliar spaces leave street-based sex workers more vulnerable to violent assault (Kinnell 2013), it also can lead to them becoming more distrustful of the police and less likely to report sexual and physical attacks (Sanders 2005). There have also been documented cases of sex workers receiving conditions attached to ASBOs which prohibit them from carrying condoms and ban them from areas where drug treatment clinics are located (Sanders 2009). The concern here is that women who need the most support will become disenfranchised from specialist services (Pitcher et al. 2006).

Young et al. (2006: 82) suggest that for some women who receive ASBOs, the presence of the order may push them towards engaging in more serious criminal activities: 'For example, one drug-using sex worker prohibited from entering particular areas, from publicly consuming controlled drugs, and soliciting or performing any sex act in public . . . was arrested and convicted for soliciting in the exclusion zone, and . . . for shoplifting, and then for street robbery'. In this situation, it seems clear that displacement may not only propel women into working in unfamiliar places, but to committing more serious offences to obtain money, once the avenue of SBSW has been cut off from them. Sanders (2009) has therefore argued that the use of ASBOs focusing on changing women's behaviours to push them to exit sex work ignores the well-being of sex-working women.

One particular problem relates to the failure of the Home Office to break down statistics at local levels – this makes it difficult to ascertain how many ASBOs are being used against sex workers in different geographic regions. A 2005 report on street-based sex work in London from the Greater London Authority [GLA] expressed particular concern about the use of ASBOs with sex workers in certain London Boroughs, including Camden (GLA 2005). In evidence provided by Camden Council themselves, the GLA report found that Camden had issued 15 behaviour orders to sex workers between 2000–05. While Camden insisted that these ASBOs that had been issued to sex workers were for substance misuse or drug related offences, the GLA expressed concerns about the implications of such an approach:

> If there is, in fact, a tendency to use ASBOs on prostitutes, this is only tackling one side of the prostitution equation. By imposing an ASBO on a woman, she can be prevented from entering a certain area, but because of her need to support her drug dependency, she will be forced to work in another area, usually a neighbouring area. Just like any other person, she will not want to move away from the people she recognises, knows, and trusts. Therefore, there needs to be a different approach to the ASBO question. . . . In the absence of definitive evidence that the use of ASBOs to displace prostitutes is becoming more widespread, we believe that more research and policy development is needed in this area.
>
> (GLA 2005: 10–11)

However, despite concerns from a range of policy makers, service providers and sex workers themselves, the dominant metanarrative in response to SBSW is still one of risk, victimisation and vulnerability. Brown and Sanders (2017: 2) discuss how these vulnerability narratives 'merge concern for sex workers' safety with anxieties about the 'problem' of prostitution'. To this extent, they maintain that the dominant discourse around sex work might be considered part of a wider 'vulnerability – transgression nexus' (Brown 2014, 2015), where classifications of vulnerability are used to indicate that an individual is at risk, but also 'to imply that they pose a risk to others and should be surveilled or controlled' (Brown and Sanders 2017: 2).

In practice then, SWSB-ers seem to have been particularly targeted with ASBOs in a number of police force areas, which has served to entrench them further into the criminal justice system under the guise of 'protection'. The fact that their 'antisocial behaviour' (soliciting) is by its very nature often recidivist, has led to sex workers often bearing the brunt of the full extent of the ASBO's powers under law (Sagar 2010; Scoular and Carline 2014; Carline and Scoular 2015; Scoular and O'Neill 2007). Sanders (2009: 515, emphasis added) regards the use of ASBOs with sex workers as an example of forced welfarism, with coercion being used to bring about behavioural change 'that is deemed by the courts to be in the welfare interest of the individual and for the benefit of the *community*'.

We argue that alternative approaches, including managed zones such as those found in Leeds, would allow sex workers to continue to work safely and recognises that sex workers (not to mention their clients) are part of the local community. Managed zones allow women to work in designated streets away from residential housing between the hours of 7 pm until 7 am without being cautioned or arrested for loitering or soliciting. The Leeds area was still policed for the safety of sex workers and all other laws were enforced:

> The non-enforcement approach and associated focus on vulnerability represented a move away from responding to sex work as transgression and public nuisance, meaning sex workers, police and support workers could get on with their work less hindered by enforcement-orientated problems. Although evidently a fragile development, this was particularly important in relation to the management of crimes committed against sex workers.
>
> (Brown and Sanders 2017: 8)

Conclusions

It is apparent that the 'danger' posed by SBSW, which has the potential to 'harm' the community, is largely socially constructed. Sibley (1995) argues that for much of the 20th and 21st centuries, marginalised or deviant groups have been subject to spatial exclusion. Hubbard (2004: 1695) discusses how this geopolitical strategy functions as a way of controlling these groups, and enforcing physical and social boundaries is here a way of removing or excluding those who are seen and labelled as 'dirty', 'disgusting', or 'undesirable'. As Sanders (2009: 520) has argued, the street-based sex worker fits into this category, being seen as both 'anti-social' and 'anti-sexual':

> she is labeled as unclean, unwanted and a symbol of decay. This iconic "whore" figure is entirely out of step with the gentrified notions of the modern city living and leisure spaces, and "deviant" groups become an easy target for removal.

As Hubbard (2004: 1699) has argued, the identification of street-based sex workers as a criminal Other 'appears an extremely effective strategy for displacing sex
work from valued city centre sites'. The removal of SBSW-ers from Kings Cross
over the past 15 years can be seen as a direct result of discriminatory and draconian urban policies that seek to remove this undesirable population to make way
for urban regeneration. As Young et al. (2006: 50) note in their report,

> regeneration was less about meaningful attempt to resolve complex needs
> within the borough and far more about obscuring complex problems. The
> main thrust of their argument was that the regeneration effort was unequal
> within the borough and produced a "gated community" that provided a "mid-
> dleclass haven".

Issues related to regeneration are not limited to sex workers, but also apply
to other parts of the community. While regeneration plans promised to create a
more socially and economically vibrant community for everyone, only a select
few really benefit from these changes. The average house price in Kings Cross in
2000 was £190,000, while in 2016 the average house price is £693,000 (Foxtons
2017). Given that only 16% of households in Kings Cross were owner occupied
in 2000 (Mutale and Edwards 2003), it seems unlikely that the 75% of households that were renting private, council or housing association properties would
have benefitted from the gentrification of their local area. Equally unsurprising
is that the three Camden wards (Kilburn, St Pancras and Somerstown, and Kings
Cross) with the highest levels of unemployment in 2000 (Mutale and Edwards
2003) are still the wards with the highest Job Seekers Allowance claimants, and
are amongst the most deprived wards in the borough with large ethnic minority populations (Camden Council 2015). While Arup's (2004) Regeneration
Strategy made clear that they hoped to devise projects that would target local
people and specific excluded groups 'to help promote local employment, jobs
and enterprise' (Arup 2004: 57), for most people living in deprivation in Kings
Cross and St Pancras, little change has materialised for them. Finally, it is not
only cruelly ironic, but deeply depressing, to note that according to the British
Transport Police, King's Cross station was still – despite the huge amount of
effort put into tackling crime by penalising some of the most vulnerable members of society – the worst station for crime in 2011, and in 2016 (Seales and
Parsons 2011; Sims 2016).

Hubbard (2004) argues that hegemonic urban regeneration policies that privilege entrepreneurial interests and favour capital accumulation 'enables private
capital to move into the vacuum left by the end of managerial, welfare-based
urban policy' (Hubbard 2004: 1697). Furthermore, he suggests that introducing
the type of legislation

> designed to tackle low-level public disorder (apparently personified in the
> figure of the street prostitute) signals an intention to tackle crime and urban
> malaise. Critics suggest that this amounts to a policy of blaming the victim
> that does nothing to tackle the underlying causes of urban crime and poverty.
>
> (Hubbard 2004: 1699)

Despite the evidence that redevelopment and gentrification has clearly not benefitted many King's Cross residents already living in deprivation, and that punitive policing measures including ASBOs have done little to help sex workers, the King's Cross redevelopment website suggests that the project is a story of community success:

> The location, the connections, the canal-side setting, the rich and varied heritage, an exciting cultural scene, a thriving business community, and a strong sense of local community. All these things come together at King's Cross to make it unique, exciting and really quite special. Come and see for yourself.
> (Kings Cross Business Partnership Limited 2017)

Walking through the council flats in Levita House, a stone's throw away from King's Cross station, you will certainly be introduced to an exciting cultural scene, with the smell of spices coming from the Bengali community that live there, or walking down Churchway lane, where you'll find a small but vibrant Mosque. This is certainly a community with a rich and varied heritage, and a few remaining locally-owned small businesses. Undoubtedly regeneration will extend out and disrupt these streets as well, turning them into more fashionable venues acceptable to the distinguished urban elite. And no doubt the few street-based sex workers who remain in King's Cross will eventually submit to the coercive salvation being offered to them, or move to areas where gentrification has not made it impossible for them to work safely. Many sex workers we spoke with from King's Cross had moved east to places like Hackney in order to work, but the recent increase in austerity approaches that has resulted in the closing of dedicated services for sex workers (as well as for other vulnerable women) has also now left them harassed by police, and vulnerable to dangerous clients (Hemery 2016). While it may be coincidence that Hackney is also undergoing a startling and rapid process of gentrification, we would argue the introduction of ASBOs for SBSW-ers in Kings Cross, and criminalisation tactics used in many other areas, are a direct result of both public authorities and private investors working to sanitise areas seen as 'undesirable' (c.f. Sanders-McDonagh et al. 2016), removing those who do not fit with the middleclass, ultra-clean image that is required for the success of neoliberal regeneration of the city.

References

2014 Anti-Social Behaviour, Crime, and Policy Act. (2014) Available at: www.legislation. gov.uk/ukpga/2014/12/contents/enacted (Accessed 10 March 2017).

Arup. (2004) *Kings cross central regeneration strategy.* London: Arup, Argent St George, LCR and Exel.

Brown, K. (2014) 'Questioning the vulnerability zeitgeist: Care and control practices with "vulnerable" young people', *Social Policy and Society,* 13 (3), 371–387.

Brown, K. (2015) *Vulnerability and young people: Care and social control in policy and practice.* Bristol: Policy Press.

Brown, K., and Moore, J. (2014) *Prostitution in Leeds: Preliminary scoping research.* Leeds: Safer Leeds and University of York.

Brown, K., and Sanders, T. (2017) 'Pragmatic, progressive, problematic: Addressing vulnerability through a local street sex work partnership initiative', *Social Policy and Society,* 16 (3), 429–441.

Camden Council. (2015). *Camden Profile*. 21 August 2015. London: London Borough of Camden.

Carline, A., and Scoular, J. (2015) 'Saving fallen women now? Critical perspectives on engagement and support orders and their policy of forced welfarism', *Social Policy and Society*, 14 (1), 103–112.

Carpiano, R. M. (2009) 'Come take a walk with me: The "go-along" interview as a novel method for studying the implications of place for health and well-being', *Health and Place*, 15 (1), 263–272.

Cooper, E. (2016) ' "It's better than daytime television": Questioning the socio-spatial impacts of massage parlours on residential communities', *Sexualities*, 19 (5–6), 547–566.

Crime and Disorder Act. (1998). Available at: www.legislation.gov.uk/ukpga/1998/37/contents (Accessed 10 March 2017).

Crown Prosecution Service. (2017a) *Anti-Social behaviour orders on conviction (ASBOs)*. Available at: www.cps.gov.uk/legal/a_to_c/anti_social_behaviour_guidance/ (Accessed 10 March 2017).

Crown Prosecution Service. (2017b) *Criminal behaviour orders*. Available at: www.cps.gov.uk/legal/a_to_c/criminal_behaviour_orders/ (Accessed 5 April 2017).

Deckha, N. (2003) 'Insurgent urbanism in a railway quarter: Scalar citizenship at King's Cross, London', *Acme*, 2 (1), 33–57.

Foxtons. (2017) *Kings cross*. Available at: www.foxtons.co.uk/living-in/kings-cross/ (Accessed 23 February 2017).

Greater London Authority. (2005) *Street prostitution in London*. London: Greater London Authority.

Hemery, S. (2016) 'Sex workers fear for their lives as London borough pushes criminalisation', *Open Democracy*. 5 July 2016. Available at: www.opendemocracy.net/sophie-hemery/hackney-sex-workers-fear-for-their-lives-as-borough-pushes-criminalisation (Accessed 23 February 2017).

Hester, M., and Westmarland, N. (2004) *Tackling street prostitution: Towards a holistic approach*. London: Home Office Research, Development and Statistics Directorate.

Hewitt, D. (2007) 'Bovvered? A legal perspective on the ASBO', *Journal of Forensic and Legal Medicine*, 14 (6), 355–363.

Holgersen, S., and Haarstad, H. (2009) 'Class, community and communicative planning: Urban redevelopment at King's Cross, London', *Antipode*, 41 (2), 348–370.

Home Office. (2003) *Respect and responsibility – Taking a stand against anti-social behaviour*. London: Home Office.

Home Office. (2004) *Defining and measuring anti-social behaviour*. Available at: www.gov.uk/government/uploads/system/uploads/attachment_data/file/116655/dpr26.pdf (Accessed 1 February 2017).

Home Office. (2006) *A guide to anti-social behaviour orders*. Available at: http://webarchive.nationalarchives.gov.uk/20100405142051/http://asb.homeoffice.gov.uk/uploadedFiles/Members_site/Documents_and_images/Enforcement_tools_and_powers/ASBOGuidance_HOAUG2006_0043.pdf (Accessed 1 February 2017).

Home Office. (2011) *Effective practice in responding to prostitution*. London: Home Office.

Hubbard, P. (2004) 'Cleansing the metropolis: Sex work and the politics of zero tolerance', *Urban Studies*, 41 (9), 1687–1702.

Hubbard, P., and Sanders, T. (2003) 'Making space for sex work: Female street prostitution and the production of urban space', *International Journal of Urban and Regional Research*, 27 (1), 75–89.

King's Cross Business Partnership Limited. (2017) *The story so far*. Available at: www.kingscross.co.uk/the-story-so-far (Accessed 23 February 2017).

Kingston, S. (2013) *Prostitution in the community: Attitudes, action and resistance.* London: Routledge.

Kingston, S., and Thomas, T. (2015) 'The Anti-Social Behaviour, Crime and Policing Act 2014: Implications for sex workers and their clients', *Policing and Society*, 1–15.

Kinnell, H. (2013) *Violence and sex work in Britain.* London: Routledge.

Lefebvre, H. (1991) *The production of space.* London: Blackwell.

Mutale, E., and Edwards, M. (2003) *Monitoring and evaluation of the work of the Kings Cross partnership: Final report.* London: Bartlett School of Planning.

Pitcher, J. (Ed.) (2006) *Living and working in areas of street sex work: From conflict to coexistence.* London: Policy Press.

Sagar, T. (2010) 'Anti-social powers and the regulation of street sex work', *Social Policy and Society*, 9 (1), 101–109.

Sanders, T. (2005) '"It's just acting": Sex workers' strategies for capitalizing on sexuality', *Gender, Work and Organization*, 12 (4), 319–342.

Sanders, T. (2009) 'Controlling the "anti sexual" city: Sexual citizenship and the disciplining of female street sex workers', *Criminology and Criminal Justice*, 9 (4), 507–525.

Sanders, T., and Sehmbi, V. (2015) *Evaluation of the Leeds managed area pilot project.* Available at: www.nswp.org/sites/nswp.org/files/Executive%20Summary%20Leeds,%20 U%20of%20Leeds%20-%20Sept%202015.pdf (Accessed 5 April 2017).

Sanders-McDonagh, E., and Neville, L. (2012) *Women's Open Space Project evaluation: Final report.* London: New Horizon and Middlesex University.

Sanders-McDonagh, E., Peyrefitte, M., and Ryalls, M. (2016) 'Sanitizing the city: Exploring hegemonic gentrification in London's Soho', *Sociological Research Online*, 21 (3). Available at: http://journals.sagepub.com/doi/pdf/10.5153/sro.4004 (Accessed 3 October 2017).

Scoular, J., and Carline, A. (2014) 'A critical account of a "creeping neo-abolitionism": Regulating prostitution in England and Wales', *Criminology and Criminal Justice*, 14 (5), 608–626.

Scoular, J., and O'Neill, M. (2007) 'Regulating prostitution: Social inclusion, responsibilization and the politics of politics of prostitution reform', *British Journal of Criminology*, 47 (5), 764–778.

Seales, R., and Parsons, R. (2011) 'King's Cross tops the Tube's list of shame as worst station for crime', *Evening Standards.* Available at: www.standard.co.uk/news/kings-cross-tops-the-tubes-list-of-shame-as-worst-station-for-crime-6435404.html (Accessed 23 February 2017).

Sibley, D. (1995) *Geographies of exclusion: Society and difference in the West.* London: Psychology Press.

Sims, A. (2016) 'London's most crime-ridden Tube stations revealed', *Independent.* Available at: www.independent.co.uk/news/uk/crime/londons-most-crime-ridden-tube-stations-reve aled-a6817261.html (Accessed 23 February 2017).

Young, T., Hallsworth, S., Jackson, E., and Lindsey, J. (2006) *Crime displacement in King's Cross: A report for Camden community safety partnership.* London: London Metropolitan University.

Index